RUSTY LABUSCHAGNE

BEATING CHAINS

Falsely Accused.
Framed.
Imprisoned.

AD LIB

To my beloved and extraordinary parents,
Wally and Peta Labuschagne

First published in South Africa in 2018 by Rusty Labuschagne

Second edition published in South Africa in 2021 by Flyleaf Publishing & Distribution

This edition first published in Great Britain in 2022 by Ad Lib Publishers Ltd
15 Church Road
London SW13 9HE
www.adlibpublishers.com

Text © 2022 Rusty Labuschagne

Paperback ISBN 978-1-802471-12-0
eBook ISBN 978-1-802470-56-7

A CIP catalogue record for this book is available from the British Library.

Every reasonable effort has been made to trace copyright-holders of material reproduced in this book, but if any have been inadvertently overlooked the publishers would be glad to hear from them.

Cover photograph by Mark Frapwell

Printed in the UK
10 9 8 7 6 5 4 3 2 1

CONTENTS

Glossary

biltong – a form of dried, cured meat, similar to jerky

braai – a barbecue or grill

droëwors – literally 'dry sausage' spruced with coriander seeds and spices

jukskei – a sport invented by ox-wagon transport riders. They used the wooden pins of the yokes of the oxen to throw at a stick planted in the ground.

kapenta – a Tanganyika sardine

kavisa (or *nchai-nchai*) – prison brew

koppie – a small hill generally made up of stacked granite boulders

kraal – a traditional African village of huts, also an enclosure for cattle and other livestock

mapolishers – prisoner staff who polished guards' boots

mielie/mielie-meal (corn/corn-meal) – a relatively coarse flour (much coarser than cornflour or corn starch) made from maize

mvumvira – stale meat in prison

Ngwebu – African beer

plough-disc braai – barbecue on a plough-disc

rondavel – a traditional circular African dwelling with a conical thatched roof

sadza (pap or grits) – a cooked maize meal which is the staple food in Zimbabwe

skwerekwere – a contraption made from a polish tin filled with burnt cloth and a toothbrush handle with a blade used for lighting cigarettes in prison

steenbok – a common small antelope of southern and eastern Africa

takkies – traditional tennis shoes

veldskoens – South African walking shoes made from vegetable-tanned leather. The name comes from Afrikaans *vel* (skin), later assimilated with *veld* (field), and *skoene* (shoes)

vlei – a long marshy depression covered with grass and devoid of trees, usually between hills or undulating ground

Acronyms

CIO – Central Intelligence Organisation

HIC – hall-in-charge

IO – investigating officer

NGOs – non-governmental organisations

OIC – officer-in-charge

ZIPRA – Zimbabwean People's Revolutionary Army

Foreword

After reading this remarkable account of tears, laughter, achievements and drama, I can assure you that you will never forget the name Rusty Labuschagne and his saga.

Russell Wayne Labuschagne, affectionately known among his friends and peers as Rusty, was brought up in an environment to be tough, proud and bush-loving, as most Matabeleland young farmer sons were. I knew his father Wally, who was respected and well-liked, from my school days in Bulawayo. I remember like yesterday hearing the tragic news of his dad's passing that rocked the community.

I'm familiar with the background young Rusty grew up in and with all the people who had an influence in his life.

I left Bulawayo to live in Durban, but on my annual trips back home I got to hear more and more about the young man: his youthful, wild escapades and what appeared to be a very successful career he was carving out for himself. The world appeared to be his oyster.

It is not for me to judge the merits or guilt of his life or the incidents recounted here – that is up to you to decide for yourself. So far as to quote from the Bible, John 8:7, 'He that is without sin among you, let him be the first to cast a stone.' But I certainly can credit, respect and admire the unbelievable courage, fortitude and resolve that he drew on to endure and survive such an ordeal.

Through Rusty's own admission, if he had his time over, there are many things he would change, as so many of us would also do when we fly the plane on our own to a crash landing, instead of letting God do the flying, arrogantly thinking that all our talent and success is of our own doing and not that of the Lord.

Rusty is now clearly in the seat of the co-pilot with our Lord at the controls and has a burning desire for his experience to be a lesson for others to learn from and to make a difference in their lives, especially the young.

There is always a winter before a summer, and with his new-found faith, undoubtedly a huge harvest awaits him.

His father and mother would have been extremely proud, as many of us are, of the manner in which he handled his adversities and through this, the man he has become. He is a true son of Matabeleland.

Ian McIntosh
Former coach of South Africa's Springbok rugby team

Preface

I want you to go back ten years in your life. Where were you ten years ago, and how much have you accomplished in the last decade? That is how much I had taken away from me when I was falsely convicted and sent to maximum security prison in Zimbabwe at a time of great political turbulence.

I have always believed in balance in life, especially in nature and God's influence. If we had no rain, we would all shrivel up and die; too much rain and we would all drown. I had to accept that principle with my experience, to get through it – I didn't have any other option.

I believe that behind every hardship is an opportunity. My prison experience gave me the chance to get to know hidden attributes about myself, and gave me time to consider some fundamental things in life.

Locked away from the world I'd known, I learned that the most important things in life cannot be bought, supreme among those being health, loved ones and friends.

But if I had to name a single attribute that got me through my nightmare, no matter how tough circumstances became, it would be never losing hope.

Hope is the anchor of your soul. It enables you to see that there is light despite all the darkness. Let your hopes, not your troubles, shape your future – and never look for hope outside of yourself. To find it, you need to look within.

Once you learn forgiveness and find gratitude for who you are, what you have and what you have achieved in life, you will experience the contentment that brings hope.

'Let everything you say be good and helpful so that your words will be an encouragement to those who hear them.' (Ephesians 4:29)

The decade of my life spent 'beating chains' taught me many lessons, and I want to share some of them with you now, in the hope that they will help you in your journey through life.

CHAPTER 1

The Gates of Hell

Stark naked, I was escorted through massive wooden doors into Khami Maximum Security exercise yard.

My hands were in cuffs, and my feet shackled. Thousands of curious prison eyes followed me, wondering what this white man was doing there, since I was the only one.

It was like entering another world. My senses were blasted by the foul smell of leaking sewage pipes and the deafening noise of a thousand prisoners continuously shouting.

Over time I would get used to this noise, a rumbling thunder that never went away.

Two guards escorted me, one on either side. Staying close to them eased my nervousness as inquisitive prisoners swarmed after us. The four guards in charge of the hall were seated on a steel-framed, wooden-topped bench.

The guards made me crouch down, naked and terrified. In front of the curious crowd of 1,000 prisoners, they bombarded me with a series of questions; my family (father of two, loving partner, fourth generation Zimbabwean), where I came from (Bulawayo), my business (safari operator), my crime (murder).

Finally, after what seemed forever, they issued me with a standard white short-sleeve shirt and a pair of drawstring white shorts – the only set of clothing allowed. Underwear was forbidden. After six or nine months, they told me, I would get a change of clothing. Looking around me, I could see prisoners walking around in tatters. If you were fortunate, they said, a red and white striped jersey, flip-flops or takkies with short white socks (brought by visitors) would be allowed.

I was informed that my prison number was 463/03 – I was the 463rd prisoner of 2003.

During roll call, your number was called, never your name. From that moment, I was just a number.

Four six three oh three.

I think it was then that I realised this was not a nightmare I was going to wake up from, or a horror movie that was going to end after 90 minutes. My being here was a mistake. I had to believe that logic and the truth and justice would prevail, and I would soon be released with an apology.

Had I known it would be ten long years before I would walk free again, I may not have made it through that first horrifying night.

CHAPTER 2

First Night

As soon as the guards were finished interrogating me, I was approached by a man named Goodmore who asked if I remembered him. Thinking that I must have just forgotten his happy smiling face, I told him that I did, but I had no clue who he was.

He was many steps ahead of me. Goodmore was a notorious armed robber. After hearing of this Bulawayo businessman coming in, he was waiting.

He led me up to our cell. It was 13 m long by 3 m wide, with a stainless-steel toilet bowl sunk into an open one-metre square cement block in one corner. It had four large steel-meshed vents on each side, two metres off the stained concrete floor. The walls were covered with chipped maroon paint up to 1.5 m, then dirty ivory to a ceiling of cobwebbed cement. There was no furniture visible anywhere. No beds, tables, chairs, cupboards, nothing – not even a mirror. (I didn't see my face for eight years.) Just cold walls, bars and razor-wire with rows of filthy blankets and hundreds of well-used water bottles and water containers on the bare concrete floor.

We were 78 in our cell. Chalk marks 33 cm apart were marked out on the walls; that was your space, and everyone kept to their territorial limits.

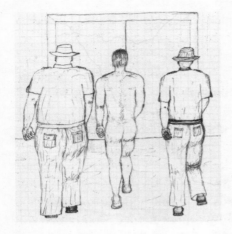

LEFT Being escorted naked into maximum security exercise yard

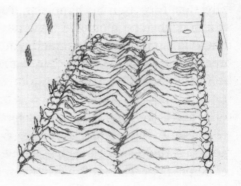

RIGHT Sleeping conditions in Khami Maximum

Goodmore showed me where I would be sleeping, right beside him. Then he offered me his better blankets and took the worn-out filthy ones I had been issued. I took a liking to him right away, and we spoke for hours that night. There were others in there that I could tell were decent men.

Friendships have always sustained me, and I would make lifelong ones during my time in prison. I would also make some serious enemies.

That first night, I learned how the sleeping conditions operated. We lay packed like sardines, all facing the same direction, with legs intertwined in the middle. When we turned over, it was all together. Lying on your back was not only impossible but also not allowed. Men going to the toilet all night would stand on you continuously.

I used two of my paper-thin, lice-ridden blankets as cushioning against the cold concrete floor, then covered myself with the third one. My clothes had to be wrapped around my toothbrush and toothpaste, or they'd get stolen; that was my pillow.

I'd always had a fear of going to prison, so this was my worst nightmare come to life. I was sleeping amongst serial killers, hardcore armed robbers, ruthless rapists as well as innocent good men. We were packed so close together, that what someone else exhaled, you inhaled. Not even the breath you took was your own. I thought, could anything be further removed from freedom than this? I had never tried sleeping on a concrete floor before. It was absolute torture in every way, but worse was to come.

Because if there is one thing every prisoner has in common, it is the need to use the toilet.

The prison was built in the 1950s. Dry earth surrounded the three-story cement block prison in the centre of the exercise yard, which was about the size of a football field, and a 20-foot white concrete wall enclosed it. There were 12 fibreglass toilets in the common ablutions of the hall, which had long been cemented into concrete blocks to enable prisoners to squat, as is the African culture. Four of them, all on the ground floor, were out of order.

Holes were blasted through the back face of each toilet bowl, to enable the plumber's spring-steel rods to slide down into the pipes during blockages. Every toilet had a jagged, tennis-ball size hole leading straight into the sewage pipes, allowing the reeking odour to flow freely out. The toilets had to be flushed with buckets (not a single toilet system worked in any prison I visited in my first eight years), and the dirt floor below was sprayed with excrement from the leaking sewerage pipes running down the walls, leaving permanent putrid puddles all around the hall. The constant wind would blow the filthy dust all around the yard. The leaking cast-iron pipes had panels cut out of them with cutting torches, to clear blockages of days gone by. The panels had long been discarded, and strips of a blanket were used to wrap around the holes that oozed continually and were forever infested with maggots.

The unsanitary conditions were unfathomable.

To add to this incomprehensible situation, the lice were everywhere: in our blankets, clothes, on the walls, in our hair – everywhere! Some were the size of a pinhead, and others grew up to five millimetres long. They bit you day and night, leaving lumps that turned to weeping blister-like sores that itched for days and often became infected. In the months that followed, no matter how often I arranged to have my blankets and clothes boiled, always for a price, within days the lice would be back. It was constant pain and discomfort, and I think the hardest thing to deal with. Bright lights were left on day and night for security reasons, which was also hard to get used to.

The ground and first floor had single and five-man cells and the top floor 16-man cells. Each one was filled way beyond capacity. Single cells had three people each, five-man cells had 13 people each, and 16-man cells had 78–82 people each. Only the top floor cells had toilets, all other single and five-man cells had cut-off plastic containers for ablutions.

With 1,000 people in this single prison and only eight working communal toilets, the rush for them in the mornings after 'unlock' was a nightmare. Every morning the plastic containers in the cells were full, and these open containers would splash everywhere in the mad rush to empty them into the toilets, creating a quagmire of human waste all over the floor, which we all had to splash through. Prisoners seem to lose all self-respect and behave like animals, but maybe it's because we were treated like animals.

I would lie there in the evenings and try to find answers for the madness I was caught up in. Some of the guys would sleep

LEFT Being questioned naked by guards

BELOW Killing lice, telling stories, playing dice games and sleeping

most of the hours we were locked up, but the majority would be either squeezing lice in their blankets, talking between each other in groups or playing some dice or card game. I tried reading magazines belonging to the other inmates, but my mind was riveted on finding a way for my release, and the turmoil of trying to figure out how I had ended up in this nightmare.

CHAPTER 3

The Good Life

L eading up to the millennium, business was booming, and life was full of the joys that love and happiness bring. My safari business was attracting customers, I was flying my own aircraft and to top it all off, I was madly in love with my beautiful fiancée, Sue.

We were building a life of dreams together. In 1998 I had purchased a 15-bed fishing resort on Lake Kariba and set about rebuilding it. It was situated in the Sinamwenda Bay, behind Christmas and Elephant Islands, east of the Ruzi River and west of Tiger Bay. Few ventured that far from either side of the Great Lake and the fishing, especially tiger fishing, was exceptional.

Over holidays and long weekends there was always a well-organised trip to one of my safari camps or the fishing resort. The pleasure I received from all the happy people around me was priceless.

The millennium party was our best ever. A group of my closest friends gathered at Triangle Estates, one of my private safari concessions in the Lowveld part of the country. It had a beautiful camp nestled under massive riverine trees on the banks of the Lundi River, overlooking a large permanent pool that was home to several noisy hippos. We invited my sisters, Bev and Lyn, and their families, Sue's family, and other close friends: 28 people in total, from six to 63 years old, all staying in my five-chalet safari camp with tents scattered in between. Some were sleeping top to toe and others on lounge furniture, which created one big happy family atmosphere.

We saw in the New Year under an enormous baobab tree, measuring 32 metres in circumference. On the millennium eve, the 14 staff I had brought for the five-day getaway set everything up in the early afternoon. The evening began with sundowners as we watched a magnificent sunset. With everyone in full party swing, the portable generator over-revved, blowing the music stereo. The sudden silence brought the dancing to a halt, but it ended up being a blessing as the staff took over and provided us with live music, which turned the night into a truly memorable event. At 9 p.m. I could see that negotiating the drive back to camp in the early hours wasn't going to work, so the men and half of the staff piled into the big truck and headed off to camp, stripped all beds of linen and mattresses and returned to the party. Everyone turned in – properly hammered – scattered around the tree at around 4 a.m., only to be woken in typical Scottish style by Stu Gilmour at sunrise for a shot of whisky each – and the party continued!

Early in 2000, Sue and I headed for the USA to market my safari business. As always, the hospitality, and our travels with the rich and famous were mind-blowing. I had a chance to introduce Sue to many of my special American friends, allowing her to see how they lived their lives and made their fortunes.

In San Francisco we visited Alcatraz prison. I remember feeling chills looking at that prison on the top of a hill with steep cliffs all around, and no way of escape. It was fascinating to see, although at the time I had no idea the role that prison bars would come to play in my life.

The 2000 season proved exceptionally productive. Over the last couple of years I had purchased two houseboats and a beautiful imported ski boat, which we placed at Ncema Dam, 40 km outside Bulawayo. Almost every Sunday and over many a weekend during summers, a crowd of our mates and those of my son, Dusty, and daughter, Sandy, would enjoy waterskiing, kneeboarding and the occasional wild party there. Their mother Mary and I had divorced two years before, so the time I had with them was precious. Although I missed seeing them every day, life was simply sublime, and I was the happiest man alive.

But all was not well with Zimbabwe. While we were living the good life, the country was placed under siege. After losing a referendum that would have given him dictatorial powers, a furious President Mugabe unleashed his 'war veterans', and the invasion of farms began. The country descended into lawlessness, chaos and a process of destruction was started which would eventually collapse the economy.

Four thousand white farmers (.03% of the total population), their families, and dependents were evicted from their farms. Many were openly murdered and when seeking refuge at police stations, were denied any security. This racially based lawlessness permeated throughout the country in every walk of life, from refusing to pay house rentals to taking over safari concessions while foreign tourists were in camp.

The majority of the population was against this anarchy, as livelihoods were being destroyed countrywide. The escalating unemployment and food shortages that followed left millions in a desperate predicament.

CHAPTER 4

I Meet My Nemesis

On a cool, bright summer's morning, I drove along in my kitted out, new, white Land Cruiser, headed for Binga District Council offices to collect the Council CEO (chief executive officer) and a surveyor. They had been sent to mark out new residential stands along the picturesque shoreline of Lake Kariba, for business enterprises in the Sinamwenda Bay area.

The beautiful bay, which was protected from severe weather by Elephant and Christmas islands, was being polluted and damaged by the kapenta fishing activity and fishing co-operatives, who were setting nets in the delicate breeding grounds of the Sinamwenda River that feed the bay. To clear the bay, all the fishing companies had been allocated new commercial stands at Chibuyu, a village site seven kilometres east of the bay. My fishing resort was the only enterprise designated to remain, as we weren't fishing for commercial consumption.

The 400 km drive from Bulawayo to Binga was a hot one. That day – 24 November 2000 – the temperatures remained in the 40 °C range. The council executive staff was happy to see me and we wasted little time leaving Binga, and after a bumpy, dusty, three-hour dirt-road drive we arrived, sweaty and tired. The resort felt like heaven: shady green palm trees, lush lawns and a sparkling pool with a cool breeze off the lake.

I sat down with the councillors and my manager Ian Borrill, and covered my future plans in depth. The CEO was totally supportive. We agreed it was imperative I help them protect the bay from poaching with nets by individuals from the nearby fishing co-operatives; doing that would go a long way to halting contamination by the growing commercialisation of the industry.

Early the next morning, the three of us took a slow cruise up the winding river through the natural fish breeding grounds, where the illegal netting was rampant. We crossed several nets spread right across the river, found smoking fires used to smoke fish and disturbed active poachers who fled on hearing the noise of our boat motor. The CEO announced he intended on reporting his findings and would push for some response from National Parks and law enforcement immediately.

The previous resort owner had had endless problems with one particular poacher, nicknamed Mekki. Despite having been convicted several times for fish poaching in the bay, he was still continually active in the vital breeding grounds. Cleverly, he would set his nets below the surface, making them very hard to spot. I had never met him, but the following day Mike Taylor, an employee of a kapenta fishing company in the bay, pointed Mekki out to me while he was marking the residential stands. At the time he was assisting in clearing bushes for better visibility, while the surveyor marked the boundary lines.

I politely introduced myself to him and laughingly mentioned that I believed he was the king of poaching in the area. Tall, thin and in his 30s, Mekki had an unruly mop of hair and scraggly beard. With a smile and relaxed body language, he denied that but asked me for a job. I said I would employ him when we started building on the stands.

I had a policy, whenever taking on a new safari area, to employ the most notorious poachers. That way we could work together; there wouldn't be any more poaching, and they knew the areas far better than we did. It worked every time. I pointed Mekki out to the CEO, but he knew of him already. He was given a strong warning that if poaching continued in the bay, all netting permits would be withdrawn.

The CEO and I spoke at length again that night, about plans to protect the bay and all looked set. Ian and his wife Pat drove the CEO and surveyor back to Binga on the morning of the 26th while I awaited a group of friends who were due to arrive that evening.

I had planned to meet them at 4 p.m. at Chibuyu fishing resort, seven kilometres from my resort on a torturous road, as they did not know the directions from there. On the way to Chibuyu, I came across Mekki walking in the same direction and offered him a lift. He was carrying a large polystyrene sack of dagga (marijuana) and offered me some. I declined the offer. We remained silent until he asked to be dropped on a well-worn footpath leading to his fishing village, which was a collection of shanties. After we said our goodbyes, he came to my car window, told me not to mention the dagga and informed me quite bluntly that he wanted my fishing resort. A little surprised, I assured him I would not say anything about his dagga and that my resort was not for sale. With real menace in his eyes he looked at me squarely and said, 'If you tell anyone, I'll kill you!' Then he turned and walked away. I drove off, thinking to myself that this guy was almost certainly 'high' and was probably just throwing his weight around. He did not intimidate me physically at all, but as I drove it occurred to me that, with the country being so dangerously, politically and racially charged, Mekki might indeed become a problem for me.

My mates arrived an hour late, full of high spirits, in three vehicles. My ever-happy uncle Lin Stanton, his gentle giant brother Charlie, and Charlie's son Matt were in one twin-cab. Matt was quietly spoken and a pleasure to be around. Sue's dad, Steve Smith, and Richie Barns travelled with Wayne Brebner ('Brebs'). Steve and Richie were both in their 50s and loved fishing and the outdoors.

Last was my childhood mate Gary Koen. He was tall and slim, a heavy smoker, and fishing mad. He came in a Cruiser with Spike Claasen.

Spike is good looking, with incredibly beautiful eyes and, being a smoker, a distinct, raspy voice. He was quite a bit shorter than me, slim with broad shoulders and short brown hair. Spike's dad Chris, and my dad had been great friends from before our birth. Having a passion for the bush, Chris had visited me regularly over the years and always brought young Spike along. The bush and way of life crept into Spike's blood, and after he completed school, his father Chris asked if Spike could work for me. Despite me being 15 years older than him, we became very close and shared terrific times in the bush. Always calm and collected, Spike had a wicked sense of humour and was as loyal as one can get. Our times together were sublime, and he became an exceptional guide.

The road being so terrible, we arrived in camp after dark to a much-appreciated plough-disc *braai* that was consumed in the traditional way: sitting in a circle around the plough disc and eating with our hands, along with several beers and *sadza* (cooked maize meal, a staple food in Zimbabwe).

We were all up at 4:30am for coffee and toast around the campfire before we hit the glassy water. The three Stantons were in one boat, Steve, Richie, and Spike in another, and Brebs and Gary with me in mine. Bream fishing, which the Stantons were always keen on, was a bit slow, but the tiger fish were going crazy, leaving the water boiling as they snapped at the surface. Often all three on a boat were locked in action at the same time, but it was tiring stuff with only one in five strikes ending in a successful catch. The tigers would hit our spinners with tremendous force, strip line off at adrenaline-pumping speed, break the surface thrashing like crazy, and shake the hook out with incredible power. The strike had to be fast and hard; otherwise, they were gone. It was a fisherman's dream day.

Late that evening while moving to a new fishing spot, I spotted two men in a boat about 200 metres away. On approaching, I noticed one was Mekki, standing shirtless with a paddle in hand, his friend seated at the opposite end.

I would learn that the friend was called Wilson, and that name would come to haunt me.

Their boat was approximately 2.5 m x 1.5 m and rectangular in shape, made of 3 mm steel plate. It had boxed-in buoyancy tanks at each end which were used as seats, and had unfinished, rough edges and sharp corners. (These details would become critically relevant later on.) They had no nets or fish with them and had obviously just arrived to check their hidden nets, as they seemed quite unperturbed.

Mekki and I spoke pleasantly at first, in English, about employment and his illegal netting presence in the bay. He protested that there were no fish in the lake, only in the river. Irascible, as at our previous meeting he went on the attack. 'If you can fish here, so can I!' he barked. Not wanting an altercation, I calmly explained that only fishing with nets was prohibited in the bay, and that we were not using nets. I told him I was going to report him to the councillor in the area as he was obviously netting and breaking the law again. Angrily he retorted that had been in this area many years and I was a recent arrival. He reminded me that I did not own the lake and reiterated his intention to 'fish anywhere he wanted to'. I decided to leave him be, and we headed back to camp.

Mekki and Wilson were part of the fishing co-operative that had grown from a few families to over eighty adults, mostly men trying to eke out a living to feed their families inland. Living in rusted old corrugated-iron structures with no ablutions in unrelenting hot temperatures, was in stark contrast to the luxurious fishing resort I had constructed only a relatively short distance away. It doesn't make poaching acceptable by any means, but they had over-netted the area outside the Sinamwenda Bay and were now destroying the fish breeding grounds in desperation.

I had worked tirelessly for my success and was enjoying the fruits of that success, but I did consider how different our lives were in comparison.

CHAPTER 5

The Incident

The following morning the happy fishermen nailed the fiery tigers again, leaving them all sunburnt and tired. While they fished, I went inland to find the councillor responsible for the area to report the confrontation with Mekki and to request help from the authorities.

While I was away the Stantons baited a spot at the entrance to the river for bream. Later in the afternoon, with tiger off the bite, we all decided to join them. Before doing so, I took a slow cruise sightseeing up the river as far as a boat could go, followed by Steve and his crew. No nets were visible, but fresh fish scales, extinguished fires and footprints were everywhere. We all took an enjoyable walk amongst the last pools among the boulders in the river before returning to try for bream.

The bream weren't active, and Spike and I soon became bored. We took my boat to try and get some tiger action going again on the open waters of the bay. As we entered the main river at full throttle, my cap blew off my head. I slowed, swung the boat around and went to retrieve it. As we approached, Spike lunged for it, but the cap sank too fast to the bottom of the river, so we continued on our way.

After about an hour, we decided to make our way back, stopping intermittently at our favourite spots as we went. At one point, while tied to a dead tree sticking out the water, we spotted Mekki and his friend Wilson about 200 metres away coming towards us. When they saw our boat, they began paddling hastily towards the shore. It was apparent he was back, rechecking his illegal nets. I asked Spike to untie us, and as he did so he noticed a net about a metre under the water. I helped him cut the net and we set off towards their boat. They saw us advancing and immediately increased their paddling to get away from us.

I was in no mood to arrest anyone and grind out the four bumpy hours to Binga police station and four hours back. Besides, the councillor had assured me the day before that he was reporting Mekki to the council officials and National Parks.

My boat stood higher in the water than theirs, so on approach I slowed to a fast drift about two metres away. The wave turbulence caused by our boat and engine tilted their boat and added to their panic. They both almost simultaneously lost their balance and jumped out into the water, which appeared to be about one and a half metres deep.

I was satisfied I had created the shock effect I hoped for and was not sorry to see them scrambling for the shore three metres away. There are plenty of crocs in that bay, which added to their anxiousness. Mekki jumped out closer to the bank and was soon able to stand and make his way out, continuing until he had disappeared into a thicket near the shore. As our boat continued past theirs, a movement to my left caught my eye. At first, it looked like a massive catfish darting to the surface, but it was Wilson who broke the surface, took a gasping breath and then was gone again. Moments later he burst out closer to the shore and after two more attempts, he was able to stand and get his breath back. I had by this time turned our boat to move closer to him, and we were preparing to help him.

Coughing and spluttering a bit, he made his way to the shore and walked off into the bush, in the same direction Mekki had gone. It was apparent that he had panicked and lost his footing, whether there was a steep shelf below or not I couldn't tell.

We checked their boat, which was empty, apart from a short, homemade knife with a handle wrapped in tyre-tube. Leaving the boat floating a few metres from the bank, we returned to our fishing party about 150 metres away around a bend in the river. We told them about our little escapade and that we did not think Mekki would be setting nets again while we were there. They said they had heard our boat and wondered what we had gone back for.

The fishing was still quiet, so we chatted and soaked up the sunset on a perfect evening. Keeping to our schedule, we all left for camp and prepared for a prearranged *braai* on a sandy beach across the bay about 200 metres from where Mekki and Wilson had abandoned their boat.

Before dark, we boarded a large raft with the chef and two waiters, smartly dressed in their tuxedos, and headed for the beach. The beach *braai* was fantastic, as always. With comfortable camp chairs in a semicircle around a blazing fire, a table covered with a starched white tablecloth, ice and glasses beside the cooler boxes, we were enjoying every moment. By 10 p.m., content, sunburnt and tired, we were all down, ready for an early morning start.

Fishing was excellent again the following morning, each boat landing several tiger fish. Later, passing Mekki's boat, we noticed it was tied to a stump on the opposite bank to where we had last seen him and Wilson run off. In the boat was a net, which wasn't there the evening before. We remarked that they must have returned to the boat after we had left.

A delicious full English breakfast awaited us at camp. While eating, a message arrived from Mike Shaw's kapenta fishing company next door to say that I was wanted there. I wasted little time, soon arriving at the thatched double-story house from which his business was run. I was surprised to see about nine men standing around the entrance to the property, all carrying either a homemade axe or a small club, and they appeared to be in a belligerent mood. At the time, farmers were being violently attacked by mobs and driven from their homes. While I was alarmed, I did not let them think I was afraid in any way. Holding my head high, I walked right through the middle of them and proceeded to the house.

Mike was waiting for me. Short, pot-bellied and a recovering alcoholic, he had an unsteady hand and seemed to lack confidence.

'Morning Rusty!' he said, puffing on a cigarette. He was dressed in faded blue boxer shorts and sandals. No shirt.

'Howzit Mike, what's going on out there?' I asked.

'Mekki says you drowned his friend yesterday evening.' He looked anxious.

'Aah no Mike, just call the police bud, I don't need this trouble!'

Mike told me he had tried the night before to get hold of the lake captain to get a message to the cops, but their radios were off. I asked what time they had reported the 'drowning'.

'Mekki arrived here at about 7 p.m. last night, maybe a bit later. It had just got dark. He told me you drowned Wilson Mudimba. I asked him if he saw you drown him, and he said no, but he knows that you drowned him. I asked if he had checked to see if Wilson wasn't at his house. He said he'd go and check, and he left. About an hour later he returned with Makore and Samuel and told me that Wilson wasn't home and that you'd drowned him. By that time lake safety's radios were off. They said they'd come back today, and I must radio for them. When they arrived this morning, Makore said that he had been a policeman once and wanted to carry out his investigations before I call the police. They wanted to talk to you before investigating.' Mike explained all of this with apparent concern.

I went off to hear what they had to say.

In days gone by, Makore had worked for both the fishing companies and me, as a night watchman against Zambian boat thieves. Mike had fired him about a month earlier, for habitually sleeping on duty. I had bought one of the neighbouring kapenta companies with Mike the year before. The deal was Mike took the fishing licences, and I remained with the assets: the property and buildings. Makore had been residing in one of the buildings during his employment with my camp staff for a brief period. As I approached the mob, Makore stepped forward to confront me, closely followed by the rest.

'Morning Makore, what's going on?' I asked.

'Mekki said you drowned Wilson Mudimba yesterday afternoon, but before we call the police, I want to go and do my investigations,' he said in English.

He looked down at his feet the whole time he spoke to me.

I told him to go ahead, and that I would be at my place during lunch if he needed me.

As I walked past the mob, they all turned to follow Makore and me. After about ten paces, with everyone now chattering excitedly behind me, Makore took me gently by the forearm and indicated for me to slow down. When we were three or four metres behind the rest, he addressed me quietly.

'Your staff stole my pots and a pan when I was working for you.'

I was taken aback. 'Makore, what pots and pan are you talking about?'

'After I was fired, I went home and left all my belongings in your building with your staff. When I returned last week, there were two pots and a pan missing,' he moaned.

Irritated at being challenged with something so trivial when I had just been accused of drowning someone, I was in no mood for compromise or compassion.

'Well Makore,' I said, 'you say you were part of the police constabulary, you must carry out your investigations on my staff. I can't just buy you pots and a pan because you say my staff stole them.'

He did not like what I said.

'Oh ... so you don't want to help me, okay ... I'll carry out my investigations on Wilson, then we'll see.'

His mouth had turned into a snarl and his eyes narrowed, but I was in no mood to back down.

'Go ahead Makore, do what you want,' I said, and made my way back to camp.

Everyone wanted to know what was going on, and I told them I was being accused of drowning someone by Mekki the poacher.

'Aaaaaah no ... here we go,' Brebs said. 'These guys want you out of here, and they want this camp, Russ. They'll hound you until you leave, or they'll burn this place down if you continue this anti-poaching pressure. That's what it's all about, I'm telling you!'

'Let's go fishing Rusty,' said uncle Lin, 'Let them do what they want. Has Mike contacted the cops yet?'

I told them about Makore who used to be a cop. 'He's doing his investigations first. When they are done, Mike will radio the cops and tell them what these guys find.'

Putting his hand on my shoulder as we made our way towards our tackle, Brebs said, 'Don't worry about it, my mate, let's go catch a fish!'

At the time I believed it could be that easy.

We had a superb morning's fishing, but upon returning to camp, we found Makore waiting with three others. He walked up to within 20 paces of us, held up a broken paddle in one hand and, gesticulating wildly, shouted: 'You killed him with this, and we found blood on a tree in the water. I'm calling the police.'

'Go, I'll be waiting here,' I answered.

And they walked off. We had lunch around the pool, tried to enjoy ourselves and had a few drinks before jumping in the boats and heading out to fish some more.

At about 4 p.m. that day, 29 November, Mike Shaw, and Mike Taylor drove up to inform us that the police had arrived. We arrived at Mike's house to find three of them in a Land Rover Defender. Surprisingly, they had an aluminium body box with them. After introductions, we left for the scene of the incident: Gary, Brebs, Spike, two police officers and me in my boat. One other policeman and seven of the mob followed in another boat with Mike.

The incident took place approximately one kilometre from camp and the scene of the supposed crime was visible from it. On arriving, we all disembarked on the far shore near the scene. Mekki stood near the water's edge, with his supporters behind him. Facing the rest of us, he told us his version of the story in Shona.

'Wilson and I were paddling out of the river when Russell drove across from that side, straight into our boat at high speed.'

He pointed to the far side where we were when we spotted them, and close to the shoreline next to him where the incident took place.

'We were knocked out of our boat into the water but managed to swim to their boat and take hold of their boat rail. Russell and his friend then began assaulting Wilson and me with their fists, forcing us to let go and swim for the shore. They drove away in their boat but turned back to help Wilson when they saw he wasn't swimming well. When they approached Wilson, he went under water and was never seen again.'

Makore then stepped forward, lifted the broken paddle above his head and said in Shona: 'And they beat him with this; there is blood on a tree over there!'

He then pointed to a line of dry, dead trees protruding out of the water across the bay. Spike, being fluent in Shona, asked Makore which tree, out of approximately 30, had blood on it. Pointing across the bay, Makore said, 'One of those trees. There was blood on one of them this morning.'

Spike listened carefully then asked Makore, 'But why would Wilson swim all the way across the bay instead of swimming a few metres to the shore here?'

Spike pointed to where he stood, which was the shortest distance to the shore from where we confronted them. Makore's reply was laughable. 'Because his house was on that side.'

With that a policeman suggested we go and see the blood. Spike and I both looked at each other, concerned they'd smeared fish blood on one of the trees during their investigations. I also asked the head policeman why he wasn't taking notes – he had a pen and paper in hand but wasn't writing anything. He said he'd report what he'd heard to his superiors. Upon reaching the tree line, approximately 140 metres across the bay, a policeman asked Makore to show us the tree with blood on it. He pointed one out, and I drove up close for Spike to hold onto it. Cutting the motor, I inspected the tree. It was about 10 cm in diameter with a few old broken branches and a maximum of one and a half metres sticking out of the water. I looked carefully at every inch of the tree and saw nothing at all.

'Are you sure this is the tree, Makore?' I asked.

'There was blood on that tree this morning,' he insisted. I glanced at Spike, and we both shook our heads as I asked all the policemen to inspect the tree, which they did in turn and found nothing. The head policeman seemed to look sceptical. He then suggested with a smile and a shake of his head that we return to camp and he would inform his superiors.

After arriving at camp, I asked all the policemen to inspect the boats. Mine was made from white fibreglass, and Mekki's was constructed from rusted steel plate with sharp edges, which would almost certainly have left a mark on impact. They all inspected both boats and found no signs of any collision. In camp, the policemen, after being offered tea, asked for beers and fishing tackle. They informed us that the sub-aqua unit would, following procedure, be arriving any day to search for a body. After two beers and a handful of tackle each, they asked when we were leaving camp. I explained we would be leaving in three days, on Friday, and they asked that we call in at Siakobvu police station on our way out as sub-aqua would have done their search by then. We happily agreed, and they left.

CHAPTER 6

Arrest

The remainder of the trip was bliss, and we were all sorry to leave on Friday morning. After a two-hour drive, we arrived at Siakobvu police station. It was a bleak facility: just a simple rectangular building, cement brick under a corrugated-iron roof in a fenced dirt yard about the size of a tennis court. Not the sort of place you wanted to spend too long in. In days gone by it had been a punishment station for badly behaved police officers.

Alongside the building was a small two-metre square hut, constructed entirely of corrugated iron, with no windows. There were no trees in the yard, and temperatures were again in the 40 °C range most of the day. We all walked up towards the entrance of the building, which had a small veranda. As we approached, I heard words over the two-way radio that will forever remain painfully clear to me. 'Have you detained those two white men yet, this is clearly a murder case!' the voice said.

Spike and I stared at each other in shock. I saw the blood drain from his face, and felt my stomach churn.

'Who is Russell?' snarled a policeman without any introductions or greetings. 'I'm Russell, officer,' I answered raising my right hand.

'Remove your shoes. Who were you with, when you murdered Mudimba?' He spat the words at me.

'I was with Russell,' said Spike, moving slightly closer. 'Remove your shoes, arrest these two, the rest of you can go.'

He motioned to another officer to take hold of us and then to our friends to leave.

Brebs visibly shaken, asked, 'So, what are you going to do with them, can we leave some food or anything with them?'

'No, you can call their lawyers. They'll know what to do,' the policeman barked.

The way he was acting, I knew we were in big trouble. We could all see that this man had a deep hatred for us.

We were only allowed a few essential toiletries – a toothbrush, toothpaste and my allergy tablets – and were escorted to the corrugated-iron hut in the blazing sun. It was like an oven, and it stank. As we were sweltering in the heat, a pleasant young investigating officer (IO) named Tshabalala called us one at a time for statements. Neither Spike nor I had ever had to write a statement before, and we were a little overwhelmed and confused. I asked Tshabalala what I should write as it was a long story and there wasn't much space on the form. He told me only to write that I denied all charges, which I did and advised Spike to do the same. That night temperatures hardly dropped, we sweated profusely and were attacked by swarms of mosquitoes. We slept on a hard dirt floor that smelled of urine on blankets that reeked of vomit.

Sadza and boiled cabbage was our dinner, which we hardly touched. They provided no lunch. Around midday the following day, Sue and her dad, Steve, arrived with some food, which we were delighted to see. Sue had notified my lawyer who would be flown to Binga on Monday morning to prepare our bail application. She was distressed and agitated about our welfare but strong during our meeting. The nasty individual who had ordered our arrest was thankfully off duty that weekend, and Tshabalala allowed Sue and Steve to stay an hour, which we dearly appreciated. For accommodation, the McBean family very kindly offered Sue and Steve their lovely holiday home in Binga for as long as they needed. Being two hours away from the prison it was as close to us as they could hope to be.

Later that day Mike Shaw and Mike Taylor arrived to inform us that the sub-aqua unit had searched for the body that morning, but had only found my cap. We were very appreciative of their concern and effort. They had driven four hours on bad roads to check on us and keep us informed. That Saturday night was another stinking nightmare. A filthy drunk man was thrown in with us, making it even more unpleasant.

The next day, at around 3 p.m. Spike and I were handcuffed and transferred in the back of a small, rattling, old pick-up to Binga police holding cells two hours away. It was a rough ride. We were jam-packed in the back with other passengers and their goods and arrived filthy, tired and demoralised, but it was about to get even worse.

CHAPTER 7

Binga Police Station

The reception at Binga police station was probably the most hostile event I had ever experienced. The police attacked us one at a time with vicious verbal abuse leaving us very shaken by the racial undertones. Mercifully, 30 minutes later Sue and Steve arrived, and we were permitted to talk to them for 20 precious minutes.

That night, Sue was permitted to bring us food, which was a godsend. Gerald Oosthuizen, bless him, had offered to provide us with free food daily from his shop in Binga, for as long as we needed it. The support from all these people was genuinely heartwarming and uplifting.

That night in Binga police holding cells was probably the worst of my life. We were packed in a cell, and throughout the night more drunks were thrown in almost every hour. We lay on a filthy concrete floor using blankets that were caked with vomit and faeces. It was steaming hot, and again the mosquitos were impossibly bad. I could not have slept more than an hour that night.

When morning finally came, we were allowed a five-minute wash under a low garden tap in the centre of the courtyard, in full view of everyone. That mattered little; it was badly needed, and I felt great for being a little cleaner. Soon, Spike was escorted by three plain-clothed men alone to a room. I was not at all comfortable about it. Some 20 minutes later, my lawyer, Mark Mellin arrived with Sue and Steve.

I had immense faith in Mark; with long straight black hair and a very long unmanaged black beard, he looked like a shepherd, but he was bright, thorough and sincere, and I was pinning our hopes on him.

My immediate concern was that they were going to beat Spike. As soon as I told Mark that they had taken Spike away, he demanded to be taken directly to his client. We followed a policeman to a room and found Spike, without shoes, sitting in the centre of a room, being bombarded with questions by the three plain-clothes men. Mark walked in and they released Spike right away.

Mark took until 3 p.m. to complete the bail application. We were escorted to court, and the magistrate then said he needed to consider it overnight. We were transferred to Binga Remand Prison. It was spotless, and the guards were very decent and helpful. All I could think was, 'When is this nightmare going to end?'

Little did I know it was only just beginning.

CHAPTER 8

Lynch Mob

The night went relatively well. There were about 40 of us in a 5 x 5 metre cell with inadequate ventilation, but thankfully there were no mosquitos, which enabled our first decent sleep in four days.

What I battled with was that we were not permitted to walk upright at all, day or night. We had to hunch over to stay below the height of a guard's eye level. This was traditionally a sign of subservience, making us look up to our superiors. When speaking to a guard, always, we had to go down on our knees or crouch very low.

Water was abundant, and there was no limit on showering, which in the heat felt beautiful. The problem was that the toilet, open for all to see, was beside the shower. Accustomed to privacy, it was tough trying to relax, squatting over a hole in a cement block with all eyes on me. Far from being polite and looking away, the other inmates stared shamelessly.

When sitting in the courtyard, we could see through the two security fences. Watching the civilian activity, with people going about their daily lives, made us desperate to be free again. We were locked up from 3 p.m. and 7 a.m. and no food was permitted in cells. There were only blankets, a dustbin full of water with a lid placed on top of it, and a plastic cup on top of the lid. We took a cup full of water, drank what we needed and if we didn't finish what was in the cup, it went into the toilet, not back in the bin – I made the mistake of doing that and was reprimanded.

The toilet was a stainless-steel round bowl, sunk into a one-metre square concrete block, with nothing around it. When we urinated, we had to stand with one leg on the floor and cock the other on the block, like a dog, and pee directly into the bowl so there was no spillage. A 'number-two' was only in an emergency, and then we had to cover ourselves with a blanket to hide and try to stifle the smell.

During the night, the inmates would talk and play cards until 8 p.m. latest. After that, all interaction was forbidden, as was smoking in the cells, thank goodness.

Going to court on Tuesday morning was extremely humiliating. It was the first time I had ever been in leg irons and handcuffed in public. Spike's mom and dad had driven down to attend the hearing, and I recall being extremely emotional in front of Chris. Since he'd been a close friend of my father, I had known him for as long as I could remember. The feeling of helplessness in front of someone I had looked up to my whole life was too much.

Mark spoke very well, but we were told that as the charge was murder, only a High Court judge could grant bail. My heart dropped. The magistrate ordered us to be remanded in custody pending an application to the High Court. Mark requested we be transferred to Bulawayo pending this appeal, but this was denied. We were to stay in Binga Remand Prison.

Mark moved fast, and a bail application was submitted the following day in Bulawayo, and our hearing was set down for Friday at 2 p.m. Sue and Steve visited daily, bringing us food from Gerald's shop and news of progress.

While trying to relax on the concrete courtyard floor on Wednesday around midday, I heard unfamiliar chanting in the distance and went to have a closer look. As it approached, initially we could only see a banner, then a mass of demonstrators and press photographers snapping away. The banner read: 'Whites kill black, they must hang!' My heart missed a beat, and my stomach churned in shock as I looked at this. They turned in unison, their chants growing louder as about 200 angry people strode determinedly towards the prison. The guards quickly ushered us into our cells and locked the doors. The following day our names were all over the news. In the eyes of the media, we were already guilty of killing an innocent man who was merely trying to catch a few fish.

Late on Thursday morning, three police officers visited us. One was Inspector Zulu, from Binga police station. They sat us down in a private room across a table from them, pen and pads in hand, and asked us to tell them what happened. In retrospect, what followed was one of the biggest mistakes I have ever made.

In a cocky manner, I told the inspector that we were not prepared to say anything without our lawyer present. In hindsight, he was considering our side of the story for the first time and a more helpful approach from me may have led to them changing their horribly distorted docket. He left, clearly annoyed.

Later that day two plain-clothed intelligence officers arrived asking us about our family history, going back as far as our parents' birth. Having by then realised my error with the inspector, we told them all.

On Friday our hearing in Bulawayo took place, and we were granted bail. However, we could only be released in Binga, 420 km away, with the original warrant of liberation from the court. The warrant was issued around 3 p.m. and Sue and Steve waited until then to feed us and bring us the welcome news. The OIC (Officer-in-Charge) at the prison was very kind and understanding. He arranged for someone to take the original bail docket to the Bulawayo police station, and they faxed a copy to Binga police station, which then verified it. Once the OIC received a copy, at around 6 p.m., he released us on condition that we would have someone deliver the original the next day. Everything went according to plan, and we all left for home very relieved on Saturday morning.

My bail conditions were to report to Hillside police station in Bulawayo twice a week. Spike was to report to Mvuma police station, close to where he lived, 320 km from Bulawayo. I was relieved to be home and have a chance to gather my thoughts while trying to get my life back on track.

CHAPTER 9

Wheels within Wheels

Roughly three months after the incident, a man named AJ Rose, a private investigator who was one of the many individuals offering help to have the case expedited, convinced me that he could have the docket sent to Bulawayo within a month. He was confident the courts would throw it out for lack of evidence. At the time the case was national news and a topic of discussion all over the country. AJ owed me quite a lot of money from a previous joint venture, but I liked him and, in a sense, trusted him to be fair with me. He claimed he knew all the policemen in the Binga area. All he asked for, at that time, was a vehicle and money for expenses. He struck me as credible, and I agreed.

In Zimbabwe, as in most African countries, the law is seldom applied conventionally. In most cases, other factors come into play, and the key is 'who knows who' and can pull the right strings. I thought this chap could do that. I didn't know then, but this decision was another grave mistake.

Upon arriving in Binga with my Land Cruiser, AJ was told by the OIC that the docket was still being finalised at Siakobvu police station. The OIC at Siakobvu, who had been so hard on us, happened to be an old friend of AJ's and assured him the docket would be complete within a month. AJ returned to Bulawayo, kept in touch on the landline phone with the OIC and drove out again after a month to transfer the docket, together with a policeman, to Binga. Unbeknown to me, by now he was stepping on toes and upsetting a few people. The OIC in Binga advised him that the docket would be forwarded to the Officer Commanding (OC) in Hwange that week.

AJ knew the OC in Hwange who informed him, after a month, that the docket had not arrived there yet. My vehicle left again for Binga, costing me more fuel and money. I started to think AJ was enjoying these sojourns at my expense and made my frustrations known.

AJ said he now wanted the money he owed me to be written off because the issue was far more complicated than he anticipated. I was angry but in a jam. I agreed.

It got worse. The OIC in Binga sent the docket back to Siakobvu, the IO there was changed, and all affidavits were redone. The new IO's name was Phillip, and he seemed very pleasant. During this period, we did indications with the police at the scene of the incident, and Phillip did the reports. My lawyer had gone to extreme measures for us to attend indications with the witnesses. He had obtained an order from the High Court, allowing Spike and I to travel to the area (as it was against our bail conditions) and he liaised with Binga police for the witnesses to be present. Mark, Spike and I drove out to camp and met Phillip and another policeman there. They had come by boat from Binga, but amazingly no state witnesses were present as was prearranged.

The police in Binga had assured Mark that they would be attending.

During indications, after we had shown Phillip precisely what happened, he asked me a question that threw me:

'Where were you when you were pulled out of your boat into the water?' Spike and I stared hard at him incredulously, and I said, 'Who was pulled into the water?'

Realising he'd said the wrong thing he looked down without answering the question. I pressed him, 'Who pulled who into the water, Phillip?'

'Mekki said he got into a fight with you both and pulled you both out of your boat into the water,' he mumbled quietly.

Spike and I were both astounded and started laughing.

'I can't believe this, are you serious, Phillip, did Mekki say that?' I asked.

He and the other officer were now laughing too, but he wouldn't say any more.

We left it at that. Months later, after bail conditions had been relaxed, I was in Binga Kwikspar Supermarket and saw Phillip. I asked for an opinion on how long it was going to be before the docket would be completed. He mentioned that he had been taken off the case and another IO appointed, which left me shocked.

'Stick to your story and all should be okay,' he said.

Although he was relaxed and appeared to empathise with us, I had nagging doubts.

Taking it all into account, I reassured myself with the belief that any judge would see through all the dishonesty. Adding to my optimism, Mark had maps made and exact distances of every detail, and he left us feeling very confident we were in excellent legal hands.

I made inquiries about Phillip having been taken off the case and discovered that Phillip had redone the docket and all the statements prepared by Tshabalala had been rewritten. He had sent the docket to Binga, who sent it on to Hwange. The docket was then sent back to Siakobvu via

Binga, and the IO changed, again. Once more, all statements and the docket were redone. This was getting ridiculous. By now 11 months had passed since the incident, and no docket had reached Bulawayo. This was not a complicated investigation so why all the delays?

One month, upon reporting for remand to the courts, the public prosecutor asked me if I knew AJ Rose, the man who was pushing for my docket to be hurried up. I said I had never heard of him, which made him smile. AJ had by now clearly annoyed people in the system all the way up to the Attorney General's office, and the docket wasn't even in Bulawayo yet. Unbeknown to me, attitudes in the police and the prosecuting authorities were hardening.

Sadly, ten months after the incident my lawyer Mark Mellin emigrated to New Zealand and a year later became a barrister there. My new lawyer was Nomsa Ncube, a very bright woman who worked for a reputable law firm. In November 2001, she applied for my passport to be released, so that I could travel overseas to market my safari business, which I had been doing annually for the previous 15 years. The High Court turned it down, but she was convinced the Supreme Court would approve it, and then we could appeal to have the case thrown out. For some unknown reason, I allowed AJ to persuade me that Nomsa was making a huge mistake and that I must take my case to Jumbo, another well-known lawyer and close friend of his, who was more influential in the justice system. He assured me his 'man' had a better plan of attack and that Nomsa's strategy wouldn't work once the case got to the Supreme Court.

Looking back, I feel this was the third huge mistake on my part. Feeling more vulnerable by the week, and listening to AJ, I didn't know any better. I trusted too quickly, I was in a whole new world and was quite bewildered by it all.

Our new lawyer, 'Jumbo' (Joseph James), was a tall, well-spoken, affable man of mixed-race descent, who was happy to take on what was by now a high-profile case, which had attracted attention nationally and internationally. I briefed him in detail, and despite all the bad blood that seemed to be flowing out of the AG's office he said he doubted very much that this would ever get to court. This was music to my ears.

Unfortunately for me, he was very wrong.

CHAPTER 10

Travesty Trial

I n early June 2002, Spike and I arrived at the Bulawayo Magistrates' court for our normal remand hearing, which we did every fortnight. Usually, this was a quick procedural process, but this time we were in for a shock. When our names were called and we came before the magistrate, we were told that we were formally indicted to stand trial for murder in the Bulawayo High Court on 9 July. Initially, I failed to grasp what had just happened – but not for long.

We were hustled down some old narrow wooden steps from the dock into the filthy crowded holding cells and told we would be held in custody until trial. We waited for two uncomfortable hours on a cold concrete floor in our smart suits, seriously sweating, before Jumbo arrived in a panic and shouted to us through the thick wire mesh that he was doing his utmost to obtain bail pending trial. It was a Friday around midday, which left him little time to prepare the application – failing which we'd spend at the least the weekend in Khami Maximum Remand Prison.

Shortly after 5 p.m. all detainees were called to board a securely barred grey prison bus. Pale-faced in shock, in handcuffs and leg irons, we boarded the reeking vehicle. We were driving out when the bus was stopped, and a tall, thin man entered and called out our names. We were remanded out of custody until trial. Our relief was indescribable.

All the assurances Jumbo had given me about this not going to trial had now been shown to be false, and the process had become irreversible. At this point, I know I should have changed my legal representative. Jumbo was an attorney and when on trial for murder in the High Court an advocate was the norm, but he continued to assure us that he was perfectly capable of defending us and securing an acquittal. To my cost, I believed him.

The day before the trial Mike Shaw came to my property in Bulawayo. As a state witness, he was barred from contact with me, so I was shocked to see him. I took him aside, away from the office under some shady trees on the lush green lawn. 'Mike, what are you doing here?' He was clearly very uneasy.

'Rusty, I'm bloody nervous for tomorrow. What must I say?'

'Just tell them the truth, Mike – don't make it sound like you are too much on my side though,' I said, as I led him back to his car.

On 9 July, my trial for murder finally commenced in the Bulawayo High Court, with Justice Kamocha presiding, along with two assessors. Neither Spike nor I had any idea what to wear, what to call the judge or how procedures went. We were instructed by Jumbo to only answer questions very briefly; if we were to elaborate at all, he warned, they could manipulate our comments. There was no evidence against us. Even so, all these instructions were quite terrifying when up against a murder charge in a turbulent political climate.

Jumbo met us outside the courthouse, and we all walked in together. The court was a magnificent sandstone structure, with finely fashioned wood-panelled walls and an upstairs gallery overlooking proceedings five metres below. The judge's bench was made of solid beams of rich red timber – very colonial. It was strikingly beautiful but intimidating at the same time.

Spike and I were escorted into the raised wooden dock in front of the judge's bench. A thick wooden rail barricaded us in there. The room was packed.

For the state, leading the prosecution was Chris Ushewokunze, a nephew of Herbert Ushewokunze who had been Minister of Health and the Minister of Home Affairs. His uncle had acquired a reputation as a hard-liner in the years immediately after independence.

Jumbo assured us the state's case was very tenuous, and this calmed us somewhat, but we were unhappy about being at the mercy of Kamocha. He had been the judge presiding over my divorce proceedings, which had commenced in mid-1997.

Only 12 days before the trial, he had this to say about me: 'While the applicant [Mary] has made a full disclosure of her income and expenditure to this court, the respondent [me] has failed to do so.' He ruled that my matrimonial estate be audited by a referee. His decision was later overturned in the Supreme Court of Appeal. It was hard for me to think that he was going to be impartial. If Kamocha had decided not to believe me in civil proceedings, what chance was there that he would believe me in the course of a criminal trial? In fairness, he should have recused himself.

Adding to my worries was the fact that at that time the eviction of farmers was in full swing. The locals in the Binga/Sinamwenda area, where the incident took place, had become politicised and there was widespread hostility in general, and particularly towards me. I was seen as something of an interloper who had interfered with their poaching rackets, and many of them were anxious to see the back of me. Kamocha had been the magistrate in Binga for many years and would have been well aware of the community campaign against me in the area.

Another complicating factor was Kamocha's recent history of finding in favour of the opposition MDC in some politically charged cases, which saw him slammed by the state-controlled media. Judges who did not toe the party line soon found themselves on thin ice, and Kamocha may well have feared for his job at the time I came before him. I may have been the perfect foil for him to ingratiate himself with the political hierarchy.

Despite all these factors, I remained confident. I knew I had committed no crime and was convinced that the truth would prevail under judicial scrutiny, and even an angry, politically exposed judge would find it impossible to convict me. Mekki was the chief state witness so as far as establishing what happened that day, it was his word against Spike's and mine, and Jumbo assured us that their version of events would not withstand a reasonable credibility test. I was also aware of the fact that only in exceptional cases was 'one person's word against another' sufficient to prove guilt beyond all reasonable doubt where no body has been presented.

The state presented their case first. There were six witnesses: Mekki, Mrs Mulamba (the presumed deceased's mother), Sergeant Ndoro (police sub-aqua unit), Samuel Mwinde (Wilson's brother-in-law), Mike Shaw and finally James Makore. The only evidence that the state produced in court was my cap, and a broken wooden paddle.

The version of events they presented was conflicting and confusing. Mekki was on the stand for an entire day and kept changing his story under cross-examination, so they called him back again the following day, and he contradicted himself all over again. But no matter how much of a mess he made of it the judge seemed to turn a blind eye to the fact that he was a ridiculously poor witness.

Mrs Mulamba initially testified that her daughter-in-law, Wilson's wife, was dead. But other witnesses claimed she had in fact moved to her own mother's home. If Mrs Mulamba didn't know her son's wife was alive, how could she be a credible witness to the fact that her son had died? It was clear that Mrs Mulamba, the only state witness produced to clarify that Wilson was dead, was also unreliable.

Jumbo applied for the case to be dismissed on the grounds of contradicting weak witnesses. It was turned down.

The defence witnesses – me, Spike, Brebs, and Richie Barns – took two days on the stand.

Murder is often referred to as *corpus delicti* in law. One does not begin to inquire whether a person is guilty of the crime until one has established that a person is dead, and that their death was caused by a crime. In a murder case, the *corpus delicti* consists of two elements: the death of a human being, and the criminal act of another in causing that death. The best way to prove the first element of the *corpus delicti* in a murder prosecution, i.e., that the victim is dead is, obviously, by the production of the body of the deceased.

There was no body.

The second element of the *corpus delicti* in a murder prosecution is, in many trials, proved by evidence from a person or persons who witnessed the event that caused the death of the deceased, for example, a witness may have observed an accused person stabbing or shooting the deceased. This type of evidence is direct evidence. It is different from circumstantial evidence, which is not directly from an eye-witness or participant in the crime. Where direct evidence requires no reasoning to prove its existence, circumstantial evidence does.

Particularly in criminal cases, 'eyewitness' ('I saw Frankie shoot Johnny') type evidence is often lacking and may be unreliable, so circumstantial evidence becomes essential. In a criminal case, the state must prove the guilt of the accused person beyond reasonable doubt.

The existence of blood on the tree was crucial to proving that there was an assault of any sort to cause Wilson's death, as was any evidence of damage to the boats. Mekki's statement alleging that he saw 'a lot of blood on the stump' was fundamental in proving the state's case. But each police officer – three in total – that attended the scene wrote affidavits confirming that they inspected the petrified tree that Wilson was supposed to have clung to when I supposedly rammed him with my boat and no blood or marks were seen. They also inspected my boat, as well as Mekki and Wilson's boat, for any blood and marks from the reported collision, and no marks were found. These affidavits were in the court with the judge, his assessors, and the public prosecutor.

Even James Makore, who was instrumental in concocting the state case, stated that he had no knowledge of our boats colliding. This crucial evidence seemed to be entirely ignored by the judge and his assessors.

The cap I was wearing on the day of the incident that blew off my head, was found by the sub-aqua unit and produced in court. I did not deny ownership of the cap in question. I also gave a perfectly logical explanation as to how I had lost it. My evidence was unchallenged. Although this was not material evidence, it did come up in testimony and

Mekki gave no less than four different versions of where, when and by whom it was found. With it being critically important that Mekki's evidence be beyond reproach if his word was to trump mine and Spike's, this series of lies and contradictions should have been enough to convince the judge that Mekki was not credible.

A broken portion of the oar was also produced at the trial. There was no evidence as to what happened to the rest of the oar, the upper handle part, or the second oar. If the evidence of the state's witnesses had been taken seriously by the police there should have been bloodstains on the portion of the oar recovered, and an attempt should have been made to locate the missing portion.

I explained to the court that what struck me as strange was that when we went to the scene with the police the day after the incident, Mekki gave his account of what happened and never mentioned blood on a tree, or a paddle being used to beat anyone.

Spike is fluent in Shona and heard every word. It was only after Mekki's version, when James Makore stepped up to give his story, that the blood on the tree and the paddle entered the discussion. And there were at least three conflicting versions of where this supposed oar was found: Mekki said it was in my boat, Samuel said he picked it up on the shore in the water, and Makore said it was picked up on the bank. Mike Shaw's evidence was the most credible – when asked about the oar he stated that he had no knowledge of it, nor had he ever seen the oar up until the court case.

In the outline of the state case, they averred that Mekki stood on the shore and watched us beat his friend Wilson with a broken paddle, as he clung to my boat rail, then I ran over him with my boat. During his evidence on the first morning, he said he was swimming backstroke away from us and watching the beating. Later he changed his position, but at no stage in court did he say that he stood on the shore and watched as the state alleged.

While I was expecting a torrid time from the prosecutor, that did not happen. He asked me for my version of events then asked me 11 questions, which I had no problem answering, and he then said he had no further questions. I found him very professional and reasonable.

Before I took the stand, Jumbo assured me the state case was hopeless and reminded me to say as little as possible under questioning. The judge seized on Mike's conflicting evidence and asked me why Mike had said I bumped the boat, and only one man ran into the bush – which he immediately corrected, saying he was confused and two men ran into the bush. This was borderline ridiculous asking me to explain someone else's testimony, but I said he must have been confused. Then I mistakenly carried on and said, 'Why would I tell him only one ran into the bush and incriminate myself?'

This was seized upon immediately by the judge as proof that I would have been prepared to lie if I had killed someone.

Then the judge started on me. He was unrelenting in his interrogation, which lasted the entire day. The two assessors played a support role for the judge and were also very much against me. The bench was clearly frustrated with the prosecutor who they did not feel had been aggressive enough and so they became prosecutors rather than impartial arbiters. From a procedural point of view, this was a massive miscarriage of justice. The judge, who is expected to listen and only ask questions when he needs clarity on issues raised, had become the prosecutor.

At the end of the day, my lawyer said there was something bizarre afoot, and he had never seen anything like it before. He said he had never seen assessors so blatantly hostile in a trial either, nor had he seen a judge behave like that.

Even though the state had closed its case, the judge decided he wanted to hear Makore's evidence and opened it again. My lawyer explained there were police witnesses who had seen what Makore had seen and were present, so this was not required, but he insisted. Makore had unfortunately left for his home 600 km away, so the trial was adjourned over three months until November.

When Makore finally appeared he went on to contradict everything anyway. But at least I had a few more months of freedom. Of course, I had no idea they would be my last free days for the next decade.

CHAPTER 11

A Judge Gets Jailed

Towards the end of 2002, while I was awaiting a verdict, my friend Ralph told me about an associate of his who owned Circle G Ranch near KweKwe, in the Midlands.

His name was Justice Benjamin Paradza. He was a war veteran who had been practising law when the president appointed him a judge. I was looking for additional safari concessions, so Spike and I went out to see the ranch and liked it immediately. I visited the judge in Harare and discussed a joint venture under which I would get the use of his property, and we agreed on a deal.

Later I mentioned to Ralph, a politically connected gentleman, that it would help me immensely if my passport could be released. I was desperately keen to travel abroad to market my safaris, which I was unable to do without any travel documents. I felt I had shown the authorities that I had no intention to abscond, having sat around for two years since the incident.

He said he would talk to the judge, which he did. I had no idea then, but I was unwittingly exposing myself to the wrath of the political hierarchy. It later transpired that Paradza could only have been fast-tracked from a lawyer onto the bench because he was related to the president.

All agreed he was a very competent lawyer, but getting onto the bench in his early forties didn't sit well with everyone.

This was also a politically charged time in the judiciary. The country's highly respected Chief Justice Anthony Gubbay had been physically threatened in his chambers by 'war-veteran' leader Joseph Chinotimba. The Chief Justice had enraged the executive, the Attorney General, and other senior politicians after a landmark ruling in favour of dispossessed farmers who had been thrown off their farms. He found their constitutional rights had been violated and ordered their properties be restored to them. This was simply unacceptable to the authorities, and when the government made it clear they could not guarantee his safety, he resigned from his post.

A government spokesman said the high courts were stuffed 'with colonial relics' and began a process to purge those who were dissenting from the political mainstream. This 'cleansing' went beyond judges seen as sympathetic to farmers, but also targeted those on the bench who were seen as too independent. One of these was Paradza.

While this was all going on, Paradza approached the other judges on my behalf about my passport, and stood on some sensitive toes. The reaction was an angry one, and some of the judges who he approached went to the minister of justice. They reported an unwanted approach and claimed that they had been offered a bribe. Paradza, who insisted that the judges had demanded money to assist him, later disputed this. Just who was telling the truth I may never know, but this interaction made my situation worse.

It appeared that Paradza was now dangerously exposed. According to the government-controlled press, he was out of favour with the president and the politicians because he was seen as too independent-minded and the senior judges saw him as a precocious upstart. In January 2003, he was arrested in his chambers, charged with obstruction of justice and jailed at Harare Central police station.

This action was unprecedented in the history of the country. Zimbabwean judges were only subject to arrest in exceptional circumstances, and this had to result in their impeachment before any other action could be taken. For a judge to be impeached the law mandated that a tribunal be constituted before presenting its findings to the president. Nothing of the sort happened.

The following day he was granted bail, and a political bombshell immediately exploded. Because the ongoing onslaught against farmers was getting international attention, the Paradza arrest also made its way into the global media. He walked out of the cells straight in front of cameras from Sky News, CNN, and the BBC, to name a few. He publicly lambasted the president, the minister of justice and the government in general. Worse for me was the fact that my name was now linked to this unwelcome tirade in every article. I was now right in the middle of the political crossfire and seen as an ally of a man who had suddenly emerged as a massive political embarrassment to a government that was under enormous pressure. Only when I met a politically connected lawyer later did I understand just how precarious my plight had become.

The lawyer explained that the knives were out for Paradza and that President Mugabe and most of the political hierarchy were determined to teach him a lesson for his impertinence. They wanted to convict him of a crime and have him jailed. The only way they could do that was to have me convicted first.

If I were acquitted, it would be much more difficult for them to make charges stick, so my guilt had become an essential requirement in settling a political vendetta. He urged me to abscond, and I refused. I reminded him that I had done nothing wrong and that everything I had worked so hard for, my family, and my future, were right here in Zimbabwe.

CHAPTER 12

Judgement Day

took a call from Ralph as I turned into my driveway. I was returning from the paradise that was my fishing resort. I badly needed the break; it had been seven agonising months since my trial and my nerves were raw from the stress, but I had worked hard on being optimistic. I kept telling myself that justice and fairness would surely prevail in the end, despite a disturbing recent precedent being set in the handing down of some very politically motivated judgements.

The message from Ralph was blunt and shattering, 'You're going to prison, Rusty, get out now!'

It made my blood run cold. Burning jets of adrenalin shot through my stomach. The questions in my head were flying. How could I run? I'd never run from anyone. I always faced my adversaries squarely and never backed down. Most importantly, I had my children, Sue and my family here. I could never abandon them. I felt I had done well in life, was no coward and was as good as my word. I had a reputation for being honourable and was not going to squander that for anything. If I ran, they'd say I was guilty, and it just wasn't an option for me. I would be running for the rest of my life; never allowed to return to the country and the people I loved while being branded a murderer. Besides, they would take all my properties, businesses, everything I'd worked so long and hard for over a period of 25 years.

The evening before my judgement, I had a sit-down dinner with my children, Sandy and Dusty, and Sue and her family. After dinner, we enjoyed a few drinks around my bar. After showering with Sue the next morning, I sat with Dusty and Sandy, who were very nervous, in the lounge stroking my favourite cat. They weren't coming to the courtroom, but I assured them I would see them later.

The courtroom was full at 9 a.m. on that hot summer's day, 2 April 2003. I kissed Sue before entering the elevated wooden dock with Spike.

The court pointed out 'that the body [of Wilson] was not recovered'. There was insufficient evidence before the court for it to draw the conclusion (to the exclusion of all other rational conclusions) that Wilson was dead.

Judge Kamocha simply did not deal with this issue in his judgement.

No matter what evidence the defence produced, the judge refused to see our side.

Mrs Mulamba, strangely, was unaware that Wilson's wife, the mother of the child she was caring for, was still alive. Wilson's wife should have been at the court to testify and face cross-examination as to the whereabouts of her husband.

Mekki gave several conflicting stories about where he was, and what he was doing when he said he saw me assault Wilson with an oar, and then drive into him while he clung to a tree stump. Judge Kamocha simply ignored all those stories and said that Mekki watched from the shore, as stated in the state's case before the trial.

Judge Kamocha ruled as follows: 'It was also the court's finding that the accused were clearly being untruthful when they denied that their boat bumped into Mekki's boat and capsized it. There is also no truth in their testimony when they said there was no scuffle in the middle of the river. Their story that both Mekki and the deceased ran out of the water is also clearly false. They said the boat was about three-and-a-half metres from the shore as they drew closer to it. That is not true and is rejected. It was in the middle of the river not less than 35 to 40 metres from the shore. That is why boats had to be used to get to the scene.'

The Sinamwenda estuary, which is situated on Lake Kariba, is some way from my fishing resort and in rough terrain that is inaccessible by vehicle. The most convenient way to get to the Sinamwenda river estuary from my fishing resort is by boat. How a judge could assume the incident was 35 to 40 metres from the shore because boats had to be used to get to the scene was beyond me.

CHAPTER 13

Findings of the Court

Mekki alleged that there was blood on the petrified tree (stump) that Wilson had allegedly clung to. In this regard Judge Kamocha, in his judgement, paraphrased Mekki's evidence as follows: 'Mekki had said there was a lot of blood which was still visible when the police examined the stump.' This despite the fact that Judge Kamocha was in possession of three affidavits from the police officers that attended the scene and searched for blood on the tree on the day after the incident on 29 November 2000. Two of these police officers were at the trial, and all the affidavits stated that no blood was seen by them on the tree stump. Judge Kamocha ignored this glaring inconsistency in Mekki's evidence and ruled that Samuel and James 'also allegedly saw some blood on the tree stump' and that 'these two supported his story'. All state witnesses gave inconsistent evidence as to the blood.

The next findings to sort through related to the boats and how they supposedly rammed together. Shaw's evidence did not amount to corroboration of Mekki's evidence. It is essential to bear in mind that Shaw was a state witness who was not impeached. The court, however, seemed to be very ready to criticise Shaw's evidence and to discount every aspect that was favourable to Spike and me. And yet the evidence of Mekki, Samuel and James were not subjected to the same criticism – the court was quite prepared to attribute inconsistencies in their evidence to their simply being mistaken.

The next issue was my green cap. The judge ruled that Mekki's evidence that the cap was found is supported by Samuel, who actually found it. Just what bearing a cap being found had on whether or not I had beaten a man to death escaped me.

With regard to the paddle, Judge Kamocha, as with my cap, ruled that, 'what was important was, not so much when and where the oar was found, but that it was found at the scene'.

Judge Kamocha found confidence in Mekki's single witness evidence in the fact that the oar was broken after allegedly striking my boat. This confidence is evinced in the following finding of the court in the judgement:

'The portion of that paddle had been broken off. Mekki identified the oar, and he testified that one of the blows, aimed at the deceased with the oar, missed and landed on the boat. The oar broke into two pieces as a result. This story accords with the probabilities because an oar without the flat portion that paddles the water is of no use to any person.'

How this accords with the probability again escapes me. I gave evidence that the police examined my boat, but no signs of damage or marks were seen on it. This evidence was not challenged in cross-examination by the state, and the policemen who inspected my boat were at the trial. I was entitled to assume that my unchallenged testimony, in this regard, was accepted as correct. The court, however, just ignored all the evidence.

I had not denied the presence of the cap or oar. There are hundreds of discarded oars on the lakeshore. What my counsel argued was that it was unsafe to draw evidential conclusions as to the commission of the guilty act on the basis of the presence of the oar and the cap, because Mekki's single witness evidence as to the location and time of finding these items was contradictory – which all pointed to Mekki having concocted the story.

The court ruled that Samuel's evidence essentially corroborated Mekki in this regard. However, Samuel's evidence in actual fact contradicted that of Mekki. All three of the state witnesses, who were present when the oar was found, contradicted each other. This was abundantly clear to the court from the following extract of the judgement:

'There is a difference in the evidence of James and Samuel in that Samuel said the oar was floating near the bank while James said it was found on the bank of the river. Mekki, in fact, told the court that it was found in the accused's speedboat.'

These contradictions should have alerted the court to the danger that Mekki's evidence was concocted – and the contradictory evidence of the three state witnesses stretches their credibility. Instead, remarkably, the court found that Samuel's evidence corroborated Mekki. There was nothing in the contradictory evidence of Samuel or James concerning the oar or the cap, that could or should have given the court a sense of confidence in the overall veracity of Mekki's (contradictory) single witness evidence.

First, the judge read out his findings against Spike. Because he wasn't driving the boat, and because I was much older than him, he had only found him guilty of assault with intent to do grievous bodily harm. That all seemed reasonable, but the fact that he had been convicted scared me. The findings against Spike personally were mild in comparison to what had been read out by the judge against us before that.

Then the judge read out his findings against me. They were vicious and delivered with venom. I went cold. He seemed to go on forever as we all waited with bated breath for his verdict. Then the words that changed my life forever: 'It cannot be said that his aim and object was to kill the deceased. He, in my view, is clearly guilty of murder with constructive intent.'

After the first part, I felt a slight sense of relief and then the second half felt like someone had stuck a knife deep into my stomach. It was all over: I was now a convicted murderer. I can still hear that gavel striking the solid bench and the echo of Sue's cry for mercy from the gallery.

Our dreams were shattered with the crack of wood on wood. I struggled for breath. I can still see the shock and devastation on the faces of my loved ones and close friends up in the courthouse gallery. Then they all surrounded me in the dock for my last minutes of freedom. To hide the pain I felt then, in what seemed a cold, lonely courtroom, I removed my suit jacket, tie, wristwatch, and silver bracelet, handed them to Spike, gave him a tight hug and said, 'It'll all be okay bud, take care of everything.' He was in total shock too.

With everyone broken, crying and crowded around me, I had to remain strong. I was always the rock, the one they turned to as a solid base to rely on. Inside though, my world was crumbling. I held Sue's hands tight as she shook uncontrollably, staring into my eyes. I assured them all I would be fine and not to worry about me, and I asked Mary to take care of our children. It was a whirlwind of emotions trying to figure out what advice to give, as they led me away, down noisy wooden steps to an empty, cold holding cell below. The last words from Sue were, 'I love you, babe,' and I shouted the same in reply as the commotion faded into silence in the fortress underground. The happiest days of my life had just ended.

CHAPTER 14

Sentencing

was down in the holding cell for about two hours. It was late afternoon when they took me out to the front of the courthouse where I was given a few moments with Sue. She told me she had just made some calls to people who might be able to help me get bail pending appeal. I was handcuffed and in leg irons. I just held her hand with one and rubbed her leg with the other, assuring her all would be okay. She was totally broken, tears streaming down her beautiful cheeks. My heart ached for her in my helpless state. I held her close for as long as I could and then they led me away.

The grey prison truck was waiting on Main Street. It was rush hour. Shuffling awkwardly down the carved sandstone stairs of the courthouse in chains was humiliating, but the next part was even worse. The first step into the back of the truck was knee high. In leg irons, I had to frog-jump up while holding only one of the rails with both cuffed hands, leaving me off balance. After falling numerous times, while guards laughed out loud and onlookers giggled on the street, I eventually made it into the back, and they slammed the heavy metal door shut.

Khami Maximum Security Prison is 26 kilometres outside Bulawayo, and we arrived after dark with stops on the way to collect other prisoners. Because I had not yet been sentenced, I was taken to the remand section. Three of us arrived together, we were handed a plate of *sadza* and half a cup of boiled cabbage, given a two-litre bottle of water and escorted to a single 1 m x 3 m cell with three disgusting blankets to share between us. I grabbed one and said I would sleep with my head to the door. I hardly slept, still in my suit trousers and shirt, my mind a mess.

At 6 a.m. we were unlocked. I asked if I could take a shower. Before leaving court the day before, Sue had brought me a toothbrush and toothpaste, but I had no soap. I asked a colossal man showering next to me if I could use his soap.

'Sure,' he said, 'but when you return from court, I want a loaf of bread.'

I used the soap, drip-dried and clothed myself in the prison-issue khaki trousers and shirt they supplied. On my feet, I wore the same socks and black shoes.

I was cuffed and loaded into a truck stuffed full of prisoners and guards and taken back to the same holding cell. It was filthy; the paint peeling off the walls and graffiti scrawled all over. I could hear the faint sounds of footsteps as people shuffled into the courthouse above.

Late that morning I was escorted up the stairs into the dock beside Spike. He was his usual warm self, but visibly concerned. We took our seats on the same narrow wooden bench. The courthouse was packed. I turned around and waved with a smile, fixing on Sue's eyes as soon as I saw her. She looked like she had not slept at all.

My mind was in a spin, thinking of the pain my family were going through. I had visions of Sandy's distraught face as Sue told her the news the day before and how anxious they must be for my sentence. I looked out of the windows high up in the courthouse and prayed to Jesus for justice and tried to visualise my mom or dad's face up in the clouds, hoping they were praying for me. I was at the mercy of a man who I could tell disliked me from day one. I hadn't felt that helpless in decades.

The judge began with Spike, read out a summary of the events and the reasons for conviction of the offence of 'Assault with Intent to do Grievous Bodily Harm', then gave a fine to the equivalent of US$10 and a sentence of four months' imprisonment suspended for five years on certain conditions.

Then it was my turn. First, the judge asked the prosecutor to tell the court what sentence he thought was appropriate. I am convinced he knew I was innocent and felt sorry for me. He suggested as he thought my offence was very close to being one of culpable homicide that a sentence of eight to twelve years would be appropriate. My lawyer then gave an impassioned, lengthy address in mitigation, which was duly noted but ignored.

The judge gave me 15 years.

My lawyer immediately asked for leave to appeal, which was granted. Before I could gather my thoughts, the gavel struck the wooden bench, and the judge left. The crowd at the courthouse was more significant than the day before and swarmed the dock for my final moments of freedom. It was heart-wrenching to see all the concerned and shocked faces. Sue held onto my hands. My darling sisters assured me they would have me out soon. All too quickly I was escorted back down to the cells, this time placed with the other prisoners. Convicted and sentenced, I was now part of the formal system.

Four stained, graffiti-filled walls, a vent and heavy bars with thick wire mesh and sand- and mud-clogged floors. All around me the harsh shouts of boisterous prisoners. I sat on the dirty step thinking of my children who needed me so badly, my beloved Sue who had given up a life abroad for me, my workers and their families who relied on me for support and my darling sisters who meant the world to me. I thought of how badly I wanted to give my children everything this world could offer. My mind flashed back to the time I borrowed a little money to buy a motorbike, so I could go to work as an apprentice and then the climb up the commercial ladder until I was able to buy my own aeroplane. I'd been making regular contributions to society as well, with donations to charities, old-age homes and orphanages. Who was going to fill that void? My reputation meant the world to me and rested squarely on the value of my word, which now all meant nothing. I have always accepted the consequences of my actions. I was not an angel by any means, but this was not fair.

I thought of those life-changing words again, 'It cannot be said that his aim and object was to kill the deceased.' So how could he convict me of murder? How did the judge see his way clear to say those words, and then convict me? His findings, correct or not, corresponded to a charge of culpable homicide or manslaughter. Much like the death resulting from a car accident caused by negligence. How could I get murder and Spike a US$10 fine?

We may as well not have bothered to go to court. I had been convicted entirely from the state outline even though nothing material alleged therein had been proved, and despite the fact that the chief state witness had been shown to be a despicable liar.

None of that mattered. With the conclusion of the court case and the drop of the gavel, life as I knew it would never be the same.

CHAPTER 15

Friends and Foes

From the time you enter prison, naked, you are government property. You have nothing, and you are in control of nothing. Everything you eat, drink, hear, say, read and write, is controlled.

Within ten days of arriving at Khami Maximum, I had a chest infection.

I had been on allergy tablets for 18 years. I suffered terribly from hay fever. Being out in the bush most of my working life, the pollen affected me badly. Whenever I didn't take my tablets, I'd get a runny nose, congested sinuses, then a sore throat and finally a chest infection. If I overtrained to keep fit or partied too hard, I'd get the same symptoms as a result.

But on entering prison, I was denied my tablets.

When you are government property, they tell you what you will take, not the other way around.

My chest infection was probably exacerbated by the filth, and the dust and germs being blown around the exercise yard. I completed a course of antibiotics and finally convinced the nurse that I needed allergy tablets daily. He allowed me only three weeks of pills, following which I developed a chest infection again. Eventually I was able to see the prison doctor, who visited once a fortnight. He was inundated with much more severe cases than mine, but he prescribed permanent allergy tablets for me. This was a blessing and significant help to my health issues that would escalate in later years.

When I arrived in prison on 3 April 2003, my notoriety preceded me. Headlines shouted: 'Bulawayo Businessman gets 15 years for Murder'. Having received considerable publicity in the national and international media was a double-edged sword. It was an advantage in a way because I would not be starting on the very lowest rung of the prison social system, but I was also a sought-after commodity and vulnerable to the slippery con men of Khami Maximum. I did not have to go to the senior prisoners; they came to me, but with their agendas.

Easter weekend was a couple of weeks away, and a select thieving mob within the prison knew of my wealth. There were no limits on the number of visitors, so my friends and family turned out in force and gave generously.

The humiliation was raw, and tears often flowed all around. I was extremely emotional and desperate to be back with them and to have my life back again. We stood across a table and were permitted to hold hands. It felt closer to freedom than I'd felt in weeks and being able to hold Sue's hand again was a blessing. She had sprayed her hands with her favourite perfume, which remained on my hands until the following day as I refused to wash it off. The yearning to be just a little closer to what I had left behind was gut wrenching.

The groceries, cigarettes, food, and drinks came in loads: large plastic bags one after the other. I was overwhelmed by emotion and relied on my new 'friend' Goodmore, to help me handle all my gifts.

While I spoke to my visitors, Goodmore would carry the bags up to our cell. In return I gave him a whole cooked chicken, two generous portions of chips, several drinks, cigarettes, sweets, biscuits and more as I trusted him; he was my prison guide.

I learned over the next few days that my trust had been sadly misplaced and Goodmore was stealing from me regularly. I found out that for every four to five bags that went to my cell, one would disappear amongst the thieves. When I confronted Goodmore, he suddenly changed cells and pretended to be sick, so he could remain in his cell, offering to look after my groceries. Being naive and trusting, I gave him another chance. The following night there was an organised casino amongst the mob in his new cell. He gambled away 203 packs of 20 Madison cigarettes and my groceries took a big knock.

I have never been a smoker, but cigarettes, referred to as 'smokes', were currency in prison; they were used to buy anything from extra food from the kitchen staff to extra blankets, and repairs to clothes by secret tailors. (We even used cigarettes to purchase players for our soccer teams – but that would come much later.) For this reason, cigarettes were among the things my friends and family brought. But when I complained about the theft, the authorities just smiled at my complaints as if to say, 'Welcome, "wet ears"!'

I remember my first evening on a cement floor; my hip bones burnt from the pressure and my shoulders ached within minutes. Within a few months, my hips had bruised black rings like hard leather and my shoulders throbbed from sleeping on cold concrete. The other guys seemed to be used to sleeping on the floor and would cover their heads with a blanket and fall asleep in no time.

A typical day included waking up at 5.30 a.m. rolling blankets and placing them neatly in your 33-cm space against the wall. There was a unique way to roll the blankets and then fold the ends that locked together, which stopped them from unrolling. Much like rolled beef ready for roasting. (What a thought that was back then!) I was quite impressed by how the prisoners did it, and I often practised often (rather than often practised) until I got it perfect.

Unlock was at 6 a.m. We sat in rows of four in our cell to be counted before being let out, leaving the prison 'staff' (who were designated senior prisoners) to sweep and clean the cell. I would head for the outside tap avoiding the urine spillage and rush of 1,000 bodies. It was not permitted to defecate in the cells. The toilets in the cells were used for urinating, and to wash clothes, unless it was an emergency. I would clean my teeth at the tap, wash up and wait outside until staff had cleaned ablutions and swept cells and the hall, which took about two hours.

Around 8 a.m. came the time to eat porridge, when it was available. Lunch was at 11 a.m. *Sadza* and relish (boiled cabbage) were carried to the entrance of the yard in 100-litre black plastic dustbins. Eight *sadza* and two relish bins were dished out with a plastic plate and a large spoon for 1,000 people; this was a very tiring hour-and-a-half of exercise for the prisoners dishing out the food.

The time before dinner at 2 p.m. we sometimes played soccer, or I just walked and talked to friends for hour after hour. Lock-up was at 3 p.m. I did not know it then, but these were good days regarding the amount of time we had outside our cells.

Prisoners did all the dishing up of food, and most of those who dished up were connected to a gang. When a new young inmate came to prison, depending on which township he came from, he was assigned to that township's gang. The senior homosexual mob would always meet to discuss which new intakes would go to which gangs' men. Then, as the new intake approached the guy dishing up the food, a signal was given, and the new intake would only receive half the normal ration of food. After passing the food bins, he would then be approached by his assigned gang 'man' and would be offered more food and better blankets if he became the man's 'wife'. Life for that new intake would become more impossible by the day until he gave in and became a 'wife'. It was repeated regularly with every member, and as the 'wives' grew older, they would take on 'wives' too, and such was prison life for 90 per cent of youngsters entering Khami Max. The 'wives' would get all the privileges that the 'man' benefitted from, like nice blankets, plenty of food if the 'man' was staff, any soap or toilet paper the 'man' won from gambling (which was rife), and in return the 'man' would have his pleasures with the 'wife' and any groceries brought by the 'wife's' visitors. They were extremely affectionate too, caring for each other like a married couple; grooming and massaging often took place openly. The guards appeared to be quite aware of all this. If the 'man' was 'staff', they would turn a blind eye, but they would thrash any others caught practising any sexual activity.

CHAPTER 16

Prison Ingenuity

The reception officer who dealt with handing out clothes would visit the hall and exercise yard regularly, and if he saw you with different clothes on from the ones that he had allocated to you, you were stripped immediately, leaving you naked to run off and find a blanket if you did not have your original garment.

Obviously, the more you washed your clothes, the longer they lasted. Old clothes were taken away as prisoners would sell their new clothes for 'smokes' and keep wearing worn-out rags. When someone in tatters was called to visitors, he was made to exchange clothes for newer-looking ones from a friend quickly, so the visitors would not see how terrible things were in jail. Some were quite meticulous about cleanliness and lice in their clothes, so it was always a drama if a dirty, rough-looking inmate was told to take some clean prisoner's clothes.

When clothes needed alterations or repair work after they had been torn while washing or playing soccer, there were certain guys secretly used for this task. Prisoners were forbidden to work on repairing garments, but there was also no repair facility provided. Tailors would operate covertly and to secure their services smokes were the legal tender.

Ironically, the guards would have tailor work done often; then, when someone was caught sewing, the same guard would beat the tailor mercilessly.

Illegal pockets inside shorts by the crotch were essential. I used to hide my shortened toothbrush in the tunnel of the drawstring, but the paste had to go into a small secret pocket that was expertly sewn by the tailors. This was because I didn't trust anyone with these items and everyone who had toothbrushes or paste did the same. The needles they used were made from sharpened wire into which a groove was cut with a smuggled razor blade. They would push the needle through the material and then retrieve the thread with the hook. Most sewing took place at about 2 a.m. when the guards were usually sleeping. Should they be caught, however, the beatings for having needles, or a razor blade, were horrendous.

We had no basins or taps in the cells, and with only one set of clothing being allowed at any one time, we had to wash our clothes in the cell toilets at night wearing a blanket. And the toilets never lost that faeces smell, no matter how often we washed our clothes in there.

It was a degrading exercise. The cell toilet would be blocked with a pair of shorts or a shirt and filled to use as a washing facility. Guys would get together usually in groups of four and take turns to wash their clothes. The washer would wrap a blanket around himself, then push the old-fashioned toilet flushing lever in to let water flow. It was so old and worn that you had to push it in hard, and the water only dribbled in slowly. Once the bowl filled up, the washer would wet all the clothes in there, line the cement block with other clothes to be washed (so he didn't spill onto people sleeping against the cement block), then hand-wash each garment on top of the cement block surrounding the bowl. Once he had washed them all and removed as much soap as he could, he would pull the plug, wash that, plug the bowl again, fill it and rinse all the clothes.

Then the clothes were hung to dry on the walls with smuggled staples from a magazine or exercise book, to dry by the next morning. The walls were constructed using cement poured into reinforced moulds; when that dried it would leave tiny bubbles into which the staples were hooked. At about 5 a.m. the slightly damp clothes would be placed on the cleanly swept concrete floor, one garment at a time, and ironed by applying several hard strokes with a prison-made sponge. Then they were folded while being stroked with each fold, leaving them creaseless and stiff.

Finally, we would place a hand towel over the pile of folded clothes and stamp on it hard many times with the heels of our bare feet until they emerged neatly 'ironed'. They were then opened gently and hung again to dry completely.

The sponge was made by buying a sack from the kitchen staff and plaiting the strands into a rope the thickness of a pencil, which was then folded in figures of '8' about 7 cm from top to bottom, multiple times. Then the centres of the '8s' would be tied together, to form bunched up '8s' in a line up to 50 cm long. Once complete, we cut the outside of all the '8s' and ruffled the ends, which would untwist and become fluffy. This formed an amazingly effective round sponge that looked like a long worm.

Every time I did the washing, I ended up rubbing the skin off the side of my knuckles which always got infected and only added to the feeling of clothes not being completely clean after washing. Bending over the toilet hammered my lower back too. Washing clothes was one of the despised chores, but was essential to retaining your dignity in there.

Many of life's habits become deeply aggravated in prison where restrictions occur. I noticed that the most evident were the craving people had for cigarettes and the desperate measures they would pursue to satisfy that craving. The allocation of a packet of ten cigarettes per prisoner weekly was a prison regulation that was discontinued in the '90s.

Although smokes were currency and valuable in prison, matches never carried the same value as they were forbidden, but there were other effective methods to light cigarettes available.

A roll of toilet paper and a bar of unperfumed soap a month (when all was normal) were our only toiletries issued by the prison. Toilet paper became valuable only because it was used to light cigarettes by plaiting three long tightly rolled strips into a rope and lighting one side. The paper-rope was stuck at one end to a wall with *sadza* and would smoulder for hours allowing guys to light smokes randomly.

Another method was to take two squares of toilet paper lying on top of each other, then roll all four corners several times causing them to tighten, leaving the centre loose. This formed a cup shape. In the centre of the cup, they would place tiny fluffy pieces of broken up toilet paper until a tennis ball sized mound was formed. With their fingers they compressed the fluffy tissue a bit while rolling the corners more, to create a pouch in a cup shape, holding the fluffy tissue.

The lights in the cells were about 2.5 m to 3 m high and uncovered. One guy would stand hunched over holding the concrete wall, while another climbed onto his back and balanced the cup-shaped toilet paper on top of the bare light. Within three minutes the tissue was smouldering, and the smokers began lighting cigarettes. For maximum benefit, all would smoke together.

The light bulbs, however, became blackened by this process. So before unlock on most mornings blackened bulbs were removed, and it was spit and polish until they were spotless again. All the cell occupants were beaten under the feet if a guard discovered a blackened bulb. This offence usually cost five lashings under each foot.

In single cells or solitary confinement, the cells were a metre wide. Inmates would stand between the walls, make a small jump and wedge their legs and arms apart against each wall, hopping three metres upwards until they reached the light, to carry out the same process.

The other method of lighting cigarettes was with *skwerekweres*. Old surgical blades or wire were bought from the prison hospital staff, although if found with one it resulted in a terrible beating. These blades or wire were bound with pieces of surgical-rubber glove (also purchased from hospital staff with smokes) to one end of an old toothbrush, protruding about a centimetre. Then pieces of old clothing were bought from prisoners who worked in admin and had access to extra clothing and burnt until black but not entirely ash. While burning, the clothes were quickly shoved into an empty shoe-polish tin and the lid closed to smother it. (The tins were also bought from guards in return for smokes.) Once cold, the burnt cloth inside was compressed to form a fluffy mat. The toothbrush, with the surgical blade or wire protruding from one end, was used to strike a concrete wall with the polish tin open, ready to catch any sparks flying off. The pros would make one strike only, leaving a spark glowing in the fluff of cloth in the polish tin to light smokes, causing little attention.

Those that were learning often got caught, as it makes a distinct sound that the guards pick up instantly. Some guards were very understanding and turned a blind eye.

When 'tame' guards were on duty all burning of cloth and preparations for their *skwerekweres* were done, as the burning of anything or being caught using a *skwerekwere* resulted in an immediate beating. Pouches were sewn on the inside of their shorts or trousers to carry their *skwerekweres*.

The big drama was hiding these contraptions during searches. Inmates very seldom took them into cells during lock-up for the evening as searches were always done first thing in the mornings before unlock, about once a month but not in any routine. They would sometimes have two searches within two days.

After lock-up at 3 p.m. every day, the guards would sleep outside in the shade or guardhouse but seldom entered the hall again. Matches were prohibited in cells as we were not trusted in any way and could set the prison alight. They were, however, always possessed by a few. The single cells on the ground floor were in rows on either side of the hall and faced each other about eight metres apart. The only way to pass matches from cell to cell was by tying a string (made from plaited polystyrene sack threads bought from kitchen staff) about ten metres long, to a ruler. The ruler was then flicked under the solid wooden door across the hallway under the opposite cell's door. Then the matches would be tied to the string and transferred to the other cell. If your neighbour needed matches, they had to go to the cell opposite, then back to the cell alongside.

CHAPTER 17

Dumusani and Dregga

You'd always have to watch your back for conniving prisoners and guards with agendas to make your life hell. Prison life was all they knew, and they resented those that made the best of it.

But there were good guys too. Friends meant everything to me in prison – both the lifelong ones outside who brought me much needed rations, and the new ones I met inside.

After my nightmare with Goodmore, Dumusani approached me to take care of my belongings. It was a sought-after position, since the guys were paid with decent food and cigarettes, which weren't available unless you had regular visitors.

Dumi was in his early 30s, always appeared happy and had a fantastic voice. He once worked for Dave Bennett, a close school friend of mine with whom I had played several national rugby tests and who was also in the safari industry. Dumi had been convicted for 'borrowing' a taxi. The taxi driver had walked across the road, leaving his car open with the keys in the ignition. Dumi headed for the Plumtree border with enthusiasm, until being confronted at a police roadblock five kilometres before the town of Marula. He made a run for cover, but the flying bullets changed his mind quickly, and he surrendered uninjured.

His sense of humour helped lift my spirits often. He would teach me Ndebele songs endlessly too, which I still remember clearly. He had some strange remedies though. Whenever he felt ill, he would drink a five-litre container of water within ten minutes, leaving his stomach bulging, until he forced his finger down his throat repeatedly and vomited it all up. It appeared to work for him, although he had to do it about once a fortnight.

The bad boy of the prison was Dregga. He tolerated no nonsense from prisoners or guards. As soon as I met him, we became friends. He was a convicted armed robber, a very senior prisoner nationally, and widely feared. We spoke for hours every day. What amazed me was his intelligence and likable manner. He wasn't only smart, full of character, and presentable but also played the only battered old guitar in prison and sang beautifully. I asked him what made him turn to criminality. He said it started as a game with petty theft because he was bored, and it got into his blood. With time, he became the 'King' and an idol to many of the younger criminals. He said he would never consider another life.

One of Dregga's daily rituals that made me warm to him was that he would bring me a one-litre jug of tea from the kitchen every morning, with sugar and milk. The guards feared him, so he did what he wanted within the maximum security confines.

From him I learned some insider facts about professional robbery. Such as, they never did a robbery without in-depth homework, and domestic workers were an essential part of a house robbery. For $100 they would get invaluable information on where a household's money was, where guns were kept, what bedtimes were and when the house would be locked up. They always watched a home for days, sometimes weeks before a hit, working out movements and the best time to strike. They would even have the dogs locked up.

Bank robberies involved bank security, a bank teller, usually the assistant bank manager, and even the bank insurance broker, all on the payroll. And of course, police, prosecutors and magistrates. I discovered over the years that all the severe trouble in prison was related to the armed robbers. They were smart, organised, and very dangerous.

After months of doing nothing but listening and learning how to survive, Dregga invited me to team up with him in a gym routine. I was not sleeping much due to the overcrowding, noise, and lice, but after a heavy workout session and reading until late into the night, I found sleeping easier.

Dregga and I would usually work out after breakfast. He would walk straight in front of all the inmates and take our breakfast rations; everyone else had to sit in rows of ten, in a separate tarred courtyard and take their rations one row at a time from a hatchway in the kitchen. Dregga was my saviour in that regard. For everyone else, feeding took over an hour, but this gave us plenty of time to exercise.

Because I stood my ground on several occasions, I slowly climbed the social order. My first benefit was moving to the corner of my cell where I only had one person, Dumi, breathing over me throughout the night. I never got used to having my personal space invaded. Although 78 per cell was average, sometimes more were added. One night we were 110 in a '16-man' cell; guys slept sitting up in a line one behind the other.

CHAPTER 18

Chaka, Zulu and Munya

Another character I became friendly with was Chaka. He was tall, wiry, and tough as nails, with a fantastic sense of humour and a huge smile of widely spaced teeth. He had been in and out of prison all his life and smoked like a train. I would often give him smokes for which he was always extremely grateful. We would walk up and down the length of one exercise-yard wall for hours daily, talking mostly about our lives. I've always been an extrovert and loved people and company. Relationships like the ones with Dregga, Chaka, and Dumi were deeply therapeutic for me, and I didn't spare my material possessions to retain these contacts. They kept my mind away from the pain of what I'd left behind. There were many moments when I would get furious, bitter, revengeful and down in there, thinking about how the authorities had manipulated the facts of my case to get me incarcerated. I would discuss it often with my new friends, but they were guilty so didn't harbour the same resentment that I did.

I helped as many as I could financially, with bail or compensation, after realising so many were decent guys who merely got lost to a life of crime in their youth. Chaka's criminal history started as a kid living with his grandmother. He was from the town of Gwanda close to where I am from and worked for Peter (Bobo) Gibbons, a great mate of mine. Housebreaking was his game, and he'd spent two heavy sentences already, with nine years to go. He had nothing outside of prison and said his only knowledge was criminal activity. For such a pleasant guy to be around, it was hard to understand.

The thieves in prison (mainly housebreaking convicts, hijackers, and armed robbers) all seemed to stick together. They were a different bunch; always scheming and distant. Few ever looked you in the eye. Two of them that I came to know very well and grew to like were Zulu and Munyaradzi. In our cramped cell they were great company, and helped pass the time with their humour and friendly personalities. Zulu was from a wealthy, prominent family and was extremely well spoken. He grew up with his aunt and became a petty thief after school. Eventually, he fell foul of the law and got a jail sentence. His dad owned several hundred head of cattle, butcheries, stores and hammer mills for grinding maize. Zulu was a habitual thief. He had spent most of his adult life in prison, and his dad had washed his hands of him. All his offences were housebreaking, and even in prison, he had been beaten regularly for stealing. He was of medium height with quite broad, slightly hunched, shoulders. He was skinny, had a deep smoker's voice and was also an excellent soccer player. He would tell me often of his younger years and achievements at school, but would always get tearful when he mentioned his dad. His father never watched a single soccer match he played at school or acknowledged any of his achievements and often favoured his siblings. His brothers all had successful careers and drove flashy cars. I pleaded with him regularly to write to his dad and tell him all he was telling me about his feelings concerning the past, and about how much he loved him. One day I got him to sit down, and we wrote a long letter together during which he cried often.

While I was walking with Chaka about six weeks later, Zulu ran up and said he needed to talk to me. We went up to our cell, and he opened a letter from his dad. He cried and cried as he read it. His dad had forgiven him and was seeing a lawyer that week to apply for an appeal for him.

His court date was granted and set in 2004. It was a particular moment of accomplishment, and that was a feeling I missed so profoundly in there. Zulu was a good man with a warm heart that lost his way as a child. Sadly, he died, in 2004, of starvation. I had already been transferred by then, so I don't know if he ever got to see his father again.

Another great character who brought me endless pleasure and often had me in stitches with laughter was Munyaradzi, commonly known as Munya. He was also short with skinny little legs, broad, muscular shoulders and a big chest that balanced an oversized head and bulging eyeballs that could swivel humorously in all directions – he was a total comic. He played the old battered three-string guitar and sang country music, which I love. I would plead with him regularly to play for me and would always have to pay him a smoke or two first. He had written many songs, which he had in an exercise book, and said he wanted to approach a recording company, but if they didn't accept him then he'd continue with housebreaking. He was from Victoria Falls and was a habitual thief, like Zulu. He had served two previous sentences and was due for release within 18 months. Because of his criminal record and having escaped once from a farm prison, he had to serve his entire time in maximum security.

The most fun with Munya was the physical side. He would always take me on, punching me in the chest and shoulders and then darting away. His huge eyes, deep frown, and rasping voice had me laughing constantly. One of the many incidents I recall with him was while exercising in my cell; he would get jealous of my time with other guys and start throwing bundles of blankets at me. The prisoners' tightly wrapped blankets lined the walls of the cells. When a bundle hit you, it was quite painful, and Munya would throw one with a loud, funny comment and take off out the cell with me after him for about three or four steps. Then I timed it perfectly, and as he took off, I threw a bundle leading him by a metre or two. As he passed the cement block of a toilet, it connected him on the head taking him off balance into the toilet with a sound like he had just been shot. We laughed and laughed with tears streaming; he was such a show-off, you couldn't help but laugh when around him. I never found out what happened to Munya in later years despite asking after him often.

CHAPTER 19

Strength

After Dregga left, I continued exercising. The other prisoners quickly warned me that it was not allowed, as guards would accuse me of trying to get stronger in order to overpower them. I told them that it was not against the law and I intended to continue. Within ten minutes, five guards came into my cell; one had three stars, a high-ranking commissioned officer, so they were not taking this lightly. They asked me what I was doing. I politely explained that I was exercising to keep fit and release stress. They said doing 'gym' was not allowed. I pleaded as persuasively as possible to just be allowed to do a few gym exercises with water bottles as weights. They blankly refused me permission, so I told them to go and tell the OIC that I refused to stop doing gym. I continued my gym routine with no further problems and soon had a gym session going with up to eight guys at a time. Others could join me, but nobody else was allowed to do gym exercises.

It showed that these guards and officers would come up with all kinds of rules to make our time as uncomfortable as possible but backed down to anyone who stood up to them.

In a way, my survival was linked to physical strength too, which I needed to maintain. Weaklings were easily abused, and I had to protect myself often. One of the more aggressive sexual predators was a guy by the name of Gasela who was one of the 'main men' in prison and was widely feared as well. I could see early on that I was probably going to have a problem with him as he made a few not so subtle approaches and it was apparent he was testing me to see how far he could go. I rebuffed him and tried to signal that he should keep his distance, but when he came at me in the hall and touched my backside purposefully, I warned him not to do that again. With everyone looking on and knowing what was unfolding I knew there was trouble coming. He swaggered away laughing, and while I hoped for the best, I was pretty sure I had not seen the last of him.

Not long after that, he touched me again. This time, he was escorted by two of his cohorts right outside his cell. They stood there smirking at me. I realised this was a decisive moment and that I had to act. I let rip with everything I had and connected him perfectly with a punch to the jaw that poleaxed him. His eyes glazed over, his legs buckled, and he crumpled to the floor.

This was much to the consternation of his escorts who had not foreseen this outcome and ran like hell. Word of that punch spread fast, and I was not interfered with again while at Khami.

There were several soccer teams, and I soon had my team, which ended up winning the tightly contested and enthusiastically supported league. Players were paid after each game and sold between clubs for smokes. No footwear was allowed, so feet were bound with strips of a blanket as the soil we played on was extremely hard and rough. Because I was a rugby player, I was the goalkeeper. It helped pass the time and kept my mind off the painful thoughts of what I had left behind.

STRENGTH

The pain of not being able to see my children seldom left me all week, but Friday afternoons were particularly tough. Only recently they had been fun-filled with friends and family as we prepared for the weekend's excursions: waterskiing, fishing or visiting one of my safari camps.

CHAPTER 20

Inside Out

As soon as my murder conviction made front-page headlines, all the banks called in my overdrafts. A quick, well-supported auction was arranged, and several vehicles, boats, and spare machinery were sold. This covered all my debts and left a significant amount over. But I was mostly helpless, and, strangely, I felt a measure of relief.

I'd been running five companies when incarcerated, and distinctly remember lying in my cell on my first evening thinking, 'This isn't so bad with no business worries whatsoever, they can have all that stress now.' Everything beyond the prison walls was out of my control, and there was little I could achieve by agonising over the successes or failures of my businesses. It made me think of how I had become lost in 'my' world, trying to build 'my' empire, neglecting the small everyday little things that I so badly missed in prison – a soft bed with fluffy comfortable pillows, a steaming hot full-to-the-brim bath, but, most of all, a warm, loving, spontaneous cuddle with my wife or children.

Lying on that cold concrete floor on my first night, I swore to myself that I would never again get lost in trying to achieve more and more instead of enjoying the journey. 'Nothing ever seemed to be enough,' I thought to myself.

While I was trying to survive, my fiancée Sue was thrown into a different situation trying to keep my businesses afloat, while doing what she could to support me and secure my release. Everyone she saw asked after me. Everything she did and everywhere she went, there were constant reminders of her terrible loss. She began losing a serious amount of weight, which she couldn't afford.

My precious children, my son Dusty, only 18 at the time, and my 16-year-old daughter Sandy, were plunged into a different whirlwind. Suddenly their dad was a convicted murderer. Friends that had enjoyed many a weekend at our home began distancing themselves, and they were ostracised at school by pupils and teachers alike. Their world had been turned upside down.

Three weeks in I had an offer from someone to start smuggling letters to Sue. I was feeling so desperately alone, pining for her and my children, and the life I had lost, that I accepted.

Paul was a slippery character, with a hunched back and bulging eyes, but he spoke perfect English and was well educated, and soon I took him into my confidence. He had been convicted of sabotage by a military court and handed a heavy sentence. The stories of his exploits involved information that I did not want to be made aware of for fear of getting into further trouble with the authorities, but I felt he was my only line of contact to Sue and my children, and I was desperate for that.

Being the cunning criminal that he was, Paul would never let me meet the guard that was smuggling for me. Furthermore, letters had to be very secretly written, as all writing required authorisation by the censor's officer (CO) and was only permitted on prison-stamped government paper.

Hi Dad

Hope you well? I'm great, working really hard. Just got off our mid-term break. Thank you so much for the money by the way it is really helping. Heard you had a bit of trouble there, hope it all works out.

Been thinking about you so much. Miss you like crazy. Can't wait for you to come out. I miss home so much wish we could just stay there, life in the world is not as great as I thought. It's very too lonely, people aren't as nice as Zimbabweans.

Can't believe that Eugene Mercuri got shot, shame his girls are devasted. I feel so bad for them.

Can't believe the whole family is spread out so much. Shel and Debs are living in Perth, Rob and Ed are in Mauritious, Lyn and Bev are in Harare, Sandy is in Durban and I'm here. Really want to be all together again.

Once a month, all prisoners were permitted to write letters all at the same time and no longer than two pages. I had no option at the time but to trust Paul and handed letters over every Tuesday and Thursday for dispatch. He would deliver replies and smokes from Sue after every run. I gave him half the smokes each time, usually two packs of 20. By that time, I had made friends I hoped I could trust, and I wrote

School is going really well. Getting good
grades all between 60-90 so not bad.
Just getting up at 5 to shower and get to
the kitchen to make breakfast is a bit of a
bitch. It's been snowing so so hard here, it's
like a metre deep now. Went snow boarding
nearly killed myself, is not at all like wake-
boarding. I still prefer water sports though.
Better go need to get some sleep or I'll never
wake up.

Love you with all my heart.

Dog

LEFT & ABOVE Letter from Dusty

letters in my cell at night. Should they search, I figured I
would flush them all down the toilet.

The runner, a guard, had Sue's number and she would
be called to meet at remote backstreet places in the city
at all hours of the night or early mornings. She would
receive my letters and hand over letters from her, Dusty,
and Sandy, along with smokes and a cash payment which

Hey Dad my Goony goon goon,

I am so much happier now that I have seen that you are ok and healthy and most importantly happy. Chukurubi looks much better than Khami, it looks more like a museum than a prison hee hee.

I hope you got all the food we brought you. They didn't let all of it in, like the Caminbear cheese and the biltong and dry wors stix, we even brought you different types of rolls like whole wheat, plain, nutty, all kinds and Aunty Lyn and I chose them. I chose your chicken, it had to be the one with the BIGGEST tail hee hee. But they wouldn't let it in. Remember how we always fought over the tail ha ha ha, you always won though. Sue knows me well now 'cause whenever we have roast chicken, she puts the tail aside for me. But don't think when you come home I will be nice and give you the tail, NO WAYS the war is on hee hee. I hope you like the fruit I picked for you, I tried to look for peaches but they didn't have any and the bananas were not ripe at all.

That glass that we had to talk through was hectic hey but I am so glad I got to hear your voice, we waited about four hours to see you but it was definitely worth it. I would do it every day if I could. There was so much I wanted to say but I am so happy at the time my mind just focuses on you and how you look and the way you move your hands when you talk and how your eyes light up, but most of all your smile I love that smile and laugh. I just remembered something, do you still point your feet on the balls of your feet when you are shitting haha?

I sprayed so much perfume on myself it was Poison Hypnotic 'cause Aunty Lyn said you would be able to smell it on the stuff we sent in, did you? School starts again soon, I am really not looking forward to it but it is better than sitting around here. Sue gets back Tuesday, can't wait I am missing her a lot but not as much as I miss you goony. She has had an awesome time and really relaxed which I think has done the world of good for her. She definitely needed a holiday, but I am sure you were on her mind constantly. She went to watch the rugby. I watched on TV, and the amount of people that were in the stadiums was unbelievable. There was not one seat visible, and you know how big those stadiums are. Last weekend's game was really good. It was South vs New Zealand, South played brilliantly, but they were all over the place with the ball. The score was 40-26 to South, man of the match was Marius Joubert. This weekend was even better, a real nail-biting match. In the first half, South kept dropping the ball, it was like a flu virus and the score was 7-0 to Australia. The second half South woke up and played like stars, especially Percy Montgomery. He was always on the ball, tackling, really on form. The score was tight, Percy's conversions were poor in the beginning but he got his kick back in the second half. The score was 23-17 to South. Australia almost scored in the last 30 seconds of the game, it was really exciting. Man of the match was Victor Matfield. I should have taped it for you but I will look for the repeats and try to tape those. Sue said it's like a giant beer fest going to a game like that. How awesome that must be, but we will see what it's like next year, hey.

was equivalent to about five per cent of the guard's salary. Unsurprisingly, Paul started wanting more and more. In prison, he wanted half the food I would get from my fortnightly visits and requested assistance for his wife in town.

Everybody sends their love, Kevin, Ryan Whytoff - Pumba says I must tell you Pumba is thinking of you and still wishes you the best of days in life at the moment and please come home soon 'cause fun is just not fun without you.

I have been thinking of Granny Peta and Grandad a lot lately. I wish they were still here. I know how proud Grandad would have been of you for the strength and positiveness you have. But mostly, for the person you have become, and a person people respect so much. He would be as proud of you as I am.

When you come home we must go to gym and stuff so I can get these Kgs off me, k? Geoff put me on the pill to regulate my periods, but it has made me put on three kgs, and now I am back to the weight I was before I started my diet, and it was going so well. The bloody bugger, so I am going off it and not taking it anymore 'cause I don't have to take it for any other reason.

I can't wait for you to come home and walk around the garden with me, and look at our bamboo trees and play with Wellington in the pool. It's gonna be so cool.

I miss you so much, Dad, but now that I know you are safe and ok I feel a lot better but still miss you so so so so so much. I love you more than anyone in the whole world, you my best friend Dad, stay strong and positive 'cause I am for you.

Love always and big hugs and kisses
Your little Goony

Always Sands
I Love you xxxxx

LEFT & ABOVE Letter from Sandy

As the weeks passed, I began receiving other offers to smuggle and on occasion I secretly bypassed Paul. After discovering who I was using, Paul snitched and told security when my next scheduled delivery was and who the runner was. They searched the guard and found four letters on him: one from Dusty, one from Sandy and two from Sue. Under pressure, instead of trying to convince them this was a one-off assignment, he told them how often he had delivered and how much he was being paid each time. They gave me a harsh warning and fired the guard. My lawyer was called in to reprimand me and explain the seriousness of my offence.

Sue was banned from visiting me until further notice.

Not being able to see someone you were head over heels in love with and had shared every living moment with for the last five years was a crushing setback.

After six weeks, thank God, this prohibition was lifted. Having that lifeline to my world cut was a stifling development, and I became extremely depressed for a while, but soon I met another guard who took pity on me. Officer Kachingwe was a fantastic, big powerful man, he was afraid of nobody and took me under his wing. Bless him, he moved letters for me until I left Khami. Without that correspondence, I'm not sure what I would have done.

CHAPTER 21

Punishment

I saw little or no evidence of any genuine programme to help reform criminals and have them leave the system better people than when they arrived. Most people left severely damaged by their experience, and few would have been able to make a success of life back in the 'outside' world.

At Khami Maximum Security, almost all the guards were from the Shona tribe, and most prisoners were from the Matabele tribe. The tribal hatred is still very evident between these two groups, even today. It was so bad that during my year in Khami Max nobody was even permitted to speak Ndebele, which is the native language of that area. If they heard you speaking Ndebele, it meant a vicious beating with their rubber batons.

Guards used 500-mm-long, 30-mm-thick, black rubber batons and sometimes a short rope attached to one end with a knot tied at the tip. Their cruelty and love of violence were shocking and terrifying.

Before entering the hall for lock-up at 3 p.m. we were made to pick up any trash and scraps of food off the dirt floor and stand in a long line. Anyone without a 'pass' (trash or *sadza*) was beaten several times across the back. At times, if they felt we were not lining up quick enough, they would walk down the line whipping every person across the back, in line or not, leaving huge welts. They were never without their batons, which they regularly swung in beating practice.

The guards showed obvious pleasure when beating prisoners, and this bothered me deeply. They would find any excuse to hit people and would argue about whose turn it was next to hand out a flogging. During a severe beating, they would even come from other halls or skip lunch; they would do anything to be part of the terrible brutality. When hungover or dealing with personal problems, they would take their frustrations out on prisoners by dishing out random beatings while reeking of alcohol.

Then there were the serious punishment beatings for stabbings, homosexuality, stealing, fighting, and the like. Prisoners were made to lie face down while lifting bare feet into the air. One guard would then beat the soles of the prisoners' feet as hard as they could swing their batons. The thud of the baton hitting feet and the screams of pain could be heard throughout the prison. The number of strokes depended on the seriousness of the offence. The smallest number was five, and it could go up to as many as 100 under each foot. The guards would exhaust themselves beating. Prisoners would crawl for days unable to walk from the swelling. Feet would swell so badly that they would ooze a thick dark fluid out from the toes and tops of their feet from blister-like sores.

If a prisoner did not lie still and take all his lashings, he was viciously attacked all over his body by guards standing around. Sometimes prisoners panicked, thinking they were not going to make it, and ran. The hysterical screaming and wailing coming from someone who believes he is being beaten to death, broken intermittently by the thumping sound of blows crunching flesh and bone, is a blood-curdling sound you never want to hear. It is burned forever into my memory.

Because homosexuality was a crime punishable by the courts, guards from the entire complex attacked offenders mercilessly. They would come by the dozen, wanting to join the frenzy of violent beatings like a pack of hyenas at a kill. It was terrible to watch. Beatings regularly left broken skin across the back, buttocks, and legs. After being beaten almost lifeless, those who were found guilty were sometimes made to roll in filthy pools of water left by leaking sewage pipes. This ended in huge welts becoming infected after a few days.

CHAPTER 22

Beware the Recruits

Any prisoner's nightmare was when the recruits for the Prison Service arrived. At Khami when they came for my first time, I remember it being recorded as the coldest day in half a century. It was around 11°C, windy and drizzling. First, they searched all the cells while everyone had to strip naked and walk into the hallways on each floor of the prison. One prisoner at a time was placed in front of a recruit. Each had to do three star-jumps. When it came to me, they would search my hair for hidden contraband as well. Then we were frog-marched in single file out into the freezing rain, completely naked. We stood there shivering while they trashed and broke everything in our cells. In the end, it looked like a hurricane had gone through the prison.

Then came the beatings. The hall-guards would teach the recruits how to beat. When the beatings started, because of instructions from high up, I was locked in a single cell, but I watched it all from the vent. The prisoners were made to lie on their stomachs in the cold, muddy pools with their feet in the air, while the recruits practised beating the soles of their feet for three hours. Thirty recruits beat the feet of 1,000 prisoners. They were shivering uncontrollably. Some suffered horrifically with their feet being totally numbed from the beatings. Those that complied and appeared humble only got five to ten under each foot. Just one is excruciatingly painful. The less compliant were beaten mercilessly. I remember one guy showing me how the thick skin under the heels of his feet had cracked from the beatings and blood was pouring through.

These recruits did not leave for three to four days and harassed us continually. When eye contact was made, we had to crouch down below their eye level as they approached. We then had to shout out our crime in detail. This would typically end with them accusing me of lying. What followed would be a, 'run and fetch me water' or 'polish my boots': anything to make us grovel. They came about three times a year and were always hell to be around.

With all the human rights abuses I was witnessing, and with the constant conflict with cruel guards, I sent a message to Sue asking to see my lawyer. When Jumbo arrived, I began explaining what I was witnessing and asked if he could bring me a copy of the prisoner's rights in Zimbabwe.

His answer totally floored me. 'Prisoners in Zimbabwe have no rights, Rusty. But if you are battling with anything, I can approach the officer-in-charge for you,' he said shrugging his shoulders.

When I explained that it was mostly about the treatment of other prisoners and the beatings, he advised me to stay out of trouble. He said to concentrate on going home and that we should not interfere with the running of the prison.

CHAPTER 23

Bail Denied

was in an unfamiliar environment trying to deal with my unimaginable nightmare. Initially, I was convinced this was going to end soon and I'd get bail pending appeal, so I didn't allow myself to get too angry or despondent, but that changed when my lawyer, Jumbo, came to see me again about four months after I was jailed.

I had asked Jumbo to apply to Prison HQ for me to receive a business visit every month, to try and have some control over my affairs at home. My request was rejected because the regulations stated that prisoners were not permitted to run a business from prison.

Up to this point, I was optimistic that I would soon get bail from the High Court, pending an appeal to the Supreme Court against conviction and sentence. Jumbo had come to inform me that the application he had presented to the High Court for bail pending appeal had been rejected.

It was a huge blow to my spirits. I remonstrated with him about what he was going to do next to secure my release, as I'd only come to him because he was supposed to be 'the man'. To my utter dismay, he was speechless. Looking at the floor while shaking his head, he said: 'Sorry Rusty, I didn't realise it was so complicated and would end like this, I'm so sorry.'

'You're sorry?' I said. 'I get ten years, and you say you're sorry!'

I felt like my world had just collapsed around me. He looked just as stressed, and I know his reputation took a knock from this outcome. I remember walking away crying shamelessly. As I passed the hall-in-charge (HIC), walking into the prison, he could see I was crying and asked if I was okay. I couldn't even answer him. I walked up to my cell, lonely, distraught and shattered.

That night I remember lying on the cold floor smelling the stink of warm, fetid breath and body odour and wondering where I had gone wrong. First, I thought, 'What have I done in my life that was so bad to deserve this?' and 'Am I not worthy of at least some justice?' Then I thought, 'Am I different to all these people in here? Are they just here to fill the gaps and do they feel this pain I am feeling?'

I relived the vivid memory of my quiet talk with Makore at the gate of Mike Shaw's house, when he asked me to replace the pots and pans that he said had been stolen by my staff. Now I asked myself if buying a few pots and pans would have saved me from this hell.

Then I thought, 'Maybe I have been put here to be protected, the country was in a political turmoil,' and that made me feel better anyway. My last slightly sobering thought was, 'Maybe I have been put here to make a difference one day?' I'd always told my children that everything in life happens for a reason. Now I had to accept that and walk my talk. I had no other option because it was too painful to think anything else.

I decided I needed a new lawyer and handed my appeal case to a prominent Harare lawyer. Jumbo agreed this was a promising idea as he was better connected. The next day during a visit, Sue informed me that the new lawyer had assured her that, for a substantial upfront payment, I would be out on bail pending appeal by November. Naively, I believed this would happen. I was not aware of how deep a political hole I was in.

CHAPTER 24

Immediate Family

Although my ancestry is European, my African roots go back a long way.

My maternal grandmother Phyllis was a Welsh nurse. She came to Rhodesia in 1933 and married Rowland Fuller, a farm manager in Matabeleland, two years later. Two children (David and Ann) were born before they moved to Sterkstroom in South Africa, where Peta (my mother) was born in 1940 and Robin, and Colin followed. Because of their Welsh heritage, Ann and Peta were selected to hand flowers to Queen Elizabeth on her Royal Tour of South Africa in 1947.

Phyllis was a frontierswoman in the true sense. She was only five foot tall, but athletically built from hard work. When Rowland died in 1951, she loaded her mother and two youngest sons, Robin and Colin, into a Willys Jeep, and drove about 2,000 kilometres to Bulawayo. (David, Ann, and Peta stayed behind at boarding school and joined them the following year.)

It was quite a feat, driving through the harsh Karoo and game-rich Limpopo basin. In those days there was no highway, just dirt roads where boundary and cattle gates had to be opened and closed along the way. Malaria and tick-bite fever took their toll, too. I remember my gran telling me how, when passing any other car during those years, they would both stop and have a cup of tea on the roadside. It was a rare chance to socialise and catch up on any news.

My paternal great-grandfather was a Scotsman named John Guthrie who came to South Africa with a Scottish regiment to fight in the Boer War when he was 25 years old. Guthrie disapproved of the way the Boer women and children prisoners were being treated in the concentration camps set up by Lord Kitchener. He secretly arranged for a horse and rations, then snuck through the camps and released all the prisoners at midnight. Fearing court martial and execution, he absconded to Mozambique (then Portuguese East Africa) with the British in hot pursuit. Through Mozambique he made his way to what was then Southern Rhodesia. There he changed his name to Westland, to avoid detection by the British authorities, and worked as a ganger on the railway line between Bulawayo and Gwelo. He returned to South Africa and married Amelia Wenzler on 2 April 1907 at St Alban's Church in Cathcart. They farmed in Nancefield (now Soweto) outside Johannesburg for many years, during which time they had six children, including my grandmother Edith (Eddie).

One night around 1918, a gang known as the 'Amelitias' attacked while John was away. A naked intruder, covered in grease – a tactic used to avoid being apprehended – tried to get through a window in the house; Amelia killed him when she struck him over the head with a coal spade. Amelia had her six children with her at the time of the incident.

The family moved to Southern Rhodesia, where John became stationmaster of the Rhodesian Railways at West Nicholson in the Matabeleland province. Amelia had two more children, but the incident with the gang member caused her many mental health problems, and John took over care of his family when she was sent to an institution in South Africa. She eventually passed away in 1966.

The Labuschagnes French Huguenots – one of only 178 families in total – who settled in the Cape between 1688 and 1691. My grandfather, Ben Labuschagne, was a giant of a man. When his father died from blackwater fever (severe malaria) in 1913, seven-year-old Ben moved to Uitenhage with his mother and siblings. Ben and his brother Johnny went to live with their uncle, Carl Bikkers, and his wife Hester. The couple never had any children of their own, so Carl adopted Ben and Johnny. Already showing his stubbornness, my grandfather Ben refused to change his name to Bikkers, which upset his stepmother.

The family trekked by ox wagon up to West Nicholson in Southern Rhodesia in 1913, where they farmed cattle, chickens, and maize.

There were very few people living in the area at the time. The original settlers in West Nicholson were Walden Edwards, Charles and Jack Rogers, and Carl Bikkers. These three families ran their cattle over a range of roughly 500,000 acres.

After ten years, the British designated all land as crown land and sections were made available to purchase. Carl bought four farms, totalling 38,000 acres, near Tod's Hotel in the West Nicholson district. At this time the community was a mere handful of tough, hard-working folk.

In his teens, my Granddad Ben often frequented Gwanda pub on horseback about 45 km away. There, he repeatedly got into fist-fights – and usually ended up beating up the policemen who tried to calm him down. Old Man Carl would then have to bail him out of jail. This annoyed his stepmother intensely, and further strained their relationship.

West Nicholson grew, and as in many other agricultural communities throughout the country, a vibrant recreational facility was established. The community would come together to enjoy golf, tennis, cricket, gymkhanas and 'bioscope' (cinema). Countrywide you can find long-standing families with similar fascinating histories who, over generations, formed a family-like bond, which really grew out of the clubs.

My dad, Walter (Wally), was born in Gwanda on 14 November 1937. Powerfully built, charismatic and energetic, he was a great water polo and rugby player. He captured the heart of my lively, vivacious mother Peta – also an excellent sportswoman, excelling in tennis and representing the national schools' side in hockey.

After leaving school in 1955, my dad was given 100 head of cattle and Lucknow Farm by his grandfather, Carl. His 10,000 acres were part of the 38,000 acres Carl had purchased. Carl was suffering from a chronic condition at this time and his niece, Freda Straagen, came up from South Africa, ostensibly to nurse him. Freda's intentions would turn out not to be so pure; the story is that Jacob, a remarkably loyal servant who had trekked from the Cape with Carl in 1913, actually cared for him.

My father was away doing compulsory national service in the Rhodesian army when Carl died in 1956. His will never appeared, which meant that the entire estate was left to his wife, Hester.

A dispute arose over the ownership of the land, during which my dad opted to work for Jack Rogers on the next-door Tshabezi Ranch, to learn more about the cattle game. In his first year there, Hester died. The disappearance of Carl's will and Hester's extensive jewellery collection became the subject of much discussion in the district. Jacob swore that there was a will, that he saw it, and that the ranches were to be left to my grandfather Ben and father Walter. There was a firm belief that the old man's will and other valuables were locked in a built-in secret safe at the homestead, but it was never discovered.

As it turned out, the ranches were divided between Jack Bikkers, another adopted son, and the niece, Freda Straagen. This shattered my dad's dreams.

I was born on 2 November 1961. My brother Barry preceded me by 13 months and my sisters Beverly (Bev), and Lynnette (Lyn) followed three and four years later respectively. We were all born on Tshabezi Ranch in a happy, loving, pet-filled home. As a family we enjoyed the pleasures of fishing, hunting, and waterskiing over weekends with neighbours and friends. It was a natural way of life: no TVs, computers, mobile phones or crime.

Those happy years, during which I revelled in the bushveld, are still vividly etched into my memory. Barry preferred mechanics and was more content in the farm workshop. With my loving little sisters still too young to venture out, I spent my entire days in the bush with the young kids whose parents worked on the property.

My dad was doing well, expanding an irrigation scheme that grew hundreds of acres of maize and tomatoes. Then one cold winter's morning in 1970, we all awoke to a life-changing shock: 400 acres of ripe Roma tomatoes ready for harvest had frozen solid. It ruined us financially.

Within months we sold up. My dad started a new project, building water reservoirs to gravity-feed watering troughs, and constructing fence-lines through undeveloped land.

We lived a nomadic existence, staying in caravans and moving from section to section. At each stop, we set up beautiful basic camps in gorgeous unspoiled bushveld where we kids slept in sleeping bags by the campfire under the stars. My dad built us 'foofy slides' – an angled cable from a steep river bank with a handle attached to a pulley that we hung onto and raced down at speed into the sand. It was pure paradise for a bush-boy.

CHAPTER 25

School Days

I was an insecure six-year-old when Barry and I were sent to board at Milton Junior School in Bulawayo, 200 km away. All my happiness came to a halt. It was brutal. Matrons and masters were cruel bullies who seemed to enjoy seeing little kids hurting from their chastisement. I was terrified of them. Being late would result in a pinch or a punch on the arm or thigh, leaving bruises for days. I missed my mom and dad terribly and used to cry myself to sleep often with visions of my mom's last frantic wave, sobbing as she drove away in the old white Land Rover. There was little compassion from any of the staff, and I could only see my parents once during the three-month terms.

The bullying and beatings made me angry at the world and, craving attention, I started to misbehave. This brought regular thrashings and punches from the masters. I hated every moment of it.

School holidays were pure bliss. My parents accommodated my boisterous behaviour happily, and our house was open to any number of friends I chose to bring back for the vacations. With my passion for the bush, I was always gone at first light and seldom returned before dark. Somehow, a distance crept in between my dad and me and this troubled me. I badly wanted his love and attention.

He was a big personality, and physically imposing. I remember so well his tanned forearms and strong hands. His green eyes had a soft sparkle, his laugh was infectious, he loved people and parties, but had strong values and principles.

People gravitated towards him, and he was always available for some rough and tumble with us kids, but I struggled to get enough of his affection and attention. I didn't get to know him as well as I wanted to and would give anything to have a beer with my old man today.

All the young men hero-worshipped him., and I was no exception. Even so, my father had his own demons. When I recall my childhood days, what stands out most strikingly are the brutal beatings. I was naughty, make no mistake, but the beatings from my dad with a three-foot stick were horrific and terrifying.

They started when I was about four years old. I recall one instance when we were told that if we visited our neighbour's ranch house, about three kilometres away, we were absolutely not allowed to get a ride back to the house with the owner. My dad was a very jealous husband and did not want our neighbour close to my mom. While walking back home with Barry, the wealthy young neighbour who fancied my mom offered us a ride in the back of his truck. We explained that we were not allowed to get a lift with him, but he assured us he would tell my dad that he insisted, and it was his idea.

After his one-hour visit, I was on the lawn and heard my dad's loud voice calling Barry and me. He took Barry by the arm and started thrashing him. My immediate thought was that the neighbour had forgotten to tell my dad, so I took off into the evening sunset. They called for ages until darkness crept up. While I was sneaking from tree to tree closer to the house, my mom saw me and took me to have a bath. We were going to a Father Christmas kiddies party at the West Nicholson Club that night, and I was excited.

Then I heard him bellow, 'Did you find him?' My father stormed into the bathroom, grabbed me by the arm, hauled me off to the bedroom and beat me mercilessly.

Barry and I would always mess ourselves all over the place and have to clean it up after our beatings. From about ten years old, though, I don't recall being beaten again.

Despite our tight financial position, my dad made sure we spent two weeks annually on the Mozambique coast. From the age of six, we travelled to the sea with families from the West Nicholson district and surrounds. It was the highlight of our year.

In most cases, we would be the only tourists on those pristine, beautiful beaches that seemed to go on forever. With all us happy, bare-chested kids piled in the Land Rovers, those were heavenly times in a precious paradise.

Our closest family friends at that time were the Rochats, Darlows, and Stantons. Rocky Rochat, Poogie Darlow and my dad were mates at school and grew up in West Nicholson together. Poogie is my godfather, and his pranks and humour drew us kids close to him. Lin Stanton, my dad's cousin, was also his closest friend.

I was extremely fond of these three men and their wives, who had known and loved me all my life. Lin was a commanding presence, but he was also easy-going and down to earth. He took a deep interest in our welfare and happiness growing up. Their eldest son Raymond (nicknamed 'Bush') Stanton and Des Rochat (Rocky's son) were my best friends, and Dianne and Wayne Stanton were as close to me as siblings. Lin's wife, Maggie, treated me like a son.

I would depend heavily on that love with what was to come.

CHAPTER 26

Tragedy Strikes

n my last month at that loathed junior school, I was rest-ing after lunch in our dormitory when the matron on duty called me down. Her tone left me uneasy.

As I walked down the worn external staircase into the courtyard, furtive glances from a few masters further unset-tled me. I removed my blazer from the rack where they all hung, and distinctly remember having a keen sense that something was very wrong. Barry, who was now at Milton Senior School, burst into the narrow passage in front of me, pale and wide-eyed, yelling, 'Daddy's dead!'

It was as though someone had stuck a knife deep into my stomach. I tried not to believe it as I ran ahead of him out to the car park to find my mom sitting between my sobbing sisters in the back seat of Grandpa Ben's station wagon. She hugged me tightly, crying uncontrollably. Our world had collapsed.

It happened on the afternoon of 22 November 1973, near the banks of the Nuanetsi River, our favourite camp-ing site. My father was repairing the kingpin on the fifth wheel of an old, well-worn five-ton trailer. With all four wheels removed, he had the frame supported on 44-gal-lon drums while using a bottle jack on one side. The jack slipped, causing the trailer to fall and pin my dad, frog-like. His lower back took most of the impact, but one of his legs was crushed entirely by the fifth wheel. Dube, our wonderful family cook, was also trapped under the trailer, but he was uninjured. The frantic workers jacked the trailer up again, pulled Dube out, and as they were about to pull my dad out, the jack slipped, doing more damage than the initial fall. They eventually managed to remove him from under the trailer while another worker, Juta, ran back to camp for help. Fortunately, he found my mom and Robin Watson, who had just flown into camp in his private plane.

They found my dad in terrible pain but quite confident and physically intact, despite his leg being badly crushed below the knee. During the flight to Fort Victoria Hospital, he mentioned that his hips felt twice their usual size and he kept saying, 'Please don't let them cut my leg off.' In Fort Vic, two doctors performed an operation on my dad's back and apparently they were happy with the procedure. My dad had a good night up until the early hours of the morning, when he suddenly passed away from a thrombosis at 3 a.m.

The cremation service was packed with mourners, and I recall seeing Lin Stanton shedding tears for the first time. We returned to the camp to pack up the last evidence of a life I'd lost forever. The West Nicholson community was generous and kind. We had to sell off movable assets and people paid over market value to help us. Robin Watson generously put $1,000 into savings accounts for each of us children, only available to us when we turned 25. Other benefactors stepped in to pay our school fees.

Mom was offered a job at Rogers Bros store in West Nicholson with a large rent-free house. Despite all my mom's best efforts to keep me home, I missed the male company that only a father could provide. To fill the gap,

I started sharing my time between visits to the Stantons, Darlows, and Rochats.

My saint of a mom devoted her life to us children after my dad's death. She grew lonely without us in West Nicholson and, after two years, she took on a job as a matron at Evelyn High School in Bulawayo where my sisters were boarding, so she could be close to them and see us.

Poogie took my dad's death badly. He had been very close to my mom and dad long before they were married and did all he could to replace the life I'd lost. When I was 14, the Darlows took me on their family holiday to Ballito in South Africa and were more caring, considerate and fun to be around than I could ever have asked for.

While we were away we heard the freedom fighters had burnt their house down. We arrived back from our holiday to a sight of complete and utter devastation. The homestead was burnt to a crisp, and they had lost virtually everything they owned. This scenario repeated itself many times during the war. It had a profound impact on me; I could not understand why good people who cared for Africans and particularly their staff, were being attacked like that.

The Darlows moved to Ripple Creek Dam, on the Bubi River, where it was my responsibility to oversee the netting of fish for workers' rations. Every morning I would head off in the little boat and outboard motor with Nyembez, Poogie's right-hand man, and retrieve fish from the nets. Another one of my duties was to keep fish poachers from netting in the dam. (Little did I know that poaching would have such an impact on my later life!) I savoured the feeling of flying across the water. The birdlife was phenomenal and the game often visible on the shoreline. The farm workers' children used to fish below the spillway, and we enjoyed endless hours fishing in the deep pools below the wall trying to outdo each other with our catches.

Most of my school holidays were spent with the Rochats, to be with Des and close to the hunting, fishing and ranching lifestyle that I loved so dearly. Rocky, a tower of a man, was exceptionally powerful, athletic and had sharp blue eyes. His strength was the stuff of legend. He could load a 200-litre steel drum full of petrol onto the back of a Peugeot pick-up, single-handedly. His ratchet-like laugh was one of a kind. His wife Gill was a honey in every way to us. She and Rocky went out of their way to make us children as happy as possible.

Rocky was a notorious practical joker, and he soon became my new idol. He was someone I looked up to in awe and craved manly attention from, as I had done from my dad. He allowed Des and me the privilege of shooting two impala a week for workers' rations and he took us fishing regularly. He would always set us targets and goals. A favourite was only allowing us two rounds to shoot two impala or betting us we couldn't camp out in the bush with anything but a .22 rifle and the clothes we stood up in for two days. Thanks to him, I learned so much about the bush that would stand me in good stead later in life. But my world was about to be turned upside down again.

We were standing outside the West Nicholson clubhouse after Sunday afternoon tennis on a May day in 1977. Rocky was about to fly his newly acquired private plane back to Mkashi Ranch. I pleaded with him to let me go with him, but he wasn't yet licensed to fly passengers and had to refuse, much to my disappointment. The rest of us kids drove home together with Gill. This was during the war, so we travelled with care with the fighting creeping ever closer to the area.

After arriving at the ranch we began to worry; light was fading, and Rocky had not yet arrived. We were all straining our ears for the sound of the engine. At last light, we mingled in the large security gateway between the airstrip and hangar. A few people heard the distant drone of what sounded like a plane and a couple of faint thuds. A neighbouring couple had a year-old daughter who always raised her finger at the sound of the plane and did so that evening when some thought they heard it. After an hour John Tedford, the member in charge at West Nicholson police station, arrived with several other neighbours. They set off in an extended line with flashlights and farm workers and made a broad sweep in the direction that some had heard the plane. It was hours before they returned. Angus Drummond walked in through the kitchen door, met Gill in the passage and said, 'Gillie, I'm so sorry, it's all over, he's gone.'

Rocky had buzzed all the neighbouring ranch homesteads to check that they were all home safe before turning into the fading light to make for home. He used a mountain silhouette to help him navigate but flew too low and clipped a tall mopane tree. He ploughed down and was killed instantly.

Rocky had provided the platform upon which I had rebuilt my life and now all that came tumbling down. I was totally broken. Lost and confused, at 15 years old, not knowing what was coming next.

So I rebelled.

CHAPTER 27

Wild Ways

My mom bought a homely four-bedroom house on three acres in Bulawayo, that became home to five dogs, three cats, two horses, one goat and many of our tight-knit friends. But my wild ways, compounded by the wild spirit of war, boarding school, and outdoor exploits, gave her endless headaches. She was little over five foot tall, fit and tough, and walked faster than most men. She had a heart of pure gold and would wake every morning and skip into our rooms singing a silly tune to wake us for school. Very rarely did she allow events to get her down and invariably overflowed with energy and happiness. She had beautiful big eyes, perfect white teeth, and powerful thighs from playing hockey.

Regardless of our tight money situation growing up, she gave us everything she had to make us the people we are today. Sacrificing relationships, accommodating endless pets from monkeys to mongooses, she gave everything to make a home feel like home should. As rebellious as I was, she was always there, whether to fetch me from a hospital after an accident or to watch me play rugby. No matter what I did, she was always there to pick up the pieces. Later in life, when I became embroiled in building my own life and career, I forgot all that she had done, and know I should have done more during her last three years battling breast cancer. It's something I live with and regret daily that can never be changed. I'm not alone; many of us forget what our folks sacrificed for us in far tougher times.

Because I was emotionally shattered, I became reckless with relationships and broke many a tender heart. I wanted affection and love from girls, but I was not prepared to risk any more emotional pain, taking what I could but reluctant to give my heart away. Alcohol became a useful crutch, and I was branded a party animal. Like my grandfather before me, I got involved in too many bar-room brawls that I'm not proud of.

During the late 1970s, the ranches around Bulawayo were all abandoned because of the war. Almost every weekend during winter, we would go out and hunt impala, kudu, and reedbuck for meat. Dube was always in the mix, enjoying the meat left over from making biltong that he prepared so perfectly. I recall many happy memories of Dube, Greg Michelson and I drinking *Ngwebu* (African beer) in my mom's garage while she was at work. It always tasted better with half a kilogram of sugar added to the 20 litres. Once, we hid the container in my mom's boyfriend's pristine Model T Ford and, due to the fermentation during the night, it exploded.

We took one look at the mess in the morning and took off into the bush for the day until things had cooled down back home. These were some of the commonly occurring memories I recall from our privileged, carefree upbringing.

Although I partied every weekend and drank too much, I also trained extremely hard daily. Greg Michelson and I trained for first team water polo (which I captained) in summer, and in winter I always led the rugby fitness and training sessions. I excelled as a loose forward, which propelled me eventually to play rugby for my country.

Many of my closest friends – including Bush Stanton – attended Plumtree School on the Botswana border, and I was determined to join them there. By this time my brother Barry had left home to start a fitter and turner apprenticeship 100 km away, and my mom wanted me home. However, when I failed my M Levels, Plumtree agreed to have me repeat them there. I loved that year at Plumtree with Bush, and much to my delight, Greg followed, and we were placed in the same boarding hostel. I passed my exams, excelled in sport and made more special mates like Max Rosenfels and Brebs, who would become part of my life forever.

Although I loved the city social life, I never stopped missing the rawness of the bush and would hurry back to the ranches for special times with Des and Bush. We were inseparable and always armed and up for any action that came with war. Our weapons never left our sides, whether sleeping, showering or relaxing.

During our last few years as teenagers, it was every young man's dream to become a soldier and be part of the war. National Service was compulsory and looked at as a transition into manhood. Most of us bush-happy guys wanted to be part of the notorious Selous Scouts. They were a special-forces regiment of the Rhodesian Army named after the British hunter and explorer Frederick Selous. Their clandestine operations required tracking and survival skills, and the most rigorous recruiting process.

Whenever asked what my ambitions were, I'd always say I wanted to join the army and worry about a future after that. Many of our young friends were getting killed in the war so I thought I'd wait and see if I survived first.

CHAPTER 28

Lost in the Hills

One day during the war, in 1979, my uncle Lin and I were on our way to check on cattle dipping on a deserted ranch when a troop of baboons crossed the road. We were about 20 km from any habitation. The baboon population had exploded, and they were regarded as problem animals then, so I took off after them with a .270 rifle – no shoes, shirt, hat or water – at 7 a.m. The plunge dip was only one kilometre away, so I reasoned that I'd walk there after I was done trying to shoot a baboon. By midday, I was totally lost, sunburnt and very thirsty. The ranch was called Bundu Hills because of the enormous granite mountains, part of the famous Matopos mountain range, that seemed to go on forever.

At around 3 p.m. I found a small natural pan with a dead giraffe in it that had died about three months earlier. The smell was almost unbearable, but I was so thirsty that I just brushed the muck off the surface and sucked in the stinking brown water. I recall the disgusting smell when I burped half an hour later, but it had quenched my thirst. By sunset, I was beside myself. I had walked non-stop with no food all day and was in a total spin. In desperation, I headed for the highest mountain I could see and climbed hundreds of metres up, but there were just mountains everywhere.

I had always felt that churches were full of hypocrites and God had enough people to worry about, so I never bothered Him. I was a tough, wild young man without any need for God. High up on that lonely mountain, I got on my knees and prayed to God for help for the first time ever.

I'll never forget the powerful feeling of lukewarm water being poured over me, and a total sense of calm that followed. I stood up, walked slowly as if being guided down that mountain, and at the bottom, about 10 metres from where the granite entered the soil, were old vehicle tracks in the long grass from the previous rainy season. My uncle Lin had shot a kudu bull there, and the labourers had cut a road in to recover it. I followed the tracks to an old fence line that took me up to the road where all the farm workers were spaced apart for miles calling for me. I knew then that there was power in prayer and a God that watched over me.

The next time I would feel this so powerfully was in prison.

CHAPTER 29

Dying like Flies

I fell into a deep slump after Jumbo informed me that the High Court had rejected my application for bail pending appeal. But soon afterwards, Sue received word that there were people on the outside who said they knew how to find Wilson, the poacher I had supposedly drowned, alive and well, and that they were able to produce him.

Naturally, I responded enthusiastically to these offers. I was told there was someone in Plumtree who knew precisely where the 'assumed deceased' lived. Money was required, and I paid it. There were a few other leads that followed, but nothing came of any of them.

Then Bruce Smith and a private investigator called James Kinnaird (aka 'King Rat') came to the house to see Sue and asked for a considerable amount of money, which they said would secure my release in a matter of weeks. They also needed a vehicle and fuel. This was provided, and James set off. He returned with affidavits from people who said they had seen Wilson. They brought the news that Wilson's family had agreed that they would confirm that the whole story that secured my conviction was fabricated, but in return for making this declaration, they wanted my fishing resort.

As much as I wanted to be a free man, I turned down this offer. Sue had someone approach the authorities about the affidavits, and was told that they wanted Wilson, not pieces of paper. Then word was received that the family would sign the declaration if I paid them what was then about US$300,000. I agreed to this proposal on the condition that the declaration was drafted and supervised by my lawyer. I wanted the affidavit signed and sealed before any money was paid.

James set off to collect the family, but when he arrived at the family homestead, the entire community was wait-ing and very hostile. Word had leaked about what was going to happen, and apparently the population was dead against it. The reception was so aggressive that James had to produce a firearm and fire two shots in the air to keep the crowd at bay. Realising the family was forbidden to leave, he returned to town empty-handed.

Having netted all the fish out of the normal fishing areas in the lake, the community was now illegally netting in the fish breeding grounds. Since the closest authorities were four hours away by road and two hours by boat, I was the only person in the area who would take action or report their illegal netting. Having me out of the area gave them free reign to continue with their illegal activities.

With the point being made abundantly clear that the community did not want me out of jail and back in the area, that was the end of that. The whole process cost me over US$42,000, and I got nothing out of it.

I had left Spike (my co-accused) in charge of my com-panies along with Sue, Debbie McCormick (who was my PA for years), Charlie Campbell and Chris Burton. We had been living the good life before prison, but soon after my imprisonment an economic crisis hit Zimbabwe, caused by the land invasions and everyone felt the impact.

Spike and Debbie disapproved of many decisions Sue made, and a rift developed between them which ended with Spike and Debbie resigning after about six months. I heard, with some irritation, about lavish nights out and dining bills being paid by my companies. It was hard visualising it all, but I felt it was easing the agony Sue was experiencing and let it go. Sue's sister Lara replaced Debbie, and Charlie Campbell (Lara's husband) became my business manager.

There was soon more unwelcome news regarding my finances. I was always anxious about promising news of my release, and when Sue came to see me in August, five months into my time in Khami, my spirits lifted enormously. It was a 'holiday visit', which meant a special holding-hands visit. But my joy did not last long. After our greetings, she broke down sobbing and explained that someone I thought I could trust had emptied my overseas account. I rubbed her hands saying that it was just money and we still had each other. We could make plenty more once I was released.

Before Christmas the year before I had given Ralph, a politically connected friend, a US$500 cheque as a gift for his trip to the UK. When he returned in January he handed the cheque back, saying he did not need to use it. This struck me as strange, but I ignored it. After my imprisonment, he faxed my US bank with details of a Japanese used car dealer's account and an invoice for two cars, with my signature. The money was transferred as requested, and more continued for other vehicles until the account was empty. It seemed that our world, no matter which way we looked, had been ripped to pieces, but I refused to let it get me down.

I lived for those visits, and I know Sue counted the days too. But the system could be unbearably cruel. Visits were supposed to be 15 minutes fortnightly. Often, after the two-week build-up, full of anxiety and excitement, Sue would only get four or five minutes and be bustled away rudely.

The visiting area was made up of five cubicles in line with a dense wire mesh that you could hardly see through, and a small horizontal slot cut out through which to look at your visitors. The mesh was caked with mud applied by cruel guards. It was always mind-boggling cruelty.

Between you and your visitors was a passage about a metre wide where guards would walk up and down during your visit. Often a guard would stand right in front of the slot, making it impossible to see your visitor until you shouted at him to move. Your visitor had a wire mesh but not as densely manufactured and without mud. As soon as we were permitted to start talking, there was a barrage of loud voices trying to shout above the others. It was tough figuring out what each one was saying.

On one occasion I was so rudely escorted away after only four minutes that I requested to see the OIC. I explained what treatment I had received and how upset my visitors were, so the OIC phoned Sue right then and there and told her she could return the next day for another full visit. That time, she brought my old mate Wayne Brebner (Brebs).

Brebs – affectionately known by his mates as the 'Mayor of Bulawayo' – is a little under six foot, heavily built with a big beer belly and shaved head. he's an incredible character who often has us all crying with laughter. I start laughing the moment I see him, but deep down, beyond the funny side, he is one of my dearest and most trusted friends.

We've been incredibly close since our days at Plumtree School. That day we had a fantastic 15-minute chat that left me on a high for a week.

Sue went through absolute hell trying to see me and get food to me or get news about me. On occasion, she would see a guard in town who recognised her, and he would assure her that on a particular day she could visit me and bring me food – he would take care of all the arrangements. She would stock up with a mountain of groceries and drive our 26 km on a bumpy dirt road only to find some surly guard at his post and the guy with whom she had made the arrangement nowhere to be found. All her efforts would have been in vain, and she would have to drive the lonely road home.

Many times, the senior authorities would call Sue to bring me something I had requested from the OIC; she would get to the gate only to be told to go away. When the goods did not arrive, I would inquire, and she would be phoned, an apology made as the superior authority had forgotten to inform the main gate, and she would come out again. It never stopped, just plain spitefulness and gratuitous cruelty, time and time again.

When I knew Sue might be coming, often from smuggled letters, I followed a bit of a ritual. If I stood on the cement block surrounding the toilet in my cell, I could faintly see out the vents and over the seven-metre walls to watch visitors coming. Although it was prohibited, my excitement always got the better of me, and I would wait for her at the vent and wave with a white lunchbox lid against the tight mesh. She could see it only if the lid was close enough to the mesh. It's difficult to describe the pleasure it gave me seeing her wave back. It was such a soul-destroying place. Several times I was caught waving and warned that I would be moved to a single cell, but the temptation was always too much.

That December on Unity Day we were permitted unlimited visitors, and 68 vehicles arrived to see me, almost all at once. It was a wonderful day. I saw the first two waves of 20 at a time, but then, due to the unusual numbers, security was called and turned out in a panic thinking I was going to be broken out. All my other visitors, over 50, were turned away. I felt desperately helpless trying to persuade the emotionless guards to please allow me just a few minutes with them. When I realised that I was fighting a losing battle, I raced up to my cell and waved to several friends who had been advised of the method with my lunchbox lid. Unfortunately, their jubilant responses tipped off the authorities, and I was moved down to a single cell. The cell was 1 m X 3 m, but for three of us. It was extremely uncomfortable, but my new cellmates, Clement and Silas, were great guys, and we were soon sharing our life stories and any humour to keep our spirits up.

I left Dumi to look after my food, cigarettes and other 'goodies' upstairs in my old cell. That night he gambled all but one packet of my 180 packs of smokes. I was furious, and soon word got out to the guards who immediately saw a chance to thrash someone. I approached them while they were questioning him and told them that I just wanted my smokes back and to please not beat him. They assured me they wouldn't.

Within 10 minutes Zulu came running into the exercise yard to tell me they were beating Dumi. I ran into the hall and stormed into the cell where all the beatings took place and saw Dumi on his stomach, with feet facing up, being beaten on the soles of his feet by three young guards. I stressed to the main guard at the door that I had asked him please not to beat Dumi. He immediately told the other guards to stop, and I walked out with a tearful but relieved Dumi.

Christmas Day was extraordinary. Sue and Michie had gathered five other close friends of ours, all in outfits for a visit. Wearing white shorts, a Father Christmas hat and a black T-shirt with the words: 'Forget Willy, Free Rusty' there was a lot of laughter. Their efforts were deeply moving and turned my day into an unforgettable memory. It's hard to express the heartwarming effect thoughtful gestures have when you are in such a desperate situation.

After Christmas, Sue brought Dusty to see me. Up till then, I had not wanted my precious children to visit, as I felt it would affect them too severely, but it was awesome seeing him again. We chatted about the dam at the house, the spray-system on the lawn, his mates, school and his life in general and were so excited to see each other that emotions never had time to take effect. But when Sandy followed two weeks later, it was a very different heart-wrenching tearful affair. For the first few minutes she was brave; then she said the impala had had two babies that week, and suddenly the tears started on both sides. Although we cried most of the 15 minutes, when she left, I felt a deep sense of elation and relief having seen my 'baby girl'.

The next time I saw my children was towards the end of March. My divorce lawyer visited me, specifically to bring them to see me. We sat across a table and spoke for 30 minutes. Seeing the pain on their faces as we talked was tough. They were hurting deep down. I was their rock, always there for support and advice, and now I was helpless.

I had a chance to ask them how they were really doing, in life, emotionally and in every other way. It was a tearful half hour, but I was able to assure them that I would be all right. I told them that the nightmare would be over soon, and life would be fantastic again. It was a bit difficult with three guards and our family lawyer listening in, but it was still fantastic.

When time was up, I was permitted to hug them. As soon as Sandy got the go-ahead, she flew into my arms, wrapped her arms around my neck and squeezed as tight as she could. I could feel her trembling with emotion, and my heart ached from her agony. It was the longest and first hug in a year. Dusty was more reserved but still emotional.

It is difficult to describe the emptiness of being stripped of your powers to care for your children who depend on you. That night I recalled the hugs and emotional trauma my children were facing, which really tore into me. I could handle the tough times, but the emotional pain that they showed was severe for me.

As the months passed by, I became deeply concerned about the death rate in prison. There were about 70 guys on TB treatment, and at least three people were dying a week. When that rate started increasing, nobody seemed to worry about it.

Initially, we were getting a tiny piece of meat twice a week, but that soon ended. There was never any fruit, vegetables or dairy. The lack of adequate nutrition triggered the outbreak of pellagra, which is caused by having too little niacin (a B-complex vitamin) or tryptophan (an amino acid) in the diet. The '4 Ds' of pellagra are diarrhoea, dermatitis, dementia and death – the last one assured within a few months if nutrition is not addressed. But there was no sign of the food shortages ending.

After some serious lobbying and on doctors' orders, I was eventually formally allowed to receive two tins of food a day to supplement my diet. This dietary supplement was only approved because meat and beans had run out, and for three months we received boiled cabbage and *sadza* only, twice a day. In September, mielie-meal supplies ran low, and the food was reduced to a cup of porridge at 8 a.m. and one meal at 2 p.m. Then mielie-meal began running out regularly. Cheap rice was provided instead and, on several occasions, served once a day without porridge. On one occasion, we received only one large spoonful of rice in 48 hours. On two occasions water ran out, and for two days we had no water to drink let alone for anything else. During these miserably hot, desperate months, TB infections spiked, and the death rate shot up as the condition of prisoners deteriorated horribly.

Out of 1,000 of us, more than 130 were now on TB treatment, and the death rate was alarming. In my year there, I started logging the deaths from April to November. I stopped at 95 for fear of being caught. Towards the end of my year, prisoners were dying almost daily, and morale was low.

Young prison officers could not afford the bus or taxi fare to town, so they relied on people dying for them to catch the prison truck taking bodies into town. Early one morning one of these young brutes, Mgopfa, ran up the stairs before unlock, shouting for any deaths that night. When he was told three had died, he jumped with joy calling out as he ran down the stairs, 'Yes, three died, we can go to town, yes, I'm going to town!'

It upset the prisoners deeply, and I lay there on the cold floor, furious at his actions, wishing that the young lout could be thrown in with us as a prisoner. We could teach him a thing or two.

Because of the shortage of transport, if we were to leave the dreaded steel and concrete fortress to visit a filthy government hospital or over-crowded courthouse, there would often be bodies wrapped in blankets on their way to the mortuary in the truck taking us to town. Stepping over two or three bodies moving up to the front of the enclosed prison truck disturbed me deeply, let alone the smell. But to the other guys going to court or town regularly, it became a regular part of prison life.

One weekend, 23 prisoners from the Khami prison complex died. Finally, news got back to HQ in Harare. An assistant commissioner arrived with his subordinates, we were addressed, and complaints were made. They moved all TB patients to another hall, but the food never improved. Some NGOs arrived after news of the deaths leaked out. The deaths were blamed on AIDS and tests were carried out on those who volunteered. In my year at Khami no fewer than 200 inmates died.

When the team of NGOs arrived to test volunteers for HIV, I convinced Chaka that we should get tested, just to have peace of mind. We were living in cramped conditions and needed to know our status. We got tested together, and when his results showed positive, this hardcore fighter cried shamelessly. When the guards asked why he was crying, and he told them, they laughed and told him he should have slept with decent women, not whores. I felt his pain deeply. We sat on the floor against the hall in the sun, and I explained as best I could that with ARVs he could live for many more years. After a few smokes, he seemed content, and we carried on walking, chatting about happier things.

In November, Sue visited me with information that there was a lawyer in Bulawayo who was very confident he could get me bail pending appeal. Soon, a young lawyer came and asked several questions about the incident, the trial, and any information about Wilson. An application was prepared, which was brought to me for signing, and it went to the High Court. I heard nothing for weeks, despite requesting the outcome many times. Sue was always told that they were still working on it. It was then revealed that the High Court had granted me bail pending appeal, but before the judge signed the warrant of liberation, word got out to the political authorities, and the bail was reversed. I was shattered, to say the least. It became apparent that my predicament had far more significant dynamics than those that I knew of.

During those lonely months, I would often watch the pigeons day after day. After they had eaten the scraps of *sadza* off the exercise yard floor, they would fly off over those high razor wire-topped walls, and I wished a million times that I could somehow just fly away with them and be free again. I don't believe there was a prisoner that didn't think that. It was the only glimpse of freedom you got to see in there.

During those food shortage months of 2003, prisoners were frail and sick. I was inside the hall with a young guard after feeding one afternoon, and it was late for lock-up. From outside the hall, Sergeant Badzi, the HIC, had ordered everyone to enter the hall immediately. He was a tall, cruel man who always had a scowl on his face and carried a passion for beating, especially when hung-over.

Unbeknown to Badzi, the gates were locked. I was on the inside with the young guard, who had not received the command to open them. They were swing gates, cuffed together in the middle. As Badzi began viciously beating 1,000 panicking prisoners outside, they pressed, panicked, against the gates. When the bulging gates were finally opened, this evil thug started beating as people broke past in a chaotic scrambling wave. He struck one of the first to pass him on the side of the head, causing the prisoner to collapse. I was standing right beside them, and the crowd trampled over the fallen man by the hundred as Badzi continued beating from behind.

When all had stampeded past, the prisoner lay unconscious in a heap on the floor. Badzi ordered two prisoner-staff to carry him to his cell upstairs. When they reached the first floor, he told them to leave him leaning against the wall beside his cell. I followed, and within minutes he was dead.

I was ordered to my cell. A wheelchair was brought over from the clinic, and the dead prisoner was speedily wheeled out with his head being held upright by another prisoner – hospital-staff – so that no one could see he was dead. The incident was never heard of again, but the thought of witnessing a murder right in front of me disturbed me for days. I hardly slept that night and wondered how many other innocent lives had been lost due to this brutal behaviour.

The censor's officers (CO) were ruthless, in every prison I was in. I received three *YOU* magazines once in Khami Max, there were seven stories in the first magazine, and all were cut out. The second and third had three stories left between them. This was a publicly acceptable family magazine. How could almost every story be removed? I made a report to the OIC about it during inspection one day. The CO called me later that day and advised me, in his usual snarling and hateful attitude, that these magazines were a privilege, and if I complained again, he would refuse their entry altogether.

The same pitiless censor's officer oversaw where our tinned food and groceries from 'outside' were stored, which was in his office in a separate administration building away from the hall but in the same complex.

My tins of food were authorised by the OIC, meaning that the censor's officer could not ignore them or have his

Peta and Wally (my mom and dad) weeks before his accident.

Interprovincial rugby champions, 1985.

My mom and Dusty.

Sandy in Mateke Hills Camp.

Dusty's first ride.

Celebrating with staff on safari.

Limpopo River, building camp, 1989.

Spike, Phinias, Kermit and me with a live python.

Bonding with nature.

Tiger-fishing with Sue at my fishing resort.

ABOVE Good times with Spike (my co-accused).

LEFT New beginnings, Nyamasikana Camp, 1989.

Richie Barns, Brebs, me, Spike and Gary Koen, the day before the incident.

Triangle Camp, Lundi River.

Enjoying life with my sister Bev.

Ray Anthony, me and General Norman Schwarzkopf, USA, 2000.

My sister Lyn and me.

TOP Sandy and me, Ncema Dam.
ABOVE Father and son, bonding time.

ABOVE Rings made in prison.
RIGHT Soccer shoes and hats made in prison.

Bangles made in prison.

own cruel way as he usually did, and this incensed him. What he didn't realise – and I dared not tell him lest he disallow it – was that I was helping several other inmates from starving, one of them being Chaka.

Chaka deteriorated after the news that he was HIV positive and despite helping him daily with food and efforts to keep him comfortable, he passed away three months later. It was an enormous loss for me, and a low few weeks followed, but I had my own life to take care of and seeing guys dying before my eyes almost daily, enhanced my determination to remain healthy and sane.

Without fail, wherever that CO saw me, be it in the hallway, exercise yard, his office, anywhere, he would order me in a scowling manner to 'crouch down'. If he saw me take offence, he would increase the time until he would attend to me, leaving me crouching for longer than usual.

The OIC at Khami was a total drunkard. Although he allowed me certain privileges, he was a ruthless individual who would regularly visit the hall the morning after a heavy drinking night. It would be clear from his filthy clothes, bloodshot eyes, slurred words, and the stench of alcohol that he had not slept all night.

During almost every drunken visit he would curse us in a long, slurring tirade, and then order D-class conditions. These were condemned section (death row) rules, which meant we were locked in cells for 23 hours a day. After two or three days, he would hear we were under D-class conditions and ask who authorised them. That happened about four times in the year I was at Khami.

I almost lost control of myself once during a visit, when a guard, with a big smile on his face, took a toothbrush that had been carefully selected and brought by Sue, and snapped the handle off. I was gobsmacked but also furious, as he'd left no handle at all with which to hold the tooth-brush. The pleasure he showed doing it, and of the pain visible on Sue's face, upset me deeply.

I later discovered that toothbrushes at Khami were considered dangerous weapons. Apparently in 1999, a prisoner at the end of his tether from cruelty by the guards, arranged for some of his relatives to assault a guard outside the prison. The news filtered back, and after several days of relentless beatings that left the prisoner unable to walk, the guards planned his fate.

The guards promised Moses, another long-serving prisoner, a reduction in sentence and other privileges if he complied with their plan.

The target prisoner and Moses were both on the ground floor in single cells. After lock-up one winter's evening, Moses's solid wooden door was left unlocked. The target was still too weak from his beatings to realise that his door was also unlocked. Around 10 p.m. Moses quietly left his cell and entered the target's cell, carrying a knife given to him by the guards. Finding the target sound asleep, Moses covered his mouth and stabbed him several times in the heart through his side.

Unfortunately for Moses, several inmates heard the commotion and there was a loud uproar and shouts of anger. Moses sneaked back to his cell, watched by all through the peepholes in their doors. No night-shift guards showed up, despite the uproar. During the early hours of the morning, a guard snuck into the hall and retrieved the knife, as planned, through Moses' peephole.

To Moses' horror, the next morning, the guards denied any involvement. He was thoroughly beaten and charged with murder, but was never convicted or sentenced. He did, however, receive all his privileges in the hall. He told investigators that he had sharpened his toothbrush and used it to stab the target – which is why the guards claimed that full-length toothbrushes were too dangerous.

Moses was very active in homosexual gangs and soccer activity in prison. He was a tall man, and always appeared unhappy. I spoke with him often, but he seemed reserved and despondent to converse openly. Towards the end of my year at Khami Max, the OIC was replaced. Paul – my original letter smuggler – and Moses requested to see him, and within a day the tins I'd been allowed through doctor's orders were disallowed. There were always inmates with hidden agendas, and Paul and Moses were part of the cynical lot we had to deal with.

CHAPTER 30

College for Criminals

M any people in this hardcore prison did not really belong in there, but even so it was a long term in hell with no real hope of ever getting their lives back together.

For example, under colonial rule, the chiefs and tribal leaders retained legal authority in presiding over certain types of offences, and these included transgressions of a sexual nature. It is traditional for fathers to receive cattle and money for their daughters from the groom-to-be. With virgins fetching a better price, anyone violating a girl before marriage was seen to be damaging the value of their property, and this had consequences.

Under Mugabe, the chiefs were stripped of this authority, and such behaviour was made a matter for the criminal courts. As a result, the prisons were full of young men who had had consensual sex with women out of wedlock, but had been convicted of rape. These trials were ridiculously unfair – the girl was not required to testify; all the courts needed was a relative (but not the mother or father) to appear in court. If an aunt claimed that her niece had been sexually violated with no bride price having been paid, then a conviction nearly always followed. And with conviction, a minimum sentence of eight years in a maximum-security facility would be handed down.

Roughly 60 per cent of the inmates were convicted rapists, and many of those were not guilty of rape in the Western legal sense of the word.

Another significant portion of the prison population consisted of men convicted of stock theft. This being the time of the land invasions, virtually all the ranchers had been driven from their properties, and a free-for-all followed to grab all the livestock. As most of the ranches went to politically connected cronies, they claimed ownership of the stock – and woe betide any arbitrary tribesman who was caught with their newly acquired livestock. The full force of the law came hammering down, and they were sentenced to nine years per animal. Some of these men arrived in prison with sentences of over 140 years for stock theft. It was terribly unfair, and these people came with no hope of any justice because they could not afford a lawyer. Coming from a cattle-ranching background, I sympathised with their situations.

The armed robbers had the most say in the gangs and were the guys who influenced staff selection the most, since they knew the guards, having spent many years, even decades, in prison. They had the most stories, and a few were excellent raconteurs. Being in cells most of the time with no radios or TV, they would regale the rest of the occupants with stories of their criminal exploits late into the night, and some were genuinely fascinating. I heard all about which judges were bribed, and from what I heard, the hardcore armed robbers all had links to judges who looked after their interests. I heard about hijackings, how to break into different vehicles, house robberies, burglaries, where to buy guns, where to buy and sell stolen property and which gangs to join. These guys became the role models for the young stock thieves and rapists. Sadly, many innocent youngsters left there, bitter, revengeful, angry, hardened and well-educated criminals with no support system once they were released.

CHAPTER 31

Holding on to Hope

Avoiding becoming depressed was a constant battle, and the only way through was to learn how to self-counsel. When I thought about Sue with another man (you get insecure in prison) or my mates on a fishing trip, it hurt in my stomach physically, so I blocked that out. The thought of staying in there another three months would also send jets of adrenaline into my stomach, causing physical pain. I had to keep telling myself I was going home that week. It was the only way to stop the pain.

I learned not to let past thoughts hurt me. The past only existed in my head; it could only come to life if I let it. To be able to find positives in all the negative aspects of life going on around me brought hope, which was a huge part of dealing with life in prison.

Having hope kept me optimistic and uplifted no matter what I was living through. What I found helped greatly, too, was to find happiness in even the smallest things that happened in there. We would laugh and fool around endlessly to keep our spirits up, and I found hanging around happy, funny guys, like Munya, was the only solution. This kept me healthy. Those who didn't remain happy would die. We watched it regularly and would often say when seeing someone really depressed, 'He's not going to make it.' Sure enough, within a month or two, he was gone.

It made me realise that life in prison or in Las Vegas is still just life; it's what you make of it, no matter where you are. I had everything I could ever have wished for before prison, and, very quickly, it was all gone.

Obviously, there were times when things would become too much. I was experiencing trauma few have ever imagined, and it was only natural for negative days, anger, hatred, bitterness and revengeful thoughts to kick in. The cruelty of the guards, people dying all around me and the predicament I had ended up in was eating me up daily. I would often lie in my cell and get so worked up that I could feel my heart racing at a ridiculous rate. I would make plans in my head for revenge on all those that had put me in there. Mekki was first. He had orchestrated, along with Makore, to rid me from his illegal poaching grounds and when I thought of him laughing at his victory, it infuriated me more. I had a deep dislike and hatred for Inspector Zulu who I knew was responsible for concocting the story against me. I'd challenge myself now and again, saying that he did come to the Binga Prison to try and get my side of the story and I had refused, but he still had no right, as a commissioned officer, to distort the facts. When I thought of the hatred and determined efforts to convict me that the judge and his assessors showed in court, it fuelled my anger more. They seemed to be venting their hatred on me. I could clearly see the menace on their faces when questioning me with snarled lips and words harshly spat out. I would have these negative attacks often in the first year, and they always left me deflated.

Then one day, after about a year, I'd had enough of all the anger, hatred and bitterness. It was draining me daily, and

I remember the exact words I said to myself walking in the prison exercise yard. I just said, 'Lord take care of them and let me get through this road that's been put in front of me. Life is a circle and what goes around comes around. They'll get what they deserve.'

Once I'd accepted that, and pushed those stresses aside, life in prison changed for me. It was like turning a switch in my mind; I just released everything and gave it all away. I had no control of the future anyway, and the sudden reality of that hit me. It was about pushing aside issues I couldn't undo and moving forward. Over time these small negative, angry thoughts kept returning, and I'd push them away until I had finally, forgiven them wholeheartedly.

On 3 April 2004, precisely 365 days after my arrival, I was relaxing in my cell chatting to fellow inmates when we were interrupted by the distinct clang of doors unlocking. I was escorted up to the OIC at 5.30 p.m. He informed me that I was being transferred to Chikurubi Maximum Security Prison at 5 a.m. the following day to be a state witness in the Justice Paradza trial.

Terrible as the conditions were, I had established myself amongst fellow prisoners and guards alike at Khami and was as comfortable as possible under the circumstances. The thought of moving, knowing I would have to start all over again with climbing the pecking order and making new friends, stressed me deeply.

I would also be 430 km – as opposed to 26 km – away from home, which would make everything much more difficult for Sue. By this time, we had established an effective communications system, and I was able to have some say regarding my business interests and the welfare of my children. I expected Sue the next day for my fortnightly visit. Wanting to save her the expense of food, fuel and time, I asked that she be notified and advised of my move, and was assured it would be done. Of course, nothing was done, and she arrived the next day, only to be told I was no longer there.

Saying goodbye to my friends was wrenching. I had suffered and survived with them and spent endless hours reminiscing, learning and laughing. They had been phenomenal in helping me through the hardest times of my life. They took me in as family, always advising on the dangers of prison life, and I did not want to leave them for a new unknown.

But when you are a prisoner, your life is not your own. I gathered up my meagre possessions and braced myself for the challenges ahead.

CHAPTER 32

Colour-coded Cellmates

When I arrived at Chikurubi Maximum in April 2004, my first impression was that everything seemed fantastic in comparison to Khami, which was derelict and filthy. Although it would change later, at the start of my stay we even had the luxury of running water.

On arrival, I was sent to the holding cell in C Hall. Chikurubi Max was built in a hexagonal shape. There were five large halls of approximately 400 people per hall, and a remand section that was half the size and held about 200 inmates awaiting trial or judgement. The other half of the remand section was the admin block, foreign prisoner cells, and the visitors' section.

In the middle of the hexagon was a large, round lawned area known as the 'centre-court'. All five halls and the admin block faced onto the centre-court. There were no windows or doors facing out, apart from the admin block.

The holding cell, like every cell in the halls in Chikurubi, was 9 m X 4 m with three solid walls, a front steel mesh grill and a gate that faced the centre of the complex. One metre of the nine-metre section was the toilet and entrance area where one prisoner would sleep. There were only six guys resident in the holding cell; it was like a transit room where new intakes and men going to court or hospital the following day would overnight.

There were six cells per floor, making 12 cells per hall and an average of 400 per hall. Aside from the holding cell, there were 33 to 36 prisoners per cell. This gave each prisoner about 47cm of space, which was a huge difference in comparison to Khami Max.

When I watch documentaries and see prisons with beds, cupboards, televisions, washbasins and other luxuries, I see how very different it was for us in Zimbabwe. In Khami Maximum there was no glass at all in prison; windows were bars with a heavy-duty wire mesh, this allowed wind and rain in at random. In Chikurubi Maximum, the cells had no windows at all, just three solid walls, floor, and roof, with the fourth wall being bars and wire mesh with a steel mesh gate. In the back wall, three metres above the floor was a very thick, glass inspection panel. All cell back walls faced out, and there was a raised walkway around the outside of the entire prison on each floor, allowing guards to inspect cells through the thick glass panel any time. On the first and second floors, after exiting the cells, there were rows of glass windows which allowed guards on opposite sides of the prison to see across the centre-court into cells for improved security. In most of these windows, the glass was missing, leaving the freezing wind to sweep into the cells.

The dining hall was just immovable concrete tables and solid red brick and concrete benches. The entire prison had never been painted; it was all cement grey and red bricks. Next to the dining hall were two toilets, then the library. Whenever a severe beating was going to take place in the halls, the offender was sent to the library. The book collection consisted of two shelves of worn out old books.

In the ranking of senior prisoners, there were yellow, blue and red stages – a little like prefects at school. Red was the highest, yellow was the lowest. Yellows were confined in the halls with other prisoners and there were about three per hall. Next was a blue stage – they could visit other halls without an escort but couldn't leave the building complex. The red stage could move throughout the prison from the halls to the kitchen and hospital.

The only red stage prisoner was Bigass Chimbizi. Bigass was a lifer and had been there for 24 years, so he knew absolutely everything about the place. All lifers were prisoners that had been on death row for murder with actual intent and were reprieved to a life sentence. He was very short, had big bulging eyes, weighed around 100 kg with a big belly and a huge bottom, hence his nickname.

Bigass was the only inmate at that time who could walk around the complex without an escort. With access to news from outside through the reception staff, he had heard I was coming and planned for me to remain in his cell for the benefits that he expected to accrue. He was a good guy, and we got on extremely well. He explained to me that being in the cell was a privilege and advised me to request that I stay there when interviewed by the OIC at my induction.

Bigass would question me endlessly about all aspects of my life. He was extremely intelligent, spoke perfect English and loved a good laugh. As he had anticipated, we shared my groceries that arrived by parcel, mainly tins of food and essentials like toothpaste and soap.

In the holding cell in Chikurubi, we also had two yellow stages, Tshotsho and Soza (a lifer). There was also Clyde, who had cancer, and Sitcha, who was responsible for the cleanliness of the cell.

Bigass and Clyde were outstanding chess players and would play almost every night on his bedding beside me. Bigass was a staunch homophobe and had Tshotsho, Soza and Clyde in there to keep them straight and avoid the temptations of homosexuality in prison. Sitcha was also straight.

Clyde was a tall, well-spoken Ndebele man, with broad, slightly rounded shoulders and beautiful teeth. He loved a good laugh and was a very likable character. He had been inside for 13 years. We became close friends and with him also being from Bulawayo, we would talk for hours about our home town. He was an armed robber and reformed – mainly due to his cancer, I think – but still associated a lot with other armed robbers.

Tshotsho, on the other hand, was not intelligent at all. He had missing teeth and a big belly, and slouched around like he had no energy. His simple thinking had him left out of many a conversation and general chat. On my first day in there, he proudly showed me newspaper cuttings of his armed robbery with a big toothless smile. He had served nine years with six remaining.

One of Tshotsho's annoying rituals was his stinking 5 a.m. bowel movement every morning, which woke everyone in a very unpleasant way. Being a yellow stage, he never adhered to the rule of not using toilets for a number two in the cells, for hygiene purposes. We never got along, and I avoided him whenever possible.

Soza played the guitar and would sing for us regularly. He was of medium height and slim build and was given a life sentence for murder. He had served nine years and was battling to stay straight. Bigass would openly warn him that he would lose his stage if he heard anything of him fooling around. Bigass had spies everywhere. I enjoyed Soza. He was quiet but smiled a lot. He was a diesel mechanic, so we enjoyed discussing machinery and mechanics. He had worked with Tommy Bawden as an apprentice. Tommy was my sister Lyn's brother-in-law, who was from a cattle and crop-farming background in the Shangani district where I had been a safari operator for 16 years.

Sitcha was also from Bulawayo. He was a good-looking Ndebele car thief, just under six-foot tall, with a healthy physique, and quietly spoken. He later joined me in my gym routine and had a pleasant nature but could be stubborn at times.

Chikurubi was a newer facility and much more substantial than Khami. It was built in the 1970s to accommodate prisoners of war during the Rhodesian Bush War, also known as the Second Chimurenga and Zimbabwe War of Liberation. Being a regular in the holding cell, I was allocated a thin lice-riddled felt mat that made an enormous difference to my shoulders and hipbones. I could at least lie on my back, although it was still on the concrete floor with the cold making its way through. The worst were the dreaded lice that never changed; they drove us insane. They were tough to kill. We had to pop them with our nails, or they wouldn't die, much like a flea. We could roll them between our fingers and thumb and squeeze hard, but if they didn't pop, they would straighten up and crawl away. It was maddening. I spent hours every day killing them; we all did.

Despite having Bigass as a connection and protector, it was still difficult being thrown into an unfamiliar environment with all these hostile strangers. He spent most of his day outside the hall, either in the kitchen, the centre-court, or visiting other halls. This took me into an interim danger zone with rival gangs often circling me warily. As a new intake and the only white person in a hall of 400 inmates, I was potentially valuable.

I was never sure what people were motivated by, but many were genuinely very friendly and helpful, which left me feeling a little more at ease. By carefully assisting here and there with smokes, and winning over officers' support, I moved into a more comfortable position socially. But I also had to be firm and robust so that the bullies realised I was not someone to be messed with.

As the news leaked that I was the gym guy from Khami Max who was a successful businessman, and that I was soon to be a state witness at a judge's tribunal, many began to receive me with warmth.

Another guy I got really close to in Chikurubi was George Chikanga. He was heavily built and nearly always wore a wide chubby smile. Although he was always happy and loved to talk, he was also a feared armed robber. He had been inside twice before and was then serving 12 years of a 19-year sentence. While serving his second sentence, which was 10 years, he was released on mysterious grounds after two years. Within a few months he showed up in court again for another armed robbery case. The same magistrate recognised him and asked why he was not in prison. A big can of worms was uncovered – it turned out George's mother was the girlfriend of a very senior politician. He was promptly given a stiff sentence and made to serve the rest of his previous sentence too.

We would chat in English about all his days as an armed robber, about his sisters in the USA and his arms caches hidden around the country that he promised to destroy when he was liberated. I met his mother, brother, and sisters during visits over the years and he met my sisters Lyn and Bev several times. We were in the same hall all the way through Chikurubi. Most of the armed robbers seemed to have weapons stored in secret locations, but I think he's one of the few who managed to leave crime behind. I would like to think some of this decision was influenced by me.

On several occasions, George got tearful with me about how much hardship he had inflicted on his mother. He had a habit of talking so fast I couldn't follow what he was saying. We would chat for hours, and I regarded him as one of my closest friends, which showed during a nasty incident in later years, where he saved me from some serious physical harm.

Another guy who used to really tear me up in my hall was old 'Sweet Potatoes'. He was tall and thin, in his late sixties with a weathered, shiny face. His real name was Matchazire, but we nicknamed him Sweet Potatoes because, before prison, he was a subsistence farmer. Every evening, his wife would cook him his favourite dish made from sweet potatoes. She always cooked extra as he loved the leftovers for lunch the next day. After one long day, he arrived home to find no sweet potatoes. When he inquired from his wife where his sweet potatoes were, she said she had given them to a visitor that morning, who he suspected was her lover. He beat her to death and was sentenced to 12 years. He was very quiet-spoken and of a gentle nature; it puzzled me that he could snap over such a small issue.

Every morning around 5 a.m., Sweet Potatoes, who was very spiritual, would wake the complex with a religious song. He had an unbelievably powerful voice and would sing a song in soprano. It would always take me to another place. It was incredibly moving, and one could almost feel the walls vibrate as he let it go. The entire prison would often be silenced as his amazing, powerful voice echoed through the halls.

CHAPTER 33

Chikurubi's Regimen

At Chikurubi Maximum, we were unlocked at 8 a.m. and cleaning staff would then clean the cells, toilets, dining hall, and yard before we were sent downstairs to the exercise yard for porridge. The prisoners ran the halls to a considerable extent; the four guards per hall just sat on a simple old bench in each exercise yard.

After taking sugarless porridge one row at a time, seated in formation on the cold, tarred floor, it was sport (if there was any on the day) until lunch at 10.30 a.m. If there was lunch, the guys would take their food and go straight upstairs for midday lock-up. If not, at 11 a.m. we were ordered upstairs and locked in cells. This was our gym time, which we thoroughly looked forward to, even if tired from sport. Unlock was at 2 p.m. and it was downstairs, line up, take your dinner and go straight up again for 3 p.m. lock-up. As water was so precious, due to a water shortage, it was carefully guarded in the containers we used for gym, and someone had to be paid specifically to safeguard the water for the hours I was playing sport.

After evening lock-up, no later than 3 p.m. was my time to have a bath in a bucket covering the stainless-steel circular bowl that was the toilet. The cell toilet had low walls blocking the sides, and I would hang a blanket for some privacy between the walls. During winter, I would heat a few litres of water using a homemade water-heating contraption to avoid bathing with freezing water.

There was no tea delivered to the prisoners at all in Chikurubi, apparently because boiling hot water in the kitchen would take too much time and pots were busy cooking *sadza*. With our hall-in-charge's (HIC) approval, we cobbled together a water-boiling device in the hall. We used two electrical wires (which were smuggled in by kitchen staff) and two lids from shoe-polish tins that were joined at the centres. They were insulated from each other by a piece of plastic or bone from the kitchen, about the size of a thumbnail. We would tie these lids together with gut made from polystyrene bags. The wires were joined to each lid and then it was dropped into a plastic water container. The short circuit through the water created heat, and we had boiling water in no time. Tea, coffee, sugar, and milk powder were generally permitted from visitors or food parcels. Those cups of tea were a treat and essential for keeping the HIC on our side.

To keep my life running smoothly and as comfortably as possible, many had to be paid, especially the HIC. Nearly all the guards smoked, and those who did not wanted coffee, tea, biscuits or sweets, which came in mailed parcels. When food parcels that were sent by relatives were not collected, my situation became very tense. I went through one period of nine months during which nothing came in, and this left me very exposed to irritable guards.

The officer-in-charge (OIC) is the man who oversees everyone and everything in a prison, like a CEO. His office is in the admin section of the prison, attached to but separate from the hall where the prisoners are housed. There are often several halls in a prison complex, to cater for the control of the number of prisoners. In each hall is a hall-in-charge (HIC), and several other guards, usually one guard per one hundred prisoners. The HIC directly influences your life in prison; he can make decisions on issues like letting you out for a drink in the rain when there was no water, without consulting the OIC. The censor's office, hospital, kitchen, and admin block each had officers in charge of those sections too.

HICs rotated monthly and were very influential as far as our welfare was concerned. They could make calls and decisions as they wished and at times, they even let the prisoner-staff stay downstairs with them to chat or suntan during midday lock-up – for a price, of course. Just three extra hours out in the sunshine felt like paradise and a break from the routine I followed for four-and-a-half years.

Protruding from a wall in the exercise yard was a brass water tap that was severely worn and leaked continuously. The only way to stop water pouring out (when there was running water) was to tie the handle down with strips of blanket. Knowing of the water shortage, it drove me crazy seeing this simple garden tap gushing water non-stop. I would conscientiously tie it up, and within a minute someone would untie it, wash his hands or lunchbox, and then walk off. I tried talking to the HIC to advise inmates on several occasions to become more considerate, but nothing changed. Then I asked the OIC while on one of his dreaded weekly inspections if I could repair the leaking tap for him. All I needed was a washer and tools. He said no; he would send the plumbers. Four-and-a-half years later when I left, the tap had still not been repaired.

There was no difference in the medical officer's mentality in Chikurubi Max to that at Khami. You were government property and didn't tell guards what you needed, they told you. It wasn't long before I went down with a chest infection and was given malaria treatment. I explained that malaria only existed below 3,000 feet above sea level and Bulawayo and Harare were well over 4,000 feet each and that I knew what my condition was, but they insisted that I had malaria. I took the treatment, which made my head feel like it was going to explode, and it seemed to work, but only for two days, then my chest was full again. After two more courses of antibiotics, I was okay and given allergy tablets daily on a three-month basis.

After three months of doing my own washing, Bigass insisted I find someone to do it for me. He explained that I was too high up in the prison rankings and if I were seen to be doing it myself, I would lose stature in the eyes of the inmates. All prisoners in the upper social order have their washing done by others, who receive benefits for their services. These were primarily food, more water, better blankets, clothes and other treats all bought with smokes or exchanged for food from visits. You never wanted to use a thief, or your soap would surely disappear along with your water. One of the biggest missions was to find a reliable, trustworthy guy. Luckily Bigass organised one for me. He selected Nyere to be my washer as he had done washing for Bigass for years. Nyere was doing 15 years for rape and had eight to go.

He was part of the toilet staff in charge of keeping all the hall toilets clean and worked like a machine. Quite short and broad but sinewy and as tough as anything, he had a long stride, causing his body to move unevenly as he walked. His heavy gumboots slapped loudly against the concrete with each step. He had a dry sense of humour, and I loved his company. He had once worked on a commercial farm and we had quite a lot in common. We would spend many happy hours in conversation. He became a big part of my life in many ways, and I promised him employment when we were out of prison. Sadly, he died before I could fulfil that promise.

CHAPTER 34

Mixing with Mercenaries

A few weeks after arriving at Chikurubi I was shackled, loaded into a van and transported into the city of Harare on my way to testify at the trial of Justice Benjamin Paradza. We ended up at the Sheraton Hotel, and while waiting in the back of the van, I heard one of the senior prison officers talking on his phone to someone involved in the trial. Eventually, he came to tell me I was not yet needed, and I was taken back to the prison.

When I arrived all the mercenaries involved with Simon Mann were sitting in reception, and I introduced myself to them. They had been arrested in March when their plane was seized after they stopped to load weapons en route to Equatorial Guinea to overthrow President Obiang Nguema. Simon, leading the operation, was sentenced to seven years imprisonment. He was kept in the foreign section, so I didn't see a lot of him but enjoyed his company when I did.

Whenever I saw him, either in reception or visiting the prison hospital, and asked how he was, he would say, 'Splendid old chap, absolutely splendid!' He was a real soldier and a tough guy. He trained hard, daily, I was told, and refused to let the system get the better of him. Like me, he was having trouble keeping a grip on his financial affairs 'outside' and was frustrated by lawyers promising and not delivering. A couple of times that I saw him, he was enraged after being let down by his lawyer who he had sent to the UK to attend to his business problems.

Kevin Woods was once in Chikurubi, but had been moved to Harare Central by the time I arrived. He was the one who gave Bigass his nickname. I'd met Kevin in Bulawayo and we'd enjoyed tiger-fishing safaris together not long before his incarceration. Kevin was jailed in 1988 for politically motivated crimes on behalf of the former South African government. He was sentenced to death and held naked in solitary confinement for five of his eighteen years of incarceration, never knowing when the door would open, and he would be led to the gallows. He was regularly weighed and measured so the hangman could prepare. Before his arrest, while working for the Central Intelligence Organisation (CIO) in Zimbabwe, he was a covert agent for the government in South Africa, with the African National Congress in exile being his primary target. Despite this, former President Nelson Mandela made numerous approaches to President Mugabe to seek Kevin's release.

Each year there was a national chess competition where inmates from several prisons would participate with the public. The two representatives from Chikurubi Maximum, Bigass and Clyde, would sleep at Harare Central Prison during that week. Every year they would return with mail and paintings from Kevin Woods for me, and I would traffick replies. Kevin was a talented artist and passed much of his time painting. His main subject was Lake Kariba sunsets. It always lifted spirits to hear from old friends. I used to stare at the paintings for prolonged periods and let my mind take me to places the rest of me couldn't go. Kevin was finally released in 2006.

Out of 2,200 prisoners at Chikurubi, the only other Zimbabweans that I had a cultural connection with were Neal Tracy and Philip 'Blondie' Bezuidenhout. Phil would end up being my saviour.

Neal was tall, thin and always dirty. He was very different to Phil and me because he was a real murderer who deserved to be in prison. He had murdered Vivienne Vassilieff in the late 1980s and stuffed her body down a mineshaft near Beitbridge. I knew Vivienne well; she was a woman from Bulawayo who owned a horse-riding school that many of us had attended as teenagers. After his conviction, he served six years in Khami Maximum before being released on mental health grounds, but he had allowed hardened criminals to influence him during that time. Within a year of his release, he had been convicted on three counts of car theft, costing him 18 years and more cases pending. On the odd occasion when I visited his hall to play soccer, we would talk. He was always very interested in the idea of breeding catfish once he was released and used to 'traffick' his ideas to me from his hall. Without outside support, however, he deteriorated physically on the terrible food rations and in 2007 he passed away. Phil and I found it hard to empathise with him. As we got to know him better it was evident that he would never reform or lead a straight life again.

When I arrived at Chikurubi, Phil was in E Hall on the opposite side of the complex. Now and again we would see each other through the windows and wave, but I only got to greet him after about eight months. I began to plot to have him moved to my hall.

Phil was a farmer from Odzi in the east of Zimbabwe who I had met briefly before prison. His family, like mine, were pioneer stock and they had been main players in opening up the area along the Sabi River, which was wild, untamed country when they first settled there. Phil's father Coen was something of a legend in the area; he only had one leg, having lost the other to a leopard he was hunting because it was killing his cattle.

The land invasions started in early 2000 and by July 2001 Phil was the last farmer in the area and under a lot of pressure from the war veterans to abandon his farm, which he refused to do. The day before his incident he was in Harare when he received word that the war veterans were beating up his labourers. Phil raced back to the farm and dealt with the problem, but the following morning, a Saturday, he received a message at his house to say that his labourers were being assaulted in his tobacco barns. He reacted immediately and put the attackers to flight before proceeding to the police station to report the attack.

The police appeared to be reluctant to help but finally agreed to investigate when it was reported that some of the victims had been seriously injured by axes and others had been severely beaten. Eventually, the injured were transferred to the hospital, and the situation appeared to cool down. After Phil's brother arrived at the farm, Phil left to visit the injured in the hospital to see if there was anything that he could do to help them. On the way, he spotted a vehicle near to where he had planted his wheat and some people who did not belong on the farm. He decided he would speak to them on his way back from the hospital. Driving onto the main tar road, he noticed the vehicle he had just seen approaching him on a parallel road and stopped to speak to the occupants. They opened the doors, however, and three of the four ran back into the wheat field while the driver crouched behind his vehicle. Phil drove closer, looking to the front and turning around to see what was happening behind him, and the next thing someone ran into his fender and then hit his windscreen. Knowing he would be attacked if he stopped, Phil kept driving and went straight to the police station to report the incident.

He was immediately arrested and held until his lawyer arrived after which they went with the police to the scene of the accident, but there was an angry mob of over 2,000 people waiting for them. The cops were nervous, so Phil approached the crowd by himself and was prepared to confront them. The police decided to take him back to the vehicle and back to the police station, after which he was transferred to the remand prison in Mutare where he remained for 14 days, having been charged with murder.

Nine months later he was put on trial before a judge by the name of Hlataswayo, who had a reputation for being very political and racist. At the end of the proceedings on the first day, it was clear to everyone that the testimony of the witnesses pointed, at best, to a conviction for manslaughter and this was reported in the press. The trial was then postponed until September of that year, and on 15 September he was convicted of murder and given a jail sentence of 15 years. The judge told Phil that he was fortunate that he was not going to have him hanged. He said that Phil missed the death penalty 'by a whisker'. He was transferred to Chikurubi prison for one night and then to the condemned section at Harare Central for 17 months, where he was locked in a 3 m X 1 m cell for 23 hours a day, before being transferred back to Chikurubi.

According to Phil, two ministers had a vendetta against him. One had stated publicly that he was going to make an example of him, and an article attributed to the other minister was published in *The Herald*, a government-owned newspaper, which described the scene as one of Phil tying one of the war veterans behind his truck and dragging him to death. He was granted leave to appeal, but for reasons that remain unclear, no appeal ever took place. It was evident that the country was now a lawless state.

CHAPTER 35

Mob Justice

The word had spread the night before that something sinister was about to happen, and all I knew was that I did not want to be seen anywhere near it, but it happened in a flash right beside me.

Although we were in the same hall, I spent very little time with Shake. He was slightly hunched, had pimples, bloodshot eyes, and wore a permanent scowl. He was forever stealing, fighting, bullying, stabbing, being beaten or involved in some sort of unruly behaviour. I did not like his character. He was quite sickly, and one could immediately pick up that he had emotional issues.

Around 8.30 a.m. one freezing winter morning in 2004, the guards were all downstairs sunning themselves in the exercise yard. Bigass had already left the hall and I'm convinced he was aware of what was about to happen. The cells were being cleaned, the upstairs communal toilets were very busy, and everyone was preparing to go down for sugarless porridge. Suddenly there was a commotion, and a mob came running in shouting from all directions like starving predators racing to a kill. I looked around wondering what on earth was going on. Yells of encouragement rang from all around. Excited men jostled for good positions to watch the attack. I was frozen and caught in the middle of it all. Noticing that they were homing in on a guy beside me, I ran for the deserted cement stairs and headed down as quickly as I could to escape the commotion. As I ran into the yard downstairs, I came toe to toe with a guard. When he saw the look on my face, he began to question me on what was happening – but the noise made it clear all was not good upstairs.

Taking their time as always, the guards made their way up with me following close behind. We found Shake a motionless wreck having been beaten senseless. Most frightening was the wild, uncontrollable frenzy all the hardcore prisoners were in. Delivering the beating had cheered them, and they walked proudly away with chests puffed out, laughing and shouting. The guards paid no attention to the perpetrators. They looked at Shake and told some of the staff to take him downstairs, then strolled back down to the exercise yard.

When an inmate was beyond reform and a hazard to officers and inmates alike, they employed mob justice. It was one of the overwhelming horrors that caused me endless nightmares and sleepless nights, on those cold concrete floors under bright lights. Shake was admitted to the prison hospital but only lasted three weeks before he died. Sadly, there are many like him, still battling in there, but entirely beyond reform.

The thought of being targeted terrified me, and I knew I had to get more acquainted with my new environment. The attack on Shake happened for no apparent reason other than the fact that he had upset some senior prisoners and guards. It was a huge shock, and quickly I realised that the only way I was going to make it through this horror was to get the solid support of the 'main man' amongst the mob in prison.

His name was Malagas. He was the most vocal and physical during the Shake attack and feared by prisoners and guards alike. He was a tall, strong, hulk of a man with a deep raspy voice from too many cigarettes. He seldom laughed, but would break into the occasional sly smile flashing a white, chipped tooth. Crime was his game, he was an armed robbery specialist who never stopped scheming about his next escapade.

It took some time for me to find a rapport with him but then the barriers came down, and we became inseparable. My food supplies from fortnightly visits and posted parcels played a huge role in winning him over. He was a big soccer advocate with his own team and hated losing. Occasionally we'd have an over-40s match, and he'd bully his way, trying to intimidate the opposition. We would talk for hours, and I soon realised that Malagas was not reformable. Not everyone in the hall was happy with our friendship, but Malagas was moved to another hall after three months, and then transferred to another prison. So, the battle for me to stay ahead continued year after year.

CHAPTER 36

Sue Drifts Away

We were only permitted to write letters at Khami once a month, but in Chikurubi if you supplied your own stamps and envelopes, there was no official restriction. The problem was that I wrote too many; the censor's officer would trash them and confiscate any international mail. I wrote 14 letters in the first week after Sue mailed me stamps and envelopes, but only three were posted. In later years the censor's office staff informed me that the officer would regularly bin a bunch of letters because he was too busy or lazy to read them.

I realised that I had to use my mind to survive now, this was as far away from the life I had left behind as I could get and there was no secret link to the outside world like there was at Khami with smuggled letters. They had control over my body and activities entirely in both places, but now without that link to Sue or my children, I had to focus on refusing to give them my mind. It was easier said than done.

When given harsh uncalled-for instructions to crouch down or roll over, I would always say to myself, 'That's fine, I'll do whatever you want, but you don't, and never will even qualify as the lowest worker in my businesses.' I refused to lower myself to be affected by them. Unbeknown to me, many mental challenges were awaiting me.

Sue conveyed her plans for Christmas Day 2004 to me with great excitement during a visit in June. For some unknown reason, I expressed my concern about all her heartache, disappointments, and sometimes futile efforts in trying to care for me. I felt she needed a break, to spend more time with her own loving family instead of driving all the way up to Chikurubi and standing in line with hundreds of other visitors for hours. She was visibly hurt. No matter how hard I tried to retract that suggestion, nothing helped.

From that day onwards, things changed. She had been through hell too, and it was showing physically and emotionally. Her warmth had faded, and she seemed less tolerant with me and my problems. Family and friends had been trying to convince her that as a gorgeous young woman she was wasting her life away on hopes and dreams of this nightmare disappearing. Sue had been to endless meetings trying to get me released, some with politicians, some with influence peddlers, and some with lawyers. She had paid a small fortune to people who had made promises but delivered nothing.

Our visits became stressed and colder as business problems worsened and family issues crept in, distancing us ever more. On one occasion she drove all the way from Bulawayo, 430 km, to find my sister had visited two days earlier, after being assured by the guard that it would not affect my fortnightly visit with Sue. They adamantly refused Sue permission to see me, despite her desperate pleas, and she drove the long miles back to Bulawayo distraught.

I could feel her drifting away even in my weekly letters. I would open them and go straight to the end to see if she had written 'I love you'. Being lonely and isolated, with all the time in the world to think, I became ridiculously sensitive to things said. One remark that either of us would make during our precious moments together would replay a thousand times over in my mind while I lay on the cold floor. I scrutinised lines in letters from her from every conceivable angle. During most of the visits I was just trying to hold onto what I had, but I knew it was slipping away.

By June 2004, I had a new lawyer, the third one. I had lost all faith in my second lawyer, to whom we had paid a small fortune to have me out by the previous November. He was also representing Justice Paradza and could not be seen to be acting for me too. On instruction, Sue had engaged two senior counsels as well: Chris Andersen from Zimbabwe and a reputable advocate from South Africa. I wanted the injustice I had suffered exposed, and I was confident this would happen at the highest judicial level in the country.

Chris came up with many angles from which to attack the Kamocha judgement. All was going smoothly leading up to the hearing, in October 2004. The appointed judge was Wilson Sandura, sitting with two female assessors. Then, a week before the set date, we were advised that, despite having had 10 weeks to prepare, the state were not ready with their response to the heads of argument. The only available date that year did not suit my South African counsel, and the next available slot was April. I had had enough by then and wanted to be home for Christmas. I instructed them to accept the date in November, without him.

The appeal was then postponed by a month, and my attorney and senior counsel were shocked when entering the courtroom to find Chief Justice Chidyausiku, Sandura and another judge with a reputation for being racist. This now left only one judge from the original bench that had been set to hear my appeal. It was a disturbing turn of events, but worse was yet to come. Even though the state prosecution conceded that the sentence I had received, was 'a bit on the high side' and that it would be in accordance with 'substantial and real justice' if the overall sentence imposed was revisited and reconsidered, 'when regard is given to the overall circumstances of this matter alone', the judges of appeal were immovable. The full bench quashed the appeal, and my conviction and sentence were left unchanged.

That judgement happened in late February 2005, and it left me devastated. Several other promises of a retrial followed and various efforts by friends in high places, but nothing materialised. All responses eventually concluded that the matter was too political.

With my last legal hope dashed, the last hope for Sue and me had disappeared too. She suggested she might move to the UK and try to earn enough to buy us a flat as an investment for our future. As much as it hurt, I felt I would still have her and that it would benefit us both, but I doubted she would go.

Regardless of these personal problems, I still profoundly appreciated all my visits and the treats they brought. I will never forget the food delivered to me on Christmas Day 2004. Family and friends had spoilt me with delicious meals they knew I enjoyed. My sisters Bev and Lyn were unbelievable. They never spared a thing. I remember being ushered into my cell for lock-up that Christmas Day while balancing a lunchbox; it fell, and two juicy chicken thighs flew out onto the filthy floor beside the toilet. I quickly scooped them up and put them back in the box. It was such a privilege to have a home-cooked meal that I couldn't let them slip away just because they fell on the dirty toilet floor.

The wellbeing of my children was a constant concern, and I missed them more than I could ever have imagined.

During my second year in prison, Dusty and Sandy left school. Dusty started a computer company, which he turned into a thriving business within a year. During that year he applied to a hotel school in Switzerland and was accepted. It was comforting for me, knowing that he was getting a qualification behind him.

The imminent Zimbabwean dollar crash made it tough for Sandy to make anything of her life at 17 years old. She decided to work for her uncle who owned several hotels in Durban, South Africa, where she soon settled in as a director's PA. She was cared for by her uncle and aunt like a daughter, which gave me immense peace of mind.

For Easter 2005 Sue had organised Dusty, Sandy and 19 other friends to visit. I confirmed the number with the censor's, security and discipline offices, and I was assured there would be no problem. She did the same with the main-gate guards and got assurances that there would be no problem with the number of visitors.

On reaching the main gate on Easter Friday, after the one-kilometre walk up to the prison, they were told by Officer Chihambakwe that we were permitted only one visitor per prisoner. They tried desperately to convince the guard otherwise, as did I from inside, but eventually Dusty was chosen to carry six large plastic bags of groceries in for me. These people had given up their Easter weekend and driven from Bulawayo to Harare, 430 kilometres, just to see me, only to have their hopes dashed by spiteful authorities.

Phil's wife and son arrived 30 minutes later, and he was only allowed to see one of them. Within two hours after that, all the other prisoners were seeing multiple visitors, but Phil and I were treated differently. The racially motivated cruelty of these sadistic guards was enough to drive you mad.

Not long after that, I was approached by the censor's officer. He was carrying a letter for me. Laughing out loud, he threw it at me and said, 'Bad luck, your big friend is dead. He was killed by an elephant!' and walked away.

I read the letter and saw my close friend Carl Bradfield had died while guiding in Senge near Gonarezhou National Park. I was too upset to react to the un-empathetic guard. Apparently, they were close to a group of elephants when the wind changed; Carl told the clients to run and, after the commotion by the elephants, everything remained silent. No shouting or gunfire took place. Carl was found dead later only metres away from where the rest of the party had left him.

Carl and I had been classmates all the way through junior school and would share hunting stories of our childhood often. I introduced him to the best booking agents in Las Vegas at the Safari Club International Convention when he started in the industry. He was a real gentleman.

Being the competitive person I am, I over-trained during that freezing winter. There were guys in my cell with flu and I picked it up, which resulted in me getting another chest infection. I was given the same antibiotics as the last time, which had no effect, and soon two more different courses followed. I was just as much to blame. Not being fit really troubled me, and as soon as I felt a bit better, I would start training again. I had this passionate drive to stay in good shape. There wasn't much else to do in there.

After the third course, I prematurely over-trained again and really went down. The next day I was due a visit, but for the first time during my stay in prison, I had to stay in bed upstairs. I asked George to see my visitor and collect my food. It was a surprise visit from Lee McNab, a close friend from Bulawayo. George was quite an intimidating guy, and said Lee seemed pretty taken aback and apprehensive about handing over my food to this hulk of a convict. George and I laughed hard about it, as he and Lee ended up having a long chat about our predicament.

I ended up taking seven courses of antibiotics in a row, was tested for TB and finally given heavy courses of cortisone continuously for two years. After recovering during those years, I started playing competitive league soccer and remained in great shape with other training and gym routines, despite my cortisone course.

CHAPTER 37

Vicious Beatings

Although Chikurubi was newer and cleaner than Khami, it was a lot more violent. During the latter part of 2005, an exceptionally cruel OIC by the name of Mudzama took over, and introduced public beatings to prisoners in cuffs and leg irons. Often 20 to 30 guards would wrestle for the baton and a chance to deliver a beating. The thud from the baton striking could be heard all around the complex, followed by screams of pain.

I was represented by a lawyer and an advocate, so they were careful not to beat me and others who had the luxury of legal representation. I was never beaten in cuffs and leg irons, but on two occasions during searches, the guards lashed me. The regimen was barbaric and brutal and made violence a way of life.

One Sunday afternoon, Mudzama was called because a letter had been written reporting that seven prisoners, all named, were planning an escape. It was homosexual gang rivalry in play with one group trying to get the better of the other one. One hall had arranged for a fancied boy to be moved from another hall to theirs by bribing officers. The hall deprived of their boy wrote the letter of the so-called planned escape.

As this happened on a Sunday, it particularly irritated Mudzama, who was busy getting drunk. Stinking of booze, he ordered both gangs to the centre-court, which was out of bounds for prisoners unless they were red stages. They were put in leg irons and handcuffed, and then the metre-long rubber beating sticks arrived from the security office. The offenders were beaten two at a time. They were laid out on their stomachs with their hands cuffed behind their backs. A chair was placed over their torso with a guard sitting in it, to stop them from turning over. Another guard stood with a foot on the prisoner's head, to prevent him from turning to see the swing coming, which would have given him a moment to try and move his feet. With legs in irons, bent at the knees and feet horizontal facing up, another two sets of irons were brought. Each one was attached at one end to each foot, leaving a free shackle on each set. The guards pulled the free shackles outwards to keep the prisoner's legs still for the beating. They were each beaten 100 times on each foot with heavy, solid one-metre batons. They would get 20 strokes, then have to shuffle around the centre-court to get the blood in their feet going then wait for their next 20 until they had received their 100.

They all crawled to their halls except one who had his leg visibly broken just above the ankle. The OIC instructed that none of those beaten were permitted to go to the hospital for any injuries. Two days later, when it was clear the broken leg was getting infected, the prisoner was taken to the prison hospital, then immediately transferred to have his leg reset and put in plaster at Parirenyatwa Government Hospital. This centre-court beating process became a standard maximum punishment under Mudzama from then on and left many broken heels and foot bones.

CHAPTER 38

Phil Moves to C Hall

It was a massive boost to my morale when Phil was permitted to move to my hall. A week after he moved, I asked to be transferred from the holding cell to his cell.

Phil was a wonderful character, making me laugh regularly with endless stories of the war years, farming days, and his life in general. We had met briefly once at a mutual friend's son's 21st birthday party on a ranch in the Chiredzi district. I distinctly remember Phil being quite cocky as he supervised the turning of the lamb on the spit. Lying there on the cold floor, he reminded me of the thundering music from my handsome vehicle full of happy folk as we drove out of the yard late that night.

He was 56 and not in great shape. I gave him a tough time and told him I was going to get him fit and young again. Initially, he was not too responsive, but then he got into the swing of it and became an enthusiastic member of my gym class. He was tough, and his tenacity earned him a lot of respect amongst the inmates.

To keep our minds off the pain of what we were all missing outside, we would train extremely hard and read up in all the *Men's Health* magazines about new exercises to try, and training programmes to follow. I slept against the grill and Phil was beside me, it was our corner and the centre of many a card game or in-depth discussion on some topic.

He was in the Grey Scouts cavalry unit during the Rhodesian Bush War and had a passion for horses. Because I grew up riding horses too, we would share many an old tale. The one story he loved was about Ernie Stock, a notorious cattle rancher from Bulawayo, who also used to breed and sell horses. One day in the 1960s, a woman approached him to buy a horse and told Mr Stock that she wanted a gentle horse as it was for her 12-year-old daughter. He said, 'My dear, I have just the horse for you.' So, the next day she drove 20 km to his farm in Figtree and there the horse was. It was by no means a magnificent specimen, but Mr Stock assured her, 'It don't look too good, but it's a fine horse and a good price.' The groom led the horse out of its stables into the lunging ring. Initially, it stumbled a bit, and the woman pointed this out to Mr Stock, but he repeated, 'Don't worry my dear, it don't look too good, but it's a good horse.' Soon it was trotting around the ring totally calm. After they had agreed on a price, the woman paid, and Mr Stock said he would have the horse delivered the next day. The following day the horse arrived, and during a short ride with the daughter, the horse kept walking into things. After a while, they realised that the horse was totally blind. The woman called Mr Stock to inform him, and he said, 'I told you it don't look too good, but it's a good horse.'

The week that I was informed of Carl's death, we were advised that there was no food until 2 p.m. again. This had been the case for over a week, leaving us all in low spirits. For some reason, that same arrogant and senseless censor's officer was put in charge of our hall for the morning. Being the cruel-minded individual that he was, he ordered all inmates to sit on the tarred floor in the blazing sun, for the entire three hours we had out of cells from 8 a.m. until 11 a.m. Phil and I point blank refused. He shouted above the guys on the floor for us to sit down and we just continued walking up and down the one wall of the exercise yard. Eventually, he signalled for us to come over to where he was sitting and asked why we were not following his orders. I told him that people were dying daily from stress and malnutrition and that walking de-stressed us. He laughed and dismissed us with a wave of his hand, but the rest of the inmates had to remain seated. It was tough not to get upset with this kind of individual.

Being laid back and a stable personality, Phil was an absolute blessing for me emotionally. Sometimes I just needed someone from my background to explain uncertainties in my head about issues at home, and Phil was incredible. Really level-headed and calm, he always gave good advice. He'd done a lot in his life and worked like a machine developing virgin land he had bought after independence, and now it was all gone.

After a few months, we teamed up with some of the mercenaries serving there. In the monotony of prison life, catching up on all their war stories, made a refreshing change.

There was one individual Phil and I were very cautious around. Joram was short, powerfully built and pure evil. He walked with his chest puffed out, his shoulders back, and permanently raised eyebrows which left his eyes wide open. His head looked too big for his body. He had been sentenced to 75 years and life for armed robberies and murder. He obeyed no rules and provided the authorities with a permanent headache.

Joram was very intelligent. He spoke Shona, Ndebele, and English perfectly and was a brilliant manipulator. An exceptional athlete and soccer player, he also had a happy, endearing side to his nature and could play on people to get them to like him. His criminal mind would then click into gear, and he would use his charm to hoodwink his target and steal.

He caught me early one morning, as I placed toothpaste on my toothbrush as I did every day, and turned around to face the toilet. Phil was sitting only a few feet away. Unlock had just begun one cell at a time, so it was chaos rushing for the toilets out of the other cells. He had arranged his gang to move about causing a bit of activity to distract me, and within 30 seconds when I looked back, as they unlocked our cell, the new tube of toothpaste was gone, and everyone was rushing out the door. He had waited and planned this for days. When I furiously raised the alarm, his whole gang were quick to step in, in support of him and loudly denied it was him. I learned quickly about jovial Joram after that. Phil was so shocked he started laughing at the audacity of it. We were supposed to be cellmates. It made Phil and me more aware of how isolated and vulnerable we were in there.

Joram had a thunderous voice and would make all the yard announcements. If I found myself anywhere near him when he was shouting orders, my ears would ring for minutes. We had our differences, but I knew I needed to remain friends with him as he had such an influence in prison.

Weeks after I had come to terms with what was going to happen, Sue advised me of her plans to go and live in the UK. She was flying at 10 a.m. on 4 May 2005, the very date we started dating in 1998.

I remember standing in the exercise yard looking over the razor wire dotted with popped soccer balls. At around 10 a.m. I caught sight of the aeroplane flying over, knowing she was on it and wishing so deeply for the miracle that would put me alongside her. Phil walked up behind me and placed his hand on my shoulder. 'Don't worry Russ, it's going to be okay, my mate,' he said. I don't know what I would have done without Phil. He was a godsend. I've always believed that people come and go in and out of our lives for specific reasons. He was a huge blessing in the most meaningful ways.

We wrote weekly, and she returned over Christmas that year, but things had changed. I felt alone and empty after that, although visits from my sisters and close friends gave me strength, I struggled not to slip into total despair. I battled to come to terms with the fact that my soulmate and the love of my life was now vulnerable to a vastly greater society thousands of miles away.

CHAPTER 39

Hard Times

t took about 45 minutes to feed 400 people in Chikurubi Max. After a year in C Hall, I was put in charge of controlling this process. Trying to bring order to 400 unruly, hungry prisoners was not easy. My semi-official position was Senior Security Staff. This led to regular confrontations with stubborn disorderly prisoners but allowed me many privileges. Importantly, it meant I no longer had to sit in formation on hot tar in the yard waiting for food or rations. If I needed to go to the prison hospital, there were no questions asked, I just went. I got the position at the request of the inmates; I had not only gained considerable respect from the other prisoners, but they did not trust any of the other inmates to be fair with the shortages of essentials, like food and water.

During my first year at Chikurubi Maximum, twice a week we would receive a single thumb-sized piece of rubbery boiled meat in a quarter cup of watery soup to go with our plate of lumpy *sadza*.

However, extra pieces were always for sale by thieving kitchen staff, who worked hand-in-hand with guards, who had already stolen what they wanted from the kitchen.

Stories from the kitchen staff about theft by the guards were shocking. The staff were escorted from the filthy kitchen, stealing by the bucketful for guards and themselves. They would pass through six security doors or gates, with everyone along the way on the take. After they had carried the two black dustbins of *sadza* to each hall, and the meat in half a bin of watery soup, they would service the five large, over-crowded halls during our 45 minutes of dishing up.

We would place orders for meat through a barred, waist-high, glassless window at the base of the stained cement staircase. A tiny chunk of meat was two smokes. For two days, deep-fried and often half rotten pieces of meat, known as *mvumvira*, that they had been unable to sell, would be made available. By late 2005, those precious little chunks of beef were a thing of the past. During early 2006, we received only rotten piglets on two occasions in one week. These came from the closing of the Mutare farm prison piggery. Due to the stench, I could not touch the meat.

Beginning in May 2005, the government ordered the destruction of tens of thousands of shanty dwellings and street stalls (mostly by bulldozers) in urban townships across the country, including the immediate arrest of some 10,000 people. The implementation of this policy, labelled Operation Murambatsvina, left an estimated 700,000 people homeless and deprived of their livelihood, and adversely affected some 2,4 million additional people. This indirectly affected the economy and had a massive effect on the supplies to the prisons. Food rations were cut to one meal a day, and the *sadza* often smelled so rancid that prisoners, even the hardened ones, couldn't eat it. It was made from the scrapings off warehouse floors, full of sand, weevils and mostly rotten. The relish was half a cup of boiled cabbage mixed with sugar beans and had a repulsive taste.

In 2005, during the Zimbabwe dollar currency crash, water started running short along with food. Our only salvation was to make *kavisa* or *nchai-nchai*. Phil knew what it was from working on crop farms where it was often made. We created it by taking leftover *sadza*, mashing it up in water to a thin porridge, then pouring it into plastic containers before adding some sort of fruit, often a banana, to give it some flavour. I would mash it up in a lunchbox and Phil would fill a bottle at a time, then add our precious water and a piece of fruit. By the morning it was a stomach-churning brew, but it tasted okay and kept us going.

We tried many different recipes and decided that banana was the best. Often the mixture would ferment too much, mainly on warmer evenings, and it would explode during the night, sending the cap flying with a loud thud and a jet of the strong-smelling fluid spilling everywhere. It was a severely punishable offence, but we were starving, and it was one of the few survival options we had. Eventually, we hung the bottles up in the toilet so that if they burst no blankets were spoilt. The condition of the inmates started deteriorating markedly, and guys were dropping all around us.

One of the saving graces of our predicament was the food parcels mailed to me from family and friends. Thankfully, a parcel was permitted in my first week in Chikurubi, after consultation with the OIC, and this paved the way for others in the years to follow. Every month without fail my uncle Allan Jones and his adorable wife Mariaan would send me a parcel. These, along with many others, were an enormous contribution to our wellbeing. One of the biggest surprises was a parcel from a woman in Canada. I had met Lori Lund once at the Houston Safari Club Convention and word had spread as far as Canada, where she was living, that I'd been incarcerated. She contacted my office, received an address for the prison, and sent many deeply appreciated parcels of food. These kind gestures kept my spirits high during such extreme hardship.

In mid-2005, the main water supply to the Chikurubi complex finally ran dry. The Chikurubi farm prisoners would carry water for us from a local dam, which collected run-off water from the city of Harare. It was a dirty orange colour, and they would carry it up to the prison in 20- and 30-litre containers. This meant manual transport of water from the dam to supply 2,200 maximum security prisoners every day.

Each prisoner was allocated one plastic cup of water a day, and that was it. That one cup of water was to drink, clean your teeth, wash your face, bath, wash clothes, wash plates and anything else you might need water for. That was our water ration for three years. Most prisoners didn't bath until it rained during our four hours out of cells – and that happened once in nine months. When it rained during our time outside, there were screams of joy from the exercise yard. Every inmate would rip off his clothes and dash into the pouring rain in the yard with soap for a bath, trying to get the best run-off stream from the roof. It was always a fun-filled event, but we didn't have nearly enough of them.

When it rained, it was also a mad rush to fill water containers, and we would line them up under each gutter pipe to fill with filthy pigeon-messy water.

Those in the upper social order, which I had reached by this time, could occasionally buy this dirty water from the farm prisoners who carried it. Twenty Madison cigarettes or a loaf of bread could buy you 20 litres of dirty water, which helped tremendously. Water containers then became valuable, as

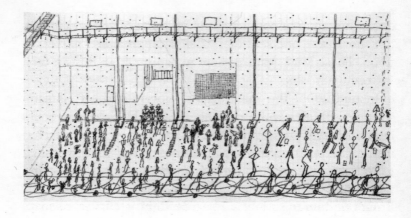

ABOVE Bathing in the rain

LEFT Washing clothes in toilets

they were not permitted to enter the prison through visitors. They were sneaked in by guards to the kitchen, then by kitchen staff to the halls, and sold to prisoners for smokes or soap rations, which were in demand by guards.

Despite this occasional natural bonanza of bathing in the rain, the guards were unrelenting in their heartlessness. If they found us with excess water during a random search, they would gleefully smash our containers with their batons or jump on them with their heavy boots and then joyfully empty any remaining water onto our blankets. It was tough to understand the twisted minds of these people as we stood forlornly watching our precious water drain uselessly away. It became survival of the fittest, and as a result of these extremely unhealthy conditions, things got horribly worse.

Being locked up for 20 hours a day, we would get incredibly thirsty. Often during our lunchtime lock-up, between 11 a.m. and 2 p.m. it would be raining, and the guards refused to let us go out for a drink or bath in the rain. The cruelty was mind-blowing.

With no running water and no deodorant, perfumed soap or cream permitted, body odours became repulsive. It was

LEFT Crouching down in front of guard

BELOW Guards smashing water bottles and emptying water onto blankets

such a mind-numbing place that some prisoners did not care about bathing and were quite happy to remain filthy.

We often heard about prisoners before they arrived in the halls, either from the guards or reception staff. There was a story that leaked out to us that there were three guys who had been sentenced to 30 years each for armed robbery and rape that were about to enter our hall. Just before they arrived, Elisha handed me a smuggled newspaper cutting with the headlines: 'They Gang-Raped My Daughter in Front of Me.'

The article went on to detail a brutal account of the three men and how they had invaded a Zimbabwean household one night. In the article, it described the brutality of the men as they beat the father of the house to a pulp and tied him up, before raping the mother and 13-year-old daughter in full view of each other. I felt sick to the bone after reading that, and when these three sauntered into our hall minutes later, like they were heroes, I battled to contain my opinion.

There were many such characters in there and having to accept that we had to coexist was emotionally challenging. Phil utterly refused to speak to them and never hid his opinion.

We were lying in our cell one morning, and the word spread like wildfire that there was a search. It always sent shivers through the prison and heightened anxiety. Phil was calm as usual and just said, 'Let them come, they can take everything.' He was a tough old man. I despised these unan-nounced monthly searches, especially during those no-water days. They would set us back to untold hardships and any minuscule bits of pleasure we managed to come up with, like card or dice games, were smashed.

I realised over time and learning from Phil that in prison there would always be people who would try to break you, and if you let them, they would. Smashing precious water bottles, or a negative word, a cold stare, or a false accusation

– these things seem simple, but they can affect you. They can break your confidence and spirit. The guards revelled in mentally torturing us prisoners. When you spoke to them, they would immediately say, *'Gara pasi'* meaning *'Sit down'* and refused to acknowledge you unless you crouched down at their feet. Initially, it really got to me; then I realised that the more upset I got, the more they enjoyed it. Phil and I learned over the years, not to lower ourselves by being affected by them. Phil had a powerful, positive mind. Often when things got really tough, and the guards could see we were rock bottom, they would laugh and ask if we were real men and could we handle the conditions, and Phil would say with a flick of his hand, 'It's a piece of cake. This? This is nothing for us,' and walk away.

CHAPTER 40

Mapolishers

I n all the prisons there are inmates who polish guards' shoes, about three in each hall. They were known as *mapolishers*. The guards would come from all sections to the halls with their polish tins, shout out, '*Mapolisher!*' and the *mapolishers* would rush over to attend to their boots. Some had *veldskoens* made from durable suede leather, and these would be starched with mielie meal. When dry, this was removed, leaving them a clean beige colour. Two of these mapolishers were Hasani and Masango.

Hasani was tall and very thin, serving 10 years for apparently raping his mother, which shocked us deeply. Phil couldn't stand him. He was not a very popular inmate and known for snitching on prisoners to the guards when polishing shoes. When guards needed info, they always talked to the *mapolishers*.

Hasani would make the most exquisite bangles and rings from plastic water bottles and bags. He would slice a plastic container horizontally several times, leaving many rings about the size of a person's wrist. Then he would cut the circles and create very clever clips to hold the bangle on once it was on your wrist. He would then take many different coloured plastic bags and stretch them while twisting them, forming long thin plastic threads of many colours.

Painstakingly, he would then bind the bangle tightly with one colour and weave other colours in periodically to write your name or create unusual patterns. He would do the same, making rings for your fingers. It showed incredible ingenuity and a talent I'd never seen before.

His other specialty was to make hats and soccer shoes, from polystyrene sacks smuggled in from the kitchen. This made him more popular with the guards and alienated from the rest of us as it gave him quite an opinion of himself. The bracelets sold for 20 cigarettes, rings for 5, hats and shoes 60 each. I have several samples and have inserted photos of them in this book.

During one of my very lonely days, I struck up a conversation with Hasani. He turned out to be from West Nicholson and on further discussion, we worked out that he was one of the schoolchildren I used to fish with below Ripple Creek Dam when visiting my godfather, Poogie Darlow. We laughed hard over incidents, recalling how they used to arrive on the trailer pulled by the tractor from the ranch HQ. Sadly, I never got to like Hasani; he had a very devious and insincere character.

Masango, on the other hand, was wonderful, in for armed robbery but fully reformed from what I could tell. He was caught on his first robbery attempt. Tall and slim, quite good-looking, with a fast-growing beard that always showed a little. We would chat for hours as he had a great sense of humour and would inform us often of news from the guards that he had overheard.

I left them both in Chikurubi and never heard what became of Hasani. Masango would surprise me many years later.

When you depend on the people around you to have your back – and not stab you in it – loyalty and sincerity become highly prized. One of my closest and most loyal friends at Chikurubi was Edmos Moyo. Everyone called him Moyo. Often prisoners would move to other halls or be transferred when causing problems in a hall, but seven of us remained in C Hall throughout my time there: Bigass, Moyo, George, Nyere, Fatso and Elisha.

I had formed my own soccer team, and Moyo became the defender and the only player who stayed with the club throughout the four-and-a-half years we were together. A tall Ndebele man of medium build, he was damn tough, quietly spoken and extremely pleasant to be around. We spoke English mostly, but Ndebele too, which I could speak before I was imprisoned. He had worked for a safari operator in Bulawayo as a tracker and was in for a murder sentence of 21 years, serving 14.

Phil and I asked him about his crime one day, sitting in the exercise yard. He told us that, while on leave after a safari, an aggressive drunk man at a beer hall was assaulting people at random and picked on Moyo. When Moyo retaliated, he picked up a brick; Moyo removed his lock-blade knife from his pocket and as the drunk man attacked, Moyo stabbed him in the shoulder. The man went down and refused help, bleeding badly. The more people tried to help him, the more he performed, pushing everyone away holding his bleeding shoulder. Police arrived after 30 minutes by which time the man had lost a considerable amount of blood. Arriving at the hospital semi-conscious, he passed away hours later. The judge ruled that Moyo, being a man active in the safari industry and aware of the dangers that a knife could cause, should have been more restrained. His sentence was unusually harsh because he could not compensate the deceased's family.

His trademark was that one of his front teeth stuck out at 45 degrees and they were all yellow. Despite his poorly formed teeth, he had a huge beaming smile and was seldom unhappy. He was a great friend who I spent hours talking to about all aspects of life, from safari work to advice about my life in general. I always found that advice from all circles gave me a broader vision and increased my options when making decisions, especially on safari with my trackers. Whenever I received a letter from Sue needing advice, I would consult several guys, and Moyo was always one of them. A stable, straight down-to-earth man.

Being a food-serving staff member, Moyo had the privilege of extra food and remained in good health. Along with his friendly personality, guards warmed to him, and I never saw him being beaten once. He was known as one of the few who was not into homosexuality, along with Bigass, Elisha and me.

He dished up *sadza* daily to every inmate in our hall for the full four-and-a-half years I was there. He had huge callouses on his hands from pushing the plate into the *sadza* 800 times a day, and also made all our soccer balls, which would take him about an hour per ball.

Soccer and volleyball had leagues as well as inter-hall competitions. The prison volleyball team, for which I was in the starting line-up, played many visiting officer teams from around the country. In 2008 I made the Prison Service calendar with a photo of me spiking at the net; this was quite an honour.

When we played sport, there were 400 of us tightly packed into a tarred exercise yard the size of two tennis courts. On the one side of the yard was the soccer pitch on which we played our five-a-side games. This was all part of a hotly contested in-house league. It was very physical because we were playing in a confined space and emotions often ran dangerously high. The pace was fast and furious, and, with walls as touchlines, the ball bounced back into play off the walls as did we, the players. Our rules were Chikurubi rules. We played with takkies that had a tightly woven net or mesh around them to add strength to the canvas. Prisoners would buy polystyrene bags from the kitchen staff and plait the plastic strings into a thin rope, which was used to weave the nets around the takkies for reinforcement. They were incredible works of art.

Teams were five-a-side and the goalkeeper played sitting on his backside using his legs only; any use of hands was a penalty. The goal posts were full plastic water containers about three metres apart, and a rope woven out of old blankets pulled tightly between the tops. A goal was under the rope and between the containers. The ball, being allowed to bounce off the walls, made the game exceptionally fast and physically demanding. After 30 minutes, we were exhausted. I enjoyed it immensely and played whenever I could.

Balls were made from blowing up four surgical gloves inside of each other; it was quite tough to blow them up. Then we wrapped the inflated gloves tightly with strips of blanket followed by wide strips of plastic from mielie-meal bags. Finally, the ball was entirely covered by a tightly woven net made from the plaited rope from polystyrene bags. They were about the size of a polo-cross ball, roughly 20 cm in diameter, and very hard but light.

Fatso was another friend of mine initially. He was from a good family, went to a great school, was well educated and an excellent athlete. Before prison, he had been supported and sponsored by a supportive white woman to compete in tri-athletic competitions in Harare. Phil never warmed to him, and they were often quite open about their dislike for each other. We slept in the same cell, often talked about sport for hours when Phil was busy reading or sleeping, and we trained together. I was also very generous with him when I had food to share.

His best friend before prison was a gardener, who, along with a domestic worker, worked for an elderly, wealthy Swiss woman in Harare. She regularly left the country for up to a month or two at a time visiting her homeland. During her absence Fatso and the gardener would regularly use her vehicle unbeknown to her, to carry out frequent petty crime like handbag and mobile phone snatching. Being old, the woman made out a will and told the maid and gardener that she had left the house and contents to the two of them, as she had another beautiful home overseas. They told Fatso about this and with his help, they promptly killed her, burnt her body in the backyard and buried the remains. It was a barbaric story that made me shudder whenever I remembered it. They then took up residence and lived 'the good life'. After about nine months of regular parties with hordes of people moving freely in and out of the house, the neighbours reported the activity to the police and made it known that they had not seen the owner for months. An investigation followed, and the gardener confessed. All three were arrested.

While awaiting trial and locked up in the remand section, Fatso persuaded the maid and gardener to take full responsibility and assured them he would care for them during their time inside. The maid and the gardener received death sentences while Fatso got 20 years of which he was to serve 12 years and 8 months.

CHAPTER 41

Healthy Body, Healthy Mind

Throughout my time in Chikurubi I was the only person out of the 2,200 inmates who had a gym routine. Generally, guards didn't allow it, but would turn a blind eye for a price (either cigarettes, tea or coffee with biscuits).

My reputation had preceded me – when I first arrived at Chikurubi, the reception staff asked if I was the gym guy, and I told them I was, and that I intended to continue staying fit. Even so, it was such a demoralising place that on many an occasion, it took all my willpower to get up and exercise. Phil was very supportive during our time together, we would push one another and keep our spirits up.

My gym classes gained popularity with the other inmates, and we were going great until the water ran out. This was a problem as we used water containers as weights for a whole variety of exercises. No water meant no weights. I would always try and buy enough so I could at least do some gym exercise daily.

As weights, we used two-, five-, 20- and 30-litre containers. We would strap four of the five-litre containers together in pairs bound together with strips of blanket, which were also worked into handles, to give us 2 X 10-litre weights to train with, too.

With these weights, all exercises were possible. Bicep and tricep moves, upright-rows, bent-over-rows. For bench-press, we folded blankets shoulder width and as high as the bench. Then we lay down and had two guys balance 30-litre containers on each hand, then another two guys placing a 20-litre container on top of those 30s. For dips, we would place the 30s shoulder-width apart on the floor, then the 2 X 20 litres on top of them and dip from the top. Pull-ups were done on the side of the toilet wall dividing the toilet from the cell, which was rough on top for grip. It was tough on the fingers but good for the forearms.

Squats were done with a person on your shoulders, lunges with weights, and calf raises on the cement block around the toilet. We improvised for every exercise using what we had. Clinging to my health while blocking out all I was missing, kept me positive and sane. Initially, I had about seven guys in the gym-training programme, but slowly they faded until just Phil and I were left.

I also read endlessly. We were allowed books brought by visitors, although of course they had to go through the dreadful censor's office. I had *The Count of Monte Cristo* sneaked in to me – it was my best read, although of course it was prohibited as it was a prison story.

Every day was exactly the same routine, day in and day out. Only Christmas Day and Easter Friday and Monday were different. On those days, we were unlocked from 8 a.m. until 3 p.m. allowing us lunch in the yards as opposed to lunch lock-up from 11 a.m. and 2 p.m.

I would spend most of my time out in the mornings playing soccer or volleyball which took up half the exercise yard, while Phil walked up and down the outer wall of the other half of the exercise yard, mostly alone. Phil couldn't run as he had broken his leg years earlier and one leg was shorter than the other, which had left him with a limp. When I was free, I'd join him. The amount of uninterrupted thinking we did was endless – from business dreams to memories, fantasies, future plans and the hope of release. Our minds never stopped.

I have always believed in visualisation, and during hours of walking or lying in my cell, I would visualise myself in every conceivable situation in life. It was always about inspiring events that made me smile and feel good. I would plan my future continuously – what car I was going to buy, how I was going to make my fortune back and help my children reach their potential, and how I could leave a legacy after my time on earth.

Much as I enjoyed looking forward, the hours of contemplation also gave me plenty of opportunity to look back and assess where I had come from.

CHAPTER 42

Building My Empire

The province of Matabeleland, where Bulawayo is situated, continued to struggle with violence after the war had formally ended and Rhodesia became Zimbabwe. Disaffected militants from Joshua Nkomo's ZIPRA (Zimbabwe People's Revolutionary Army), continued attacks on farming communities. Despite the ongoing instability, displaced farmers and ranchers started to move warily back to their abandoned properties. Unfortunately, the war years had taken their toll on the wildlife, and there was extensive work to be done in helping the land and its game to recover.

When I finished school I had considered becoming a veterinarian, and then to study Agricultural Management. Unfortunately, my mom couldn't afford the tuition fees, so my uncle Lin encouraged me to learn a trade in Bulawayo.

I started as an apprentice fitter and turner on 3 January 1981, doing all the dirty work that new boys did. The same year I joined Old Miltonians Rugby Club, playing beside great players like Rob Halstead and Neville Jenkinson. Our coaches were ex-World XV captain Bucky Buchanan and ex-national captain Lou Corbi. The highlight of my rugby career would come later when we played two tests against Italy in Harare and Bulawayo.

Although rugby was in my blood, the more I trained and played the less time I had to do those longed-for ranch excursions with my close friends. Mary (Muffy) McDonald, my future wife, was invariably along on those trips. During those special sojourns driving through beautiful deserted ranches, we camped where we liked and shot what we needed for food and biltong. It was a wonderful time for us, but it was also sad in that properties that had once been pristine and vibrant were now derelict.

It was during those trips that Mary and I developed a unique bond. Slowly, in this blissful environment, I opened a barricaded heart to her.

We started dating seriously towards the end of 1981. This was during the peak of our ranch trips that were fuelling my passion for bush-life away from the claustrophobic confines of the workshops where I was hemmed in trying to become a tradesman.

In June 1982, when I was peaking as a rugby player and a member of the national squad, I was offered a job on Nuanetsi Ranch where I had experienced some of the happiest days of my life as a young boy.

While I loved the game of rugby, I also loved the bush and that was where I wanted to be. I couldn't do both. I consulted Bucky, Lou, and Robbie, my rugby mentors, and was relieved to receive their blessing.

I traded in my old Yamaha motorbike for a short-wheelbase Land Rover and headed for Nuanetsi Ranch. Mary and I planned to marry in October – against the wishes of her parents and the advice of many of my friends. She was 19, and I was just shy of 21.

I loved every minute back on the ranch. Learning all about the safari industry was exciting, and I had a chance to visit all the sites we frequented as children. The first person I ever employed was Hadhlani, who I nicknamed Kermit, because he reminded me of Kermit the frog with his bulging eyes and infectious laugh. He was born in Chikombedzi in the Chiredzi district not far from Nuanetsi. He was just out of school and roughly my age, and we formed a friendship close as family.

Another member of the skinning-shed staff at the safari camp that I got along very well with was Kermit's deaf brother, Hasani. He had a fantastic way of communicating with huffs and puffs mixed with grunts, head-shaking and an array of hand signals. We managed to communicate easily despite neither of us having any training. Our chats were invariably filled with laughter, smiles and hand slaps.

Very few well-known game ranches entertained any sort of safari hunting. On other private land, game was seen as a means of feeding labour and numbers were controlled as they competed with cattle for food. In the Gwaai Valley near Wankie National Park, for example, sable antelope were shot as ration meat for the labour, while lions were shot on sight. On every cattle ranch, leopard and cheetah were considered vermin and a bonus was paid to section managers for every leopard trapped and shot.

After Mary and I married, I obtained a job with Dan Landrey in the Matetsi Safari Area near Victoria Falls. It was a beautiful area divided up into state-owned concessions. I worked several months there before being sent to run a camp on the banks of the Zambezi River in the Chewore Safari Area.

This was wild Africa at its best. It was remote and unpopulated; my team and I were the first civilians back in the area since the war ended. The place was teeming with animals that held no fear of humans. A leopard chased an impala ram right through camp one morning, lions walked unfazed between tents regularly in daylight and vehicles were charged daily by the black rhino. Large tuskers roamed the game-rich floodplains at ease, and in front of the camp was brilliant fishing. It was heaven on earth to me, but not for long.

I went down with a bout of malaria that almost killed me and ended up losing seven kilograms in a fortnight. I had no treatment for a week, throwing up any medication I took and hallucinating about being stampeded by herds of buffalo. I was going down fast; then the staff cleared all the vegetation around my tent as part of their belief system, and within two days I was on the mend. I was very weak for weeks but completed the task of building a lovely tented camp and conducted several successful safaris. To my great disappointment, Dan decided to replace me, and I was back looking for another job. When nothing in the safari line came up, I headed back to Bulawayo and joined National Tyre Service as a sales representative. This was not where I wanted to be, and we spent most weekends in the bush, fishing and enjoying the outdoors.

Bulawayo in those days was a party town, and I was not going to miss any of the action. Mary was not as outgoing as me, and this strained our marriage. She wanted us to be home alone, and I wanted to be out having a good time with my mates. Suddenly I missed the freedom of bachelorhood.

I also found this burning desire to please everyone and to be loved by all. I'm not sure what led to it during my upbringing, but I always wanted to be the best at, and have the best of, everything. Be it a game I was playing, my job, car, house, partner – everything. Even if all seemed perfect, nothing appeared to satisfy me for long. I had an innate desire to always improve on what I had.

Mary was a beautiful person, and a loyal and constant supporter. She worked exceptionally hard to help us build our lives, but my apparent discontent distressed her. Being in town was not good for us. I was a flirt, and unsurprisingly, this enraged her. On occasion, she would viciously attack me, which I thoroughly deserved.

Once we were back in the bush though, all was happy again. Before too long I was given the opportunity to work in a safari venture on a new concession, with Billy and Chloe Edwards and Ian and Sue Lennox. I would be based at camp and assist with conducting safaris. This was a blessing for Mary – it kept me away from the distractions of town as I lost myself again in my love for the outdoors.

I felt at home in the bush and more convinced than ever that this was where my heart was, and with it my future. That season with Ian and Sue was fantastic. When the safari season ended, I returned to Bulawayo. Mary was pregnant, and my intuition kept telling me this is not where I was meant to be.

My childhood friend and cousin, Bush Stanton, was speculating in cattle. After a cattle sale in Shangani on 18 December 1984, Bush was returning to Bulawayo when he was killed in a head-on collision. It was a huge shock to us all, and hit my uncle Lin hard.

Towards the end of 1984, Brian Ross offered me the opportunity to build and manage a new abattoir. The job would give me a steady income and enough time to play rugby again, so I accepted. I bought a house and played a full season, which included several test matches for Zimbabwe.

On 27 January 1985, our precious son Dustin (Dusty) entered our world, bringing a new vibrancy and purpose to our lives. Dusty was a delightfully happy baby, and Mary was a devoted mother, but fatherhood came as a bit of a shock to me. I was not expecting the sleepless nights, but did my best to help.

While fatherhood and family life appealed to me deeply, my exposure as a national rugby player and the constant travelling placed a continuous strain on our marriage. I played hard that year but had to withdraw due to a neck injury towards the end of the season.

Being out of action gave me opportunities to help safari operators based in Bulawayo, and with the abattoir running smoothly, it was time to move back into the safari industry.

CHAPTER 43

Trust and Teamwork

Wayne Grant was a former Rhodesian Army officer I had known since school. He took me under his wing, and I worked with him through the 1986 season while aiming at setting up my own safari company. Kermit was back in his element and soon sent for his brother, Hasani, who was a phenomenal skinner. We made a fantastic team.

The approach to wildlife was changing, and a few landowners began their own safari operations on their properties. A handful of us chose to try and build game numbers up on private land to make it attractive for hunting safaris. We figured if we could bring about seven wealthy American and European hunters out annually to hunt sensibly, we could generate enough income to survive while boosting wildlife populations. We operated according to strict rules; only male trophy animals were taken, which were invariably over their prime, and we did not shoot out of breeding herds. The meat went to the camp staff, ranch labour and, sometimes, hungry local tribespeople.

Landowners soon realised the value of wild animals; with income generated, we funded anti-poaching units, fed wildlife during droughts and started reintroducing game that had been shot out over the years. This was obviously a long-term process, and I wanted to devote my life to the development of wildlife in our beautiful country.

That season with Wayne was brilliant. We worked exceptionally hard building safari camps and in December 1986 we went on a three-month marketing trip to sign up clients for the following season. We travelled to seven states in America, including Hawaii. Wayne gave me a proportion of the new clientele and allowed me free use of his camps and concession areas.

During this trip our precious daughter Sandy was born. Our family was now complete, and I was on my way to realising my dream of working for myself in the safari game. The problem was I was spending over half the year away from home.

After a successful 1987 season, I needed to find new hunting concessions and start on my own. It was tough, as banks refused to lend me money without a track record. I ended up borrowing US$10,000 from a friend to build and outfit my first safari camp.

From 1988 onwards, I obtained my own safari areas consisting of 120,000 acres on Debshan Ranch in Shangani and three large cattle ranches in the Mateke Hills in the Mwenezi district. Kermit sent word to all we had worked with to join us, and we ended up with 14 staff members. It was the beginning of a fantastic loyal, dedicated team of trackers, skinners, and chefs. Seeing these wonderful men again, willing to support me as an upstart, was heartwarming.

In my almost obsessive desire to make landowners aware of the value of conservation, I crisscrossed the country addressing far-flung communities. This was not entirely altruistic; as a safari operator, I had no livelihood without wildlife. It was imperative for me to protect and build up the wildlife numbers on private land, which made up a significant proportion of my quota.

In April 1988, my first client, a man called Howard Nations, arrived from Houston. Mary went out to the airport to collect him at 6 p.m. They drove into our driveway and pulled up next to our Land Cruiser. Beside it lay the engine innards: crankshaft, pistons, cylinder head, rocker shaft, all set out on the floor, with me next to it in dirty coveralls, full of grease. After our greetings Howard asked, 'Where's our safari vehicle?'. I recall the disbelief on his face when I told him this was it and I'd have it going by 5 a.m. At 3.30 a.m. I took it for a test drive, had a nap, and we left at 5 a.m.

On the second day of the safari, while cruising slowly through the bush, smoke started coming out from under the bonnet. The engine spluttered a few times then stopped, 20 km from camp. I sent Howard off on a walk and went to work. Removing the tappet cover, I found a seized rocker-shaft and realised that no oil was being supplied to the rockers. Using brute force, I stripped the shaft completely. By the time Howard returned I was removing the last bit of mud I'd used as sandpaper so the rockers could move freely on the shaft. The head gasket had been incorrectly placed the night Howard arrived, blocking the oil feed. We had no more trouble for the remainder of the safari. These practical skills would stand me in good stead in the hell I would find myself in later in life.

Our client base increased and my reputation spread. Mary ran my office from home and would drive out to the camps at all hours with the children, delivering supplies and sometimes spending the night. During those years I worked like a machine with my fantastic team. They would work way into the night at times, never complaining, but I cared for them like family and always led by example, even with the toughest jobs.

There was one young member of the staff named Modrick who I took a particular shine to because of his dedication, loyalty, and eagerness, which stood out above the rest.

I was learning invaluable skills from these men. One of the older trackers, Gombise, had the most fantastic eyesight I had ever witnessed. He could spot and identify game miles away that I had to look carefully at through binoculars to identify. That's when I started to realise that the Zimbabweans who grew up in the bush had natural senses that way outdid ours in every way.

Early on I learned that without a happy, motivated crew, safaris were not as successful or enjoyable; my staff were the blood in the veins of my operation. On safari, we spent every waking hour with our trackers. Survival depends on a commitment to one another in times of danger. These brave men invariably walked in front on tracks without weapons while I relied on their instincts and special bush skills to take us to our quarry and warn me when danger lurked. Being armed, I was the point man on whom they relied when a weapon was needed. Through those years I formed a bond with my trackers and gun bearers that I share with no others.

CHAPTER 44

Business Booms

At the end of 1988, my big break came. I signed a lease for the hunting rights in the Malipati Safari Area and adjoining areas. It was a massive area surrounding three-quarters of Gonarezhou National Park with a large quota at an excellent price.

For the first time, banks were happy to lend me money, and in no time, I was flush with a thriving business and purchased a more upmarket house in Bulawayo. To keep control of the business, I was spending over 200 days a year in the bush, six weeks in the USA, and was marketing and expanding fast. With my increasingly impressive track record, the Land Bank loaned me money to purchase Angus Ranch, in the Chiredzi district. It was a gem of a property – 40,000 acres of prime cattle-ranching country with sweetveld on fertile soils. The icing on the cake was when the Cold Storage Commission loaned me finance to buy 820 head of cattle.

Despite all my new acquisitions, my drive for conservation increased. I had three active anti-poaching units in different hunting areas and on Angus Ranch, and was active in feeding game on Triangle Estates and Mateke Hills. The game was making a strong comeback. My safari business was booming and after a drought that year, I bought a 12-ton Schramm air drill for drilling water wells and founded Matabeleland Drilling & Contracting.

All was going fantastically until late 1989, when my mom was diagnosed with breast cancer. It was an enormous shock to us all, but after a successful single mastectomy and with her cancer in remission, she found visiting my camps a real joy.

One evening on the banks of the Mwenezi River in a tented camp, the lions came in roaring. They were so close the tents shook from the sounds. Mom was sleeping with Dusty, who was only four. In the morning she told us how they clung to one another for comfort and prayed hard as the tents vibrated from the roaring.

She was a devout Christian, as is my sister Lyn. I had always questioned religion, but still believed in God from my experience when I got lost during the war. It gave my mom deep comfort knowing that I was a believer. My life in the years that followed was a whirlwind. When I had spare time, I'd want to do things with Dusty and Sandy. My mom was craving my support and attention in the insecure situation she was in and I did not see that. I had plenty of time to regret this deeply, when I looked back on that time during my years in prison.

CHAPTER 45

First Time in Jail

During the mid-80s there were a few dissidents from the war that turned into outlaws, murdering mostly white farmers. They were primarily from the ZIPRA forces that had lost the elections that gave Robert Mugabe the presidency. The retaliation by Mugabe's forces was to murder 20,000 Matabele (which is where the ZIPRA forces came from), and enforce martial law.

We were at our main camp, Nyamasikana, on the sandy banks of the Nuanetsi River, in Malipati Safari Area. It was a Sunday, and we were making last-minute preparations for our first client of the year when a government vehicle drove into camp.

The government officials informed me that I was under investigation, and drove me back to Chiredzi, two hours away, while Mary and the children followed with an escort. At Chiredzi police station I was detained in cells, and they held Mary, Dusty, and Sandy for five hours in the charge office before releasing them.

At 11 p.m. I was transferred to Central Intelligence Organisation (CIO) holding cells in Goromonzi, near Harare, arriving around 4 a.m. It was a large barricaded yard about the size of a football field, with approximately 12 separate concrete blocks spaced evenly in two lines in the yard. Each block was a cell, 2 m X 3 m and 3 m high, with solid steel double doors in each cell. It was totally empty inside except for a 10-mm-thick felt mat and three blankets. In one corner was a hole six inches in diameter, being the toilet, which was flushed once a day from outside. There were no windows, only vents, and it was so dark I couldn't even see my hand. At 9:30am each day, I was given a plastic plate of baked beans, two slices of brown bread and a cup of water. That was it for the day. After they flushed at 10 a.m. (you had to time your movements) I was escorted alone, with the sunlight blinding me, for a cold outside shower. Whenever I asked what I had done, they would just say, 'You're under investigation.'

In other nearby cells, I could hear crying and pleading. Whenever my lawyer called, he was given different locations of my whereabouts, day after day. During this time, all four camps on my concessions and our house in Bulawayo were thoroughly searched. I would lie there for hours wondering what on earth I had done that they considered so wrong.

On Wednesday morning, the day before my clients were due to arrive, an intelligence officer visited and asked me several questions about spying for South Africa. Seeing that I was totally unaware of anything, he arranged for an interview with his boss several hours later.

The security manager on my Shangani concession was a man by the name of Van der Riet. I had reported him as a suspect for poaching on the property; he had stolen several stationary water-pump engines on the ranch and a hired car in which he absconded for two months. When he was arrested, he concocted a story that I was a spy for the apartheid government, which obviously seemed plausible because I had safari camps in Malipati and on the Limpopo River, bordering Kruger National Park in South Africa.

When they tumbled to the conclusion that I had absolutely nothing to do with these activities, I was released and dumped in Harare to find my own way home. I arrived just in time to collect my first client the next morning. It was a rude reminder of a capricious system of law enforcement that I would see more of in the future.

Despite that rocky start, the 1990 season proved the most productive period of my career. Safari camps were full, cattle were doing well, and the drilling rig was busy. Things were moving fast, but with harsh interest rates on loans, I was losing myself in controlling it all. I was never home. Mary employed her mother to help in the office, and was too busy to visit camps regularly as she had before. Our relationship suffered.

There was financial pressure on all of us, and my stress release, when home, was to bury myself in unconditional love for my children, neglecting my wife. The truth is, my success in the safari industry and business world gave me confidence, Dusty and Sandy now provided the deep secure love I'd craved as a young man, and the formerly minor differences between Mary and me soon became significant issues. The gap between us increased over the years.

To compound these problems, the contract to renew our main concession in Malipati Safari Area was not renewed for the '91 season. At the same time, the Lowveld experienced a severe drought; although we spent tens of thousands of dollars on feeding game, we lost significant numbers of animals on all of my concessions. I had to move all the cattle 600 km away up to Mashonaland, where there was grazing, and my cash flow took a hit.

My mom's cancer returned in late 1992. She had another mastectomy and more chemotherapy and battled for months against the disease.

During that time I needed extra money to stay afloat. Somewhat reluctantly, I established a joint safari venture with Joshua Nkomo, the then vice-president. An Austrian safari operator had gone into a joint venture with Nkomo and acquired several concessions for their VIP clients. The company needed professionals to conduct the operations, and I was approached. My involvement attracted a lot of negative publicity – the vice president had the power to demand quotas from any areas without the usual tender process, which upset many safari operators. After a year, I terminated my participation.

It seemed my life was one big crisis; I was torn between trying to repair a failing marriage, paying my bills and worrying about my beloved mother's health. From the time her cancer returned until her passing on 30 November 1993, Mom needed my reassurance and help, but I was battling with my own issues. Her last years will forever remain painful to me.

I was on a marketing trip to Austria when I received a call from my sister, to say Mom wasn't doing well on chemotherapy treatment and wanted to see all her children. I boarded a plane that night and was at her bedside the next morning. She held on bravely until we were all there. We said a prayer together, and within two hours, she was gone. It was tough to witness, but she was at peace with death before she went. The energetic little lady with the huge heart who made us all feel so happy and loved lives on in her children, grandchildren, and great-grandchildren.

I thanked God that she didn't have to witness the years of my incarceration.

CHAPTER 46

My Business Turns

t broke my heart, but I sold Angus Ranch and all the cattle, along with the drilling company, in 1994 and 1995. This took care of all the debt, leaving a substantial surplus.

Shangaan tribesmen are renowned for their tracking ability. From a young age they herd cattle and would have to track the missing beasts. They were also the last tribe legally allowed to hunt with bows and arrows, for which tracking skills were essential.

Kermit had been a skinner since 1988, but now I asked him if he could track. He was only too happy to give it a try and turned out to be an outstanding tracker – except that he was terrified of elephants.

On one occasion while walking in the Zambezi Valley, we came upon three elephant bulls fast asleep on their sides, which is quite unusual. I saw them before Kermit did because he had his head down looking at the tracks. The grass was long, and we were close. When I tapped him on the shoulder and indicated for him to look up, he got the fright of his life and tried to run past me. Not wanting him to make too much noise, I held his overalls tightly as he kicked up dust trying to get away. In the commotion, the elephant woke up and then we all had to take off!

We went through many dangerous times together. I remember following Kermit through a tunnel in a thorn-thicket after a wounded leopard. This was close to a suicidal situation, but he always stayed calm and was exceptionally brave. There was complete trust between us. Rom and Gombise became Kermit's assistant trackers, and the four of us formed a talented, loyal bond that would last decades.

Life without debt was beautiful and gave me a chance to think of investment opportunities. Two magnificent properties caught my interest. One was a 34-acre plot with an old homestead, three stone-and-thatch cottages, four stables, nine staff quarters, a recently built massive warehouse, and an excellent borehole. The other, a breathtaking 72-acre piece of undeveloped terrain. I jumped in and purchased them both in 1995 and 1996.

In early 1995, I also bought a five-seater single-engine aeroplane, and after a six-week course in Harare, I obtained my PPL (private pilot's licence). With concessions from the Zambezi Valley on the northern border with Zambia to Triangle Estates in Chiredzi in the deep south, it was a godsend. I loved flying, and it allowed me more time at home, instead of being on the road. During the dry safari season, it was a pleasure; once the rains started though, it became a little dangerous, and the risks increased with my penchant for taking chances in inclement weather.

On one occasion, I flew to Harare and only finished my business commitments at 5 p.m. With a lawyers' meeting awaiting me back in Bulawayo, I was pushed; it would be dark before landing in Bulawayo and I wasn't night- or instrument-rated.

In an irrational moment I figured, 'Stuff it, I'll fly.' With my flight plan and refuelling done, I only got airborne after

6 p.m. My ETA was around 7.20 p.m. way after dark. Over Zisco Steel, near KweKwe in the Midlands, the light faded but there were enough visible lights on the ground to make out roughly where I was going. However, being September with bushfires and dust in the air, there was a terrible haze that hampered visibility. About 15 minutes before my ETA, the Bulawayo ATC (air traffic controller) asked if I had entered their air space yet.

They were expecting Air Zimbabwe, Flight 003, five minutes after me, so they needed to know exactly where I was. My reply was that I would be on time, but I wasn't sure. A few minutes later, to my right and in the distance, I saw a huge glow. Thinking I'd gone off course, I altered direction and headed straight for it. Ten minutes later, the glow turned out to be a bushfire. Doing an about turn, I retraced my path, now in total darkness. The ATC asked again for my position. I told her that I was on track but couldn't see the airport lights. Then she asked what my 'some instrument' reading was. I said, 'I'm sorry that "instrument" isn't working.' When asked about another 'digital reading' I gave the same answer, and the Air Zimbabwe pilot admonished me for not being 'au fait' with my night instruments.

Air Zimbabwe landed, but I could still not see the lights of Bulawayo, and it was 10 minutes past my ETA. With my father-in-law on the phone to the ATC, she was now apparently in a spin, and I was seriously worried – I had 15 minutes' fuel left! Doing a wide circle, I eventually saw what I prayed were the lights of Bulawayo, far away. I had flown right past the city. By the time I got over town, picked out and followed the airport road and saw the flickering lights the controller had on for me, I had five minutes' fuel left.

I landed after dark for the first time ever. I was terrified I'd be called in and found out for flying without night rating.

I hastily parked my plane in the private hangar, jumped in my waiting pick-up and headed home.

The following morning after a busy day in town, I drove into our yard and stopped the car. Mary marched up, handed me a fax and walked off without a word. It was from the head of the Aviation Department in Harare. It read: 'Due to you inconveniencing Air Zimbabwe Flight 003 on 30 September 1995, at 7.20 p.m. a complaint has been lodged against you. You are to report to room 31 at our headquarters on 12 October 1995 at 10.30 a.m.' My heart fell into my stomach.

I walked around the garden thinking, how on earth was I going to get out of this one? Half an hour later, with a smirk on her face, Mary walked up and said, 'It's a joke!' I did not see the funny side. 'It might be a joke to you, but it's very serious to me! That aircraft cost a fortune, and I desperately need it now you know how much I love flying!' She just burst into laughter.

I looked hard at the fax again, still not registering clearly. It appeared so legitimate. Then the relief! The fax was from Rich Huntley-Walker, an old friend from Plumtree School, not the head of Civil Aviation. Being a pilot too, he had a letterhead, and all the details, so he knew what he was doing. He and I had a good laugh on the phone. It was a brilliant con but a tough one!

CHAPTER 47

Endings and Beginnings

Mary and I could always compromise on our differences. But this slowly dissipated, and our marriage deteriorated to the extent that our unhappy times at home were now affecting Dusty and Sandy. In November 1996, I decided to move onto the 34 acres alone. We tried unsuccessfully to patch things up over Christmas that year, but it was effectively over between us.

Having never lived alone before, it was a struggle at first. I craved company and didn't even have my faithful dogs or favourite cat. The large property was home to 23 healthy impala, two duiker, a steenbok, many scrub-hares, flocks of noisy guinea fowl and a few francolin, so having an untrained dog was out of the question. It was like living on a farm out in the bush somewhere but surrounded by residential suburbs. I loved the quietness, except that I had no one to share it with. But the freedom to now move where and when I liked was liberating, and I soon fitted in to the social circles.

My biggest heartache was not being allowed to see my children. I missed them terribly. For the first three months after leaving, the only access I had to them was on a school sports field where they were participating.

All through our marriage, I was never permitted to take either of my children in a vehicle alone with me – Mary said I was an irresponsible driver, and to keep the peace, I complied. The one and only exception was shortly before I moved out permanently. Dusty, who was almost 12, was permitted to accompany me to Shangani Safari Camp for a memorable bonding weekend to supervise repairs to buildings there.

The 1997 season turned out to be extremely busy, making it challenging to spend time with my children. After enduring six painful months of being apart from them, Mary heard of another woman and me, and the divorce papers arrived. This was the start of a seven-year legal wrangle.

My priority was visiting rights. Following a month of correspondence, through Mary's domineering lawyer, dinner together with the children every Thursday night, from 5 p.m. to 9 p.m. was permitted. It took seven more months of haggling and frustration before being granted a weekend together every month. The pain of not being allowed that unconditional love from my own children, was agonising.

Thankfully, the restrictions actually brought Dusty, Sandy and me closer and we began fighting, as one, for more time together. Soon they were allowed every second weekend at my home. We spent some of the happiest times I can recall during those weekends – waterskiing and kneeboarding at Ncema Dam, on fishing trips and parties with all their mates at our house. They were difficult, but magical years.

I'd been emotionally unsettled for years, but this didn't stop me trying to find that special soulmate. If I were ever to let anyone in again, she would have to be an extraordinary woman.

Around Christmas of 1997, I was shopping one day in Makro Hypermarket, dawdling along absentmindedly, when I noticed a striking young woman pushing a shopping trolley between two aisles. I stepped back to sneak another look and I liked what I saw.

A week later, while cooking at a *braai* on the lawn outside the clubhouse at Ncema Dam, this gorgeous, long-legged creature arrived with a friend of mine. In all my travels I've seen my share of beautiful women, but Susan Smith was the most striking girl I'd ever laid eyes on. She was tall, with dark hair, a beaming smile and beautiful tawny eyes. She was living in London, but on vacation visiting her folks. Standing there, turning steaks and trying to act casual, I knew I needed to play this one perfectly.

We chatted briefly, and both felt instant chemistry, but I was seeing somebody else at the time, who was due to move to Dubai in a couple of weeks. During that unforgettable, fun-filled evening, the seeds were planted.

At Ivy League the following weekend, I was hurrying from the bar to the dance-floor, tipsy, and there she was in the hallway. It was a spontaneous, instant reaction. Without saying a word, in the noise and dim light, we enjoyed a long, passionate kiss – then headed off in opposite directions like naughty kids. She'd floored me; I was smitten but cautioned myself to slow down.

Days before departing for Cape Town on a 'Golden Oldies' rugby tour, I was refuelling at a petrol station when I noticed her alone in the driver's seat of a flashy car. With nothing to lose, I asked if she would wait for me until my return. It was an arrogant request, make no mistake, but she was being pursued by every eligible guy I knew. She agreed and when I returned we had our first romantic dinner date. The attraction was frightening, we couldn't seem to get enough of each other and were inseparable after that. Within four weeks, she had moved in with me, living in one of the thatched stone cottages on the property.

Dusty and Sandy adored her and treated her like family, right from the beginning. We would often drive to Shangani Camp and collect driftwood for the garden at home or net fish to stock our little dam in front of the house. They were terrific, precious times that helped us all become exceptionally close.

My darling sister Lyn was also living in Bulawayo, and spent a lot of time with us. Lyn inherited my mom's quick walk, never stopped talking and seemed as if she was always busy doing something. She and I shared a special bond that grew stronger by the year.

Sue didn't work, so we were together 24/7. She accompanied me on safaris, we went on fishing trips, we exercised together – everything. Months after we started dating, I began building my house. The stone cottages were rondavels, but two were joined by thick stone sidewalls with one roof over them. The plan was to build up, and extend the building forward. As the house developed, we altered plans and turned it into something unique and gorgeous. All doors and windows were fashioned from Rhodesian teak; tiles and fittings we brought from Italy and it all blended well with the stone and thatch. In one corner of the lounge, an enormous dry leadwood tree and massive boulders were brought in from Shangani Camp to give it a real bush look.

It took 18 months to build during which time Sue and I very happily lived in the remaining rondavel. Over the years we acquired several pampered puppies, two spoilt cats, and a tiny pet squirrel. I also introduced three magnificent sable antelope, three beautiful bushbuck, and two steenbok onto the property. My life couldn't have been any more perfect. I was in heaven, living in an earthly paradise and head over heels in love.

All that changed in an instant, from an unexpected encounter in a fishing boat on a river.

Over time, I saw my life from a very different perspective in prison. Being removed from the rat race we all get caught up in, I better understood the mistakes I had made, the money I had wasted, opportunities I had lost and people I had neglected.

Having these uninterrupted times gave me a completely different vision of where I wanted to go and what I wanted out of life. I realised that life is not about your assets and wealth alone, it is about your journey and the people in it.

I learned many valuable life lessons from uneducated but intelligent old farm workers in prison too. Their way of life, hard-earned wisdom and laid-back outlook on life, was so very different but real. It gave me much valued inner peace.

CHAPTER 48

Running on Empty

On the regular days at Chikurubi Maximum, after unlock at 8 a.m. the 30-odd cleaning, security and toilet staff were allowed downstairs. None of the other 400 inmates per hall were allowed downstairs until cleaning of the hall was finished, which took around an hour, after which we were all locked downstairs.

Within that hour, every day – except on soccer days, or if we were sick – Elisha and I would run the steps.

Elisha was an exceptionally well-spoken, hardcore armed robber. He grew up in an affluent family and was schooled at Prince Edward School in Harare. He had been in and out of prison his whole life but had access to a top advocate who kept getting him out on bail pending appeal.

He was of medium build, bow-legged, with a bit of a paunch. We both shared a passion for fitness and would push each other extremely hard.

Others from our respective soccer teams would periodically join us for training.

The stairs rose 13 steps half-way up to the first floor, then doubled back for the remainder of the 13 steps. The same for the next level, 26 steps per floor. We would start with two slow jogs from the top floor down one-and-a-half storeys, 39 steps, and then back up. Then it was pyramids:

always jogged downhill except on sprints, which were fast up and down without holding hand rails for support. One circuit was five times down and up at slow pace, four times down and up at medium speed and three times down and up at a sprint. Then we would start again: no rest from the warm-up until the end. We would do six circuits in shorts and takkies, which left us saturated in sweat and exhausted.

I was incredibly fit, working out with my improvised gym routine every lunch break too. Soccer days were Tuesdays, Thursdays, Saturdays, and Sundays. Volleyball was on Mondays and Fridays. Drama was on Wednesdays, which was very boring for the sportsmen, but the others loved it.

Elisha and I stopped training for a few months when water and food became a severe problem before June 2006. Then we decided we would start training again, just to keep sane, but our food rations were not enough, and we both broke out in a bunch of terrible boils. They lasted several weeks, then we were at it again.

For 17 hours during night-time lock-up, only urinating was permitted in the cells for hygiene purposes, unless it was an emergency. So after unlock at 8 a.m. each day, there was always a stampede for the hall toilets, which soon had queues of bursting guys waiting.

The stench that permeated throughout the entire complex was indescribable. No toilets had doors, and none flushed. The toilets were just stirred to a 'sludge' with a pole when overflowing, and pushed down like a mudflow, followed by any filthy water.

There were eight toilets per 400 prisoners. Like all the rest, I would wait in line, then climb up on the cement block to do my business, and there would be 80 pairs of eyes glued on me, waiting for me to finish. Talk about stage fright! My white bum stood out like a sore thumb.

Dignity was non-existent. If Nyere was not around to ram the mound of excrement down with the pole he used, we would have to half squat over a stinking heap of excrement, which protruded above the toilet lip by up to 30 centimetres. A more degrading manoeuvre you could not think of. Worse still, we had not been issued toilet paper for months, so others had used pages of the prison-issue Bibles, which were visible in the pile of excreta. It was the most soul-destroying place.

After cleaning, all would go downstairs, and the gates leading upstairs were locked to prevent sodomy, marijuana smoking, and stealing.

Visiting reception, censor's or any other department was always a problem because they invariably said there were not enough guards to escort you. The standard rule was at least three guards in each hall at all times. But when the centre-court beatings took place, it was full of guards from every department jostling to get in on the beating frenzy, often leaving halls totally empty. The pleasure they derived from being part of this brutality was extremely disturbing. It still troubles me when I try to understand the world we live in and the cruelty with which some people treat others.

That cruelty extended to our visitors. Usually, on Easter and Christmas holidays, depending on the OIC, there was no limit on the number of groceries or visitors allowed in. During Christmas of 2005, my beautiful sister Lyn and her daughters Tara and Kassie, brought me several bulging bags of food and goodies. The eagerly awaited bounty had to be passed through a dirty open barred window and carefully checked item by item by an officer before being passed on.

Most guards would allow shaking hands and were polite to visitors. In her excitement, while holding my hand, with a seemingly pleasant guard at the window, Lyn pulled me close and pecked me on the lips through the bars. This caught the officer entirely off guard, leaving him perplexed, so her daughter Kassie quickly followed in case he changed his mind. However, when Tara did the same, the officer completely lost it. He promptly stopped the transfer of goodies, told me to hand back what I had in my hands and ended the visit. My poor sister and two nieces left sobbing. I was left with only half the groceries they had so generously bought for me. I was absolutely gutted. For days, I could not shake the anger and sadness I felt, despite Phil's encouragement to let it go. We savoured every little packet of goodies from them.

That Christmas we enjoyed tins of fish, olives, blocks of cheese, crackers, dried fruit, chips, dips, peanut butter, marmite, muesli, nuts, energy bars, powder energy drinks, biltong, biscuits, rusks, pickled onions, chocolate, sweets, nougat, fresh fruit and freshly cooked food for the day. There were about six bags of food, and then lunchboxes of fresh food. My favourite was prawns and rice (which Lyn always put in), and a roast leg of lamb with potatoes and veggies. I found that any food with sugar didn't agree with me, so she would make sure that all goodies were sugar free, even the chocolate.

Outside of special holidays, the regulations were one visitor fortnightly per inmate for 15 minutes. There was a list of groceries that they were allowed to bring, displayed for them at the main gate. The list changed depending on the OIC at the time. If anything was brought in addition to what was stipulated, it was disallowed. The list was as follows:

2 x 20 packs of cigarettes
2 x loaves of bread (without butter or margarine)
2 x 300 g plastic bottles of peanut butter
1 x packet of sweets (candy)
1 x packet of biltong (jerky)
6 each of any fruit
1 x box of biscuits
1 x bar of non-perfumed soap
1 x 50 ml of petroleum jelly
1 x roll of toilet paper
1 x toothbrush
1 x toothpaste

The boxes that the biscuits came in were always removed, to prevent inmates from making cards to gamble. The staff assigned to visitors would collect the empty boxes, and they would be secretly sold back to prisoners in the halls for cigarettes or soap. The cruelty experienced by visitors was shocking as well.

One of my closest friends in the safari industry, John Sharp, had another unpleasant experience. John is about four years my senior, just under six feet and built like a cart-horse, so you would have expected a bit more respect for him.

One day he drove the 430 km from Harare from Bulawayo to visit me. Charlie Campbell, who was looking after my safari company told him what he should buy, how he should carry it into the prison, and what to expect.

John bought the supplies and packed everything into a bag with wheels that he could drag the long route from parking past all the checkpoints. At this first gate, he was questioned about his relationship to me. Knowing that only relatives were allowed to visit, he told them he was my brother. The second checkpoint was the same, and by the time he approached the third he was grateful that he could pull the bag instead of having to carry it.

The third checkpoint was a building about fifteen foot square. It had windows on two sides, with heavy steel bars set into the concrete, to secure them. Some people loitered about outside in some sparse shade. Inside this fortified building an overweight woman in a prison guard's uniform beckoned for him to approach the window. 'Show me the food,' she growled. He handed over the items, one by one. She made him open the peanut butter jar and motioned for him to remove some of the contents with his finger and eat it. Then she ordered him to eat some of the biltong. He reached into the packet, searching for the smallest piece, while telling her that he did not want to eat a starving man's food. She reached into the bag, scooped out a huge handful of the biltong and stuffed it all into her mouth! John told me he seethed with anger – what kind of person was this that would steal a prisoner's food? Mumbling through a full mouth of food, she asked for the name of the prisoner he had come to visit. He was told to join the other waiting visitors. While he sat on a vacant bench, wondering whether I would see any of the supplies he had brought, a young kid approached the food cage. In his hand he carried four little buns, still joined together from the baking tray. As he handed them through the bars for inspection, the overweight woman broke off two of them and, beckoning to a small, well-dressed little girl on the outside, probably her daughter, she handed them over. 'As the little girl began to stuff them into her mouth,' John said, 'something died inside me. I will never forget the look on that young man's face as he watched this privileged little girl eat half the meagre offering intended for his incarcerated father.' We had a good 15-minute visit, but John could never bring himself to visit me again.

I'll never forget seeing an old woman wailing uncontrollably during the Easter Friday holiday visit in April 2006. She was quickly ushered off to the reception area by the guards. She had come a long way from the rural areas to see her husband and had probably covered a lot of the road on foot, and she had brought him a pile of food only to be told he had died six weeks earlier. There were so many deaths that the authorities couldn't keep up with what was happening. If nobody responded to the address given when entering prison – mostly because the country had turned into chaos with the Zimbabwe dollar crash and food, fuel and communications falling apart – then the bodies were set aside for pauper's burials.

CHAPTER 49

Each to His Own

One thing I learned very quickly in prison was to mind my own business at all cost. Whenever someone reported an offence to a guard, he would end up getting worse treatment than the offender. If the guards did not turn on him, then the inmates did. This was especially so with homosexuality which was very common in prison. During midday lock-up, while we were doing our gym, there would always be two or more couples actively involved in the corners under blankets no matter how hot it was. Phil was from the old school, and he despised them for this behaviour, but we were well advised not to intrude. Homosexual activities were especially prevalent in lifers and long-serving prisoners, who would often have several youngsters (wives) each.

I often asked the active homosexuals, how they could do it so often. Every night and most afternoons they would have some sort of sexual intercourse with their lovers. They said that they would only penetrate infrequently, but mostly it was between the legs. They would also build themselves up until close, then end off between their partner's legs. We would laugh and tell them they were crazy as most of them were married with children, but they saw it all very differently. Inmates were often extraordinarily jealous and protective of their 'wives', who were forbidden to so much as talk to some of the other promiscuous prisoners. They would watch their 'wives' like hawks, follow them to keep an eye on them and violence often followed if orders were ignored. One guy marked a one-metre-square box on the floor of the exercise yard and made his 'wife' sit in there the entire time out of cells because the kid was so promiscuous.

Gideon was a recent arrival. He was a really rough-looking 30-year-old, who had been living on the streets. He never followed any rules, was invariably disorderly during feeding time, and often tried to sneak back for a second helping of food. He had been warned several times by the hall-in-charge to start complying but brushed away orders with contempt. Phil and I would often warn him about his unruly ways and the beatings that he hadn't yet witnessed. The prisoners had had enough of him. He was also a common thief, which was what pushed the authorities into action.

It was prohibited to go up the stairs during our three-hour unlock period in the mornings and one hour in the afternoons, as prisoners could steal from the cells if they were not locked. Gideon had made a habit of being one of the last each day to come downstairs before the grilled gate leading into each floor was locked. This was so he could see if the gate was locked or not. One morning, the gate had been opened as a guard was having his hair cut by a prisoner on the first floor and he'd forgotten to lock it after he had finished. When we went up at 11 a.m. for lunchtime lock-up, almost every cell on the first floor reported a theft.

Gideon had hidden a big haul of toothpaste, Vaseline, soap and Mazoe orange juice concentrate under the blankets used to clean the toilet area each day. This was at a time when we had had no running water for ages. These

First cuddle in seven years with my daughter Sandy.

Celebrations all round with Sandy and Lyn.

My freedom party with my children – April 2013.

ABOVE Reunited with my special mate Max.

RIGHT My 50th with my children.

Lyn and her special man, Ed New.

Bonding with Dusty, Victoria Falls.

Myself and Phil, reunited as free men.

Jesse, bonding with Granddad.

Home sweet home.

A kudu bull in our garden.

Sandra, the love of my life.

Jesse – priceless.

Our second grandson, Jay Rusty Pigors.

Introducing Sandra to free-roaming rhino.

The smiles say it all.

Happily married!

Daniel, me and Gideon.

Newly-weds, with Dayne, Sandy, Jesse and Dusty.

Closing speaker in Sun City, South Africa.

disgusting blankets were left on the filthy shower floor each day after the toilet staff, armed with rubber gloves and gumboots, had used them to clean the floors. They were covered in what looked like slimy glue from never being washed.

The stench in those halls was so revolting that I battled not to vomit every time I went upstairs past the bathroom area. How Gideon expected to get away with this was beyond me. He was quickly found and escorted down to the library.

Being the senior security staff, I was permitted to wait downstairs until they had dealt with him. Guards from other halls were quickly informed by the centre-court guard that there was action in our hall. I braced myself as the stomach-churning screams began, then after about five minutes of beatings and wailing, suddenly, with bursts of laughter, the guards came flying out of the library almost falling over one another. Gideon had totally lost it; he was sitting naked in the centre of the library on the shiny concrete floor, eating the faeces that he had extracted from himself, leaving his face a brown stinking mess. The beatings were so horrific that prisoners would do anything to prevent them from continuing, but this was a first. It was a horrible sight and clearly apparent that Gideon was absolutely mortified. Being entirely new he did not realise how severe the punishment beatings were and got a huge shock. He changed his attitude for a while but then went back to stealing again.

CHAPTER 50

A Living Hell

From the beginning of 2006, with no running water in Chikurubi, diarrhoea became a deadly and out-of-control problem. The inmates received only one meal a day of boiled cabbage and *sadza*, which made us extremely weak and thin. We were losing significant amounts of weight through starvation. There was no salt or oil in the little food we received, and my parcels were not making it through. By this time the Zimbabwe dollar was around one million to one US$, and things in the country were catastrophic.

Once a week the OIC would visit all the halls for complaints and inspection. On a hot summer's day in desperation, I asked Mudzama if he would allow my visitors to bring me raw potatoes, butternut, and gem squash that the dietician had agreed to cook for us because the boiled cabbage was not agreeing with me. He refused, and when I asked what I could eat with the *sadza* because I was starving, he said, 'The kitchen staff can bring you salt, you can eat *sadza* and salt.' I was gobsmacked and helpless.

Not only did I not get any more food, but this request was apparently seen as insolence and, after six months together, my dear friend Phil was promptly transferred to A Hall where I was unable to visit him. A directive followed from the OIC saying we were not to be seen together under any circumstances. Our friendship annoyed many guards, which was just plain racial cruelty.

It was a terrible blow, but we had to keep on going. I missed Phil terribly, especially during the 17-hour lock-up from 3 p.m. to 8 a.m. I had many great friends in there that genuinely cared about me, but Phil and I were the only ones from a similar cultural background. We laughed at the same jokes, his accent and way of describing things made me laugh, and he made my life before prison seem not so distant.

Despite the order, I paid smokes to continue seeing him. Fortunately, a new OIC came after six long months and Phil was moved to one of the large halls next door to the one I was in, making it easier to see him.

In June 2006, the prisoner death rate from malnutrition and disease was so high that the prison HQ started allowing relatives to deliver food to their loved ones daily. It was the most sensational news. My dear sisters Bev and Lyn stepped in immediately. Unbeknownst to me, they were selling furniture and scraping money together from wherever they could to pay for food for Phil and me. After several months of Lyn feeding us daily, Bev visited and explained that Lyn was battling financially. Lyn eventually sold her pottery business and with help from my safari business, was able to keep us going for four more long years.

Because the authorities were afraid Simon Mann and the mercenaries might be sprung from prison in some military-style rescue, a rule was implemented that forced cars to be parked one kilometre away from the maximum security complex which made it a long walk for my sister to carry the packages every day. It took an exceptional person to feed us for four more years and without Lyn's devotion to us, I do not think we would have survived the conditions. I believe our bodies were only able to withstand all the sickness and disease because we were relatively well-nourished.

Very few relatives could afford to feed their loved ones daily, and I helped as many guys as I could afford to, but the hunger continued for most. Lyn was a saint of a little sister; I could never have wished for better. It wasn't only the delicious food, but also the knowledge that it was in her hands only hours before, that helped my mindset. Just feeling that little bit closer to the free world was a massive boost to morale and hope.

Being so far removed from the world and only having a few minutes every fortnight to talk was difficult, but the fact that I was now being fed by them daily gave me a chance to get a little more information and news. It was always a painfully upsetting time, seeing them hurting so badly, witnessing me in that helpless state. I had always been the strong, solid, supportive brother, as was expected, but now the roles were reversed. The system had brought me to my knees. When I went into prison, I was flying high, full of confidence, making plenty of money and continuously helping people financially. When you go to jail, they set about breaking you physically and mentally. I tried extremely hard to withstand it, but my spirit, my soul, and my confidence were severely damaged. I was smart enough not to let them get to me too much, but under those conditions, it was impossible not to be affected.

Makorudzo was a young security officer who came to Chikurubi around 2005. He always looked angry, and his top lip was in a permanent snarl. When he spoke, he spat out his words in contempt of everyone. His mission in prison was to control everyone everywhere, including guards. He particularly disliked Phil and me would often enter our hall and, on seeing us together, he would bark the order, 'Come here!'

We would have to crouch down at his feet as he questioned us on random and, invariably, frivolous issues.

'Why are your clothes so clean?'

'Who are you paying to do your washing?'

'Where did you get hot water for tea?'

It was continuous harassment that often pushed me to the limit.

Not long after Phil left, I was escorted to the prison hospital by a junior guard, and on our way back we bumped into Makorudzo passing the reception area. '*Gara pasi!*' he bellowed – 'Sit down!'. I was physically sick, and sick of him, and being in leg irons and handcuffs. I decided I was not going to crouch down. He strode angrily up to me and bellowed at me to get down, but I did not flinch, stood firm and upright and looked him straight in the eye from very close as he glared at me.

'When I tell you to crouch down, you crouch down,' he bellowed. 'I'm not crouching down today,' I said calmly.

'When I give you an instruction, you obey them,' he shouted.

'Wearing that uniform doesn't make you right Makorudzo,' I said quietly. 'Today I'm in cuffs and leg irons and will not crouch down just because you want to see me crouch down. No other guard or officer tells me to crouch down when I am being escorted except you. Now leave me alone.'

He was totally lost for words and backed away. I watched him as he went a short distance then turned, stared at me menacingly and said, 'You will pay for this.'

I just said, 'That's okay.'

He was true to his word. His hounding of me became more severe, especially during searches, when he would make it his business to go through my belongings thoroughly, making loud remarks about each item and confiscating as much as he could. I had been allowed UNO cards by the censor's officer, and they had brought Phil and I lots of pleasure over the months. Unfortunately, he knew this, so it was with a big smile that he took them away. I appealed to him on the basis that they had been approved by the censor's officer, but he dismissed my pleas.

Not long after that, I had gone to the hospital in Harare to have my eyes tested, he came into our hall and decided to confiscate all bags made from polystyrene sacks, which were bought from the kitchen staff. Almost every decent prisoner kept their meagre possessions in these homemade bags with drawstrings to close the tops. My bag was against the high wall of the exercise yard where we all left our bags, and because Phil had been transferred by then, Moyo was looking after it for me.

Makorudzo instructed all prisoners to go and sit on the tar in the yard. This interference in the halls often upset the guards in the halls, but because he was a security officer, the guards were afraid of him. All guards and officers were up to some sort of skulduggery, and it was the job of the security officers to control this. When Makorudzo got to my bag, after searching all the bags along the wall, and confiscating every bag, the prisoners told him that it was mine and that I had gone to the hospital. He promptly ordered a prisoner to open it and empty all the contents out onto the tarred floor and took my bag. He then started going through my belongings, taking what he felt was not allowed in prison, then told Moyo to take what was left back to my cell when lock-up time came.

When I returned, I felt terribly dejected. Everyone was too afraid to take responsibility for my belongings as Makorudzo had put a large number of items in a bag to take away. All the prisoners were seated on the tarred floor some distance away watching him. Should I claim some things were missing, then Makorudzo would insist they must have been stolen by the prisoner who took my remaining goods upstairs. Which was precisely what happened. My goods were left on the floor until lock-up when the HIC told Moyo to collect them and take them up to my cell. Luckily, Moyo made a list, in front of the HIC, of what he was taking upstairs.

There were tubes of toothpaste, bars of soap, a bottle of unopened peanut butter, four packets of Madison cigarettes and a bag of milk powder missing. The following day I was escorted to reception and made a report to the authorities, who were very happy to help me. Makorudzo, to my surprise, arrived in our hall moments after I had returned. He came to me looking sheepish, explained that he would never take anything from me and that my missing supplies were stolen by the prisoners. I just said I wanted it all back or replaced. He made everyone sit on the floor and harassed them for ages. I never got anything back, but Makorudzo backed off a bit after that.

He finally got some sort of a comeuppance. During the water shortages, he antagonised a soldier taking water from a garden tap that they all shared. The soldier was not taking any of his bossiness that day and gave him a good hammering which delighted us all and most of the guards.

Geza was another very prominent guy in my prison life at Chikurubi. He was short, sinewy and walked with a limp from a bullet wound during the war as a Rhodesian soldier. His knowledge of Rhodesian history was unbelievable. He knew all the dates and places of events and people in our country's past, better than anyone I knew. With his raspy voice, he would chat for hours about the war and how he was shot in the thigh. He had been inside for 17 years for armed robbery and rape.

Despite his crime, he was a good man with a jovial manner and another guy I would like to think I convinced to turn his back on crime and start leading a decent life. After his release in 2008, his wedding photo and an article appeared in the government newspaper. The heading in the press was: 'Armed Robber Reforms.'

One famous prison story from many years previously involves Geza. He was in a fully loaded prison vehicle, returning from the court during the early hours of the night, and the vehicle overturned, injuring several of the occupants. If I remember correctly, it was at Khami prison complex, and the incident was in a remote area on the prison farm leading up to the complex. While some guards ran for help, others were attending to the injured. Geza was uninjured, and so were some of the female prisoners in the vehicle. Being the wild character he was, Geza sneaked in a quickie with one of them – initiated by her, according to Geza and witnesses. The woman became pregnant, hence the discovery of the escapade. We often ragged him about it, and he would just laugh as if it was a great achievement. He was a wonderful personality and a real no-nonsense guy that I missed after he left prison.

CHAPTER 51

Dead and Dying

As a senior security staff member at Chikurubi, I was put in charge of vetting sick guys for admission to hospital, which was a 300-metre walk, out of the maximum security area. Only five per day were permitted, which meant, many critically ill guys were refused permission to go to the hospital, and often died in the halls as a result. I asked permission from the HIC for George to help me daily as my Shona was not that great at that stage. I could speak Ndebele and Chilapalapa, but I was still learning Shona. Once I made my choice, approval was given by the HIC, and they were handcuffed and put in leg irons to be escorted to the hospital.

Vetting these sick inmates was always tough; they would beg to go to the hospital because they were genuinely ill. On many occasions, George and I informed the hall-in-charge, that certain inmates were not going to make another day and pleaded to have them added to the group. He would just tell us that the number was up, and they would have to go the next day. In most cases, they died that night.

The cruel treatment at the prison hospital was staggering. I recall countless incidents where prisoners were shown little concern and terrible treatment. Prisoners dying meant absolutely nothing to a nurse. They spoke about the dead and dying like they were talking about trash. All medicine was prescribed by nurses, which made matters worse. Despite the massive number of dying prisoners, the prison doctor only visited the prison once every fortnight for a morning.

During a troubled time of diarrhoea in Chikurubi when guys were dying daily, there was a healthy young kid named Tendai in my cell that suddenly became seriously ill. I liked him; he was tall and pleasant with a great physique.

He slept at the far end of the cell where most of the homosexual activity took place. I slept at the front against the steel mesh opposite the toilet. The kid would try and walk, stumbling over everyone and messing along the way with no bowel control. Geza would shout, 'Tambaira, tambaira,' meaning crawl, each time as he tried to hurry. He would crawl on his hands and knees and explode into the toilet almost hourly. I gave him a toilet roll, as he didn't have any, and he eventually slept on the floor beside the toilet. The following day George and I requested that he go to the hospital as one of the five allowed per hall.

The HIC refused Tendai. For some reason, he looked a bit better that morning, but he was still walking bent over; others could not even walk. That night was horrible. I made the kid a sugar and salt solution to help rehydrate him and gave him another toilet roll, but at 3 a.m. he died beside the toilet after hours of absolute agony. It was just another needless death thanks to a system that had fallen apart. I called Geza after I couldn't hear him breathing and we carefully wrapped him in a blanket, not wanting to get contaminated, and placed his body at my feet. That night, two other guys died as well. It was really demoralising.

Periodically the commissioner of prisons or the assistant commissioners would visit the prison, and one day an assistant commissioner visited. We were all in our cells during lunchtime lock-up, and he moved from cell to cell asking for complaints. When he approached my cell, I felt an atmosphere of nervous apprehension from guards and inmates because they were worried I was going to say something that was going to incriminate someone. I politely asked if there was anything that he could do about the death rate in prison. Clearly shocked at my audacity in addressing such a sensitive issue, he looked at me for a long anxious moment, then, before turning away, said, 'We don't give up that easily' and walked off. I was totally blown away.

Gastrointestinal diseases, combined with the lack of adequate nutrition, showed in the outbreak of pellagra and AIDS symptoms. Pellagra caused chronic pain, and then the skin would darken, dehydrate and peel off the body. It usually started on the neck and ankles before spreading. Because the victims were untreated, they became unsteady on their feet, and then they seemed to lose their minds. In the final stages, they could talk but it was unintelligible. The disease got so bad in Chikurubi that an entire hall – E Hall – was converted to a pellagra hall.

There were several deaths per week per hall – in addition to the 120-bed prison hospital being constantly full of dying inmates. Due to there being no running water, the halls were exceptionally unhygienic everywhere you looked, with a permanent repulsive stench. An old three-wheeled trolley (one wheel was missing) would go around each morning on the walkway which connected all the halls and collect bodies each day.

One cold winter's morning, when the trolley arrived in our hall, there were three bodies wrapped in blankets beside a cement pillar. Next to them was a very sick half-naked prisoner. The two hospital staff, in gloves and masks, under instruction, placed the bodies on the trolley and advised the nurse, who was chatting to a guard, that they were ready to leave. George and I then pleaded with the nurse to please have the sick prisoner taken to the hospital, as he was not going to make it. The nurse turned and instructed the hospital staff to load the sick prisoner on top of the carefully stacked bodies. I could not believe my eyes. They left with the wobbly trolley and semi-conscious prisoner perched on top of the pile of corpses. Other prisoners, flabbergasted, just started laughing as the trolley left the hall.

CHAPTER 52

Makro's Comeuppance

After being given no toilet paper for four months, someone finally found their voice during a weekly inspection and asked the new OIC, Inspector Makro, when we could expect our allocation. He was told by the OIC that there was no water or paper, so the prisoners must train themselves to be like him and his wife and go to the toilet only twice a week. This would save water and toilet paper. This came from the OIC of the largest prison in the country; it was incomprehensible. I complained to him that same day that our letters were not arriving at their addressed destinations. His blunt response was, 'If we don't like what's written in them, we tear them up and burn them.'

Any complaints about food or water were shot down with, 'It's worse outside so be grateful you don't have to pay for yours.' The frustration and desperation that set in while dealing with this mentality are hard to describe.

The new OIC, Makro, decided the first thing he was going to do was bring our well-known prisoner, Joram, to heel. Homosexuality was an offence punishable by the courts in Zimbabwe but Joram, being a lifer, without any hope of release, had many wives in prison. The regular officers accepted this situation as they feared Joram. During one of the many horrific and barbaric centre-court beating of homosexuals, Makro decided in his first introduction to it, that he was going to settle an old vendetta with Joram. He ordered Joram to be escorted into the centre-court in cuffs and leg irons. Despite Joram's pleas for forgiveness, Makro laid into him in the usual manner, brutally beating him under the feet. Joram bellowed with the pain, pleading with all his utmost persuasion. When Makro was satisfied, he decided he would further demonstrate who was in charge and moved Joram to the FB1 Section, away from his wives, still in cuffs and leg irons.

FB1 section was an enclosed, hangar-like dormitory, consisting of 12 individual cells with thick wire mesh gates for observation. Six of them faced each other. Each cell had its own toilet, a metal bowl sunk into a cement block.

After three days, Joram had laid his plan. He had saved his faeces for three days in his trash can, which was a plastic 5-litre container with the top cut off, and covered it with a strip of a blanket to prevent others from smelling his waste. As the unsuspecting guards unlocked at 8 a.m., Joram was ready. He reached into his trash can while running after the guards, extracted as much of his faeces as possible and wildly attacked, hurling handfuls of his stinking excrement at them, sending them screaming in every direction. When his ammunition ran out, with wide, wild eyes and constantly bellowing, he dropped his shorts and reached with his fingers into his rear for more. He chased the guards while holding his shorts at his knees with one hand and reaching for more with the other. When that supply ran out, he rushed into other cells and extracted handfuls from those toilets before resuming his pursuit all the while demanding his return to his hall. He was utterly uncontrollable, having lost all his senses and fear of any consequences. As there had been no running water for years, the smell remained in the hall for weeks before enough water was carried in by farm prisoners to clean up properly.

That afternoon Joram was put in leg irons, handcuffed behind his back and escorted to the first floor of the admin block to see the OIC. While waiting outside his door, he struck again. Bounding like a demented springhare to the enormous glass windows overlooking the centre-court, he head-butted the clear glass pane, shattering it and sending glass cascading down onto the walkway to the halls. Before they could contain him, he bounded to the opposite side and repeated the same there, smashing the huge window to the entrance hall below.

They returned him to his cell in FB1 under orders from the OIC, who decided to use another approach. He was formally charged with destruction of government property and expected to pay the costs. This meant he had to appear in a criminal court before a magistrate. Once again, he had a devilish plan. Knowing there were reporters present he laid a public complaint against the OIC, charging him with detailed sexual harassment, which was highly embarrassing and completely unexpected. Joram had played an ace! The OIC conceded defeat and Joram returned to his hall and his wives. Adding insult to injury, the reporters published the claims, which obviously did not do Makro's career any favours.

CHAPTER 53

Gambling and Losing

Prisoners would secretly repurchase boxes from the censor's office staff and use a red and a blue pen – which the staff would steal for them at a price as well – to painstakingly make a deck of cards. The cards they produced were works of art: perfectly designed and beautifully coloured.

During monthly searches, it was always a challenge to try and line up to be searched by the most understanding officer to enable guys to keep their cards or dice. Gambling was a huge addiction in prison, but not my game. Often guys would come back from a visit, during which their loved ones had left groceries that had taken months of savings to buy, and they would gamble the whole lot away in a morning.

The three main stakes used for gambling were smokes, rations of soap, and a ration roll of toilet paper. Anything could, however, be used and the price was always determined by the owner of the cards, who was always paid for providing the cards. After our monthly rations – which we sometimes did not get for months – the exercise yard would be a buzz of gambling activity for three hours. This would then continue in the cells for lunchtime lock-up. Gambling activity increased after a holiday when inmates would have plenty to gamble with. Instead of soccer or volleyball games, the exercise yard would have up to ten circles of prisoners gambling feverishly. When guys got desperate, they would gamble even their groceries, towels and shoes away.

This, of course, all depended on the HIC. Some would turn a blind eye or call for an occasional smoke or bar of soap. Others would walk around collecting tax from each circle, while others would confiscate everything from everyone. Cruelty was deeply ingrained in some of them, which tested the inmates' tolerance to the limit. We would get the occasional, infuriating officer who would allow gambling one day and confiscate everything the next. If any resistance were shown, the officers would crack down, generally through a random search that would see many of us lose precious contraband. Most of the time, we just had to suffer the cruel capriciousness in silence.

There were often gambling nights arranged when four or five inmates with influence would organise to sleep in the same cell. They would gamble from lock-up at 3 p.m. until unlock at 8 a.m. without respect for anyone's rest. These nights would regularly end in disputes, which woke inmates and ignited tempers.

Dice were made from bones bought from kitchen staff, who would save them from the meat they had cooked for officers. These bones were broken and ground on a rough piece of cement floor or wall, into cubes. Then tiny circles were scratched on the sides, and black ash was mixed with Vaseline gel smeared on, which would leave the black dots.

There was a game played with dice and four markers each, where the markers were moved around a board, from start to finish. Four could play at once individually or in pairs, racing around and eliminating one another if you landed on your opponent's position. The board was marked by pen on the inside of someone's white prison shirt. Many a happy hour passed playing this game with regular challenges between teams in our cell.

I was not a gambling man, but that didn't mean I couldn't lose in love.

In October 2006, Sue visited after obtaining special permission to enjoy 30 minutes as opposed to the usual eight to ten minutes. She had been in the UK just over a year by then. She looked gorgeous and radiated love and affection during our conversation. It felt like my old Sue was back and I bubbled inside.

On my birthday that November a beautifully worded card touched me deeply, but something in the extra-affectionate wording left me a little concerned. I was not sure why, but my gut told me something was not right. The fact she did not return to see me over the festive season that followed, but flew to Durban in South Africa with a girlfriend instead, worried me deeply. My intuition told me all was not as it should be.

When my manager Charlie – who was also Sue's brother-in-law – visited in February 2007 and I asked after Sue, he frowned and said, 'Did you not receive her letter?' By the expression on his face, I knew there was bad news coming.

He said he would tell me later and continued with a business discussion until I heard the words that numbed my mind: 'Sue has moved on Rusty.'

He told me she was putting the past behind her and had dreams and aspirations she wanted to follow.

My mind was in turmoil. I reminded myself that she had stood by me for four years, but I had to understand the stress and pain was too much for her. I was gutted thinking about the fact that we were about to get married when cruelly ripped apart, still madly in love. Now I lived in a world where there was no food, no water and people were dying all around me. My emotional link to the person I wanted to live for, had been severed and the person I breathed every breath for was gone. I was totally broken.

I never thought I would bounce back from that. I never thought I would ever recover, or ever find or feel joy in my life again after that. I felt a deep burning pain and was hollow inside. I had handled everything the prison system had thrown at me, but this news felled me. I sobbed uncontrollably.

The only person in the world who I knew could help me was Phil. I was desperate to see him, but he had been moved away from me. It was an almost impossible task, but bribing heavily and taking a considerable risk, I was taken to his section that day. Phil was calm, strong and controlled. He could see my pain. I distinctly remember him standing in the barred, glassless elevated window above me and saying in his kind, convincing, manner, 'Don't worry, Russ, she'll be back ... It's just a phase she's going through, she'll be back my mate.' His words were heaven sent. He was my saviour in a time of desperate need. He gave me the strength to believe and the strength to battle on.

Sue's letter arrived soon after Charlie's visit, explaining everything. I remember flicking straight to the end, expecting a miracle, but there was no 'I love you.' I felt broken. But there was nothing to do. She had to get on with her life. I gave her my blessing and wished her all the very best, she was a good person and had suffered terribly, too.

My appetite vanished. I doubled up with abdominal pain and ate nothing for three days. Within a week I had a chest infection, and after two weeks I had piles. After five weeks of non-stop antibiotics, I weighed 76 kg, having lost 11 kg. I had been heavier at school. The chronic stomach pains continued. I don't think I realised how terrible I looked until Phil saw me again at the hospital five weeks later and his shocked expression startled me. A broken heart was killing me, and he could see it. He spoke very gently, but firmly, looking deep into my eyes after I had poured out my heart over Sue again.

'Russ, listen to me, my mate, very carefully; you are going to die if you don't let her go! Look at all these guys dying, do you want to be one of them?'

I could see his desperate concern, and only then did it strike me, that I had more in life to live for. Without a doubt, those words from Phil saved me.

I then reminded myself that I had my beautiful children, a supportive, loving family, and loyal friends, all waiting for that special day of my release.

What I learned from that experience was that sometimes, we all give up on something, and, as soon as we do, we lose an integral part of ourselves. I could have given up, it was a living hell in there, but thanks to my friend Phil I didn't. No matter how dreadful things seem in life – never give up. Never lose who you are, because the moment you do, a part of you will die.

I started recalibrating my mind. I took the very few negative aspects from my relationship with Sue and blew them up. I told myself that it was never going to work, and I had been deluding myself. I kept repeating this to myself over and over. Slowly, over a period of six months, I could feel the physical pain going. Sue and I wrote two more letters each, but it was too painful to continue hearing from her. I decided I had to let go completely.

That Christmas in 2007, she got engaged, fell pregnant and then gave birth to a gorgeous daughter, which was what she had always wanted so badly. My spirit and determination to stay healthy and survive eventually returned.

A year after she told me she was leaving me, I was a healed man again.

CHAPTER 54

Hope on a Wing

No matter how low I went, I kept looking for meaningful ways to make a positive contribution, even though my place in the world was in one of its hellholes. For my own peace of mind, I wanted to feel I could still be of some use in some way, no matter how small.

When the Zimbabwe currency crashed, the economy collapsed, and food was so scarce, that even the guards were starving. I used to watch the pigeons at the prison carefully every single day. Thinking they were safe, they would lay their eggs high up in the gutters of the halls. The guards, always looking for food, would regularly catch the poor brooding pigeons off their nests, which infuriated me.

One evening around 9 p.m., the night shift guard approached our cell with a struggling pigeon in his hands. While a few inmates were congratulating him, I took 10 cigarettes from my stash of smokes (never a smoker myself but this was the prison currency), stood up, walked over to the wire mesh between us, and asked him what he was going to do with that pigeon. In the silence of the cell, he proudly said, 'I'm going to eat it.' The other inmates burst out laughing, knowing that the thought of killing the innocent bird upset me a lot. I had expressed as much, many times. Knowing that he was a heavy smoker and would be susceptible to a bribe, I asked him if I could buy the pigeon from him for 10 cigarettes.

He looked at me, then at the pigeon and asked to see the cigarettes. After showing him the smokes, he immediately agreed. I then said to him, 'Go to the window and let the bird go.'

In astonishment, he looked at the window, then back at me.

'How do I know that you'll give me the cigarettes after it flies away,' he said.

'I will, I'm going to stand here in front of everyone as my witness, with the cigarettes, and once you release the bird, I'll give you the smokes,' I said.

The prison guard walked over to the window and released the pigeon into the darkness. It was a moment of uplifting magnificence as we watched that pigeon fly away to freedom once more.

I gave him his 10 cigarettes. It gave me a profound sense of fulfilment, knowing that in some small way, I was able to make a difference in this beautiful world, under those terrible conditions.

CHAPTER 55

Shame

There was a prisoner that Geza and Phil despised openly, and I hardly ever spoke to. He never slept in our cell, which was a blessing. His name was Shame; short and stocky, he had a permanent snarl on his lips. His eyelids covered the top half of his eyes, which gave him a particularly sinister look. With multiple convictions for armed robbery, he was particularly cruel to the new inmates. I don't think I ever saw him smile. He was beyond reform and a frequent visitor to the centre-court.

By 2007, we had been without running water for two years, and I'd just recovered from a severe chest infection. Elisha and I were both off the steps training and spirits were low. When there is no clean water to just have a drink because you are thirsty, is a frustration that is indescribable. Even the guards were short of water, which made them more aggressive and unreasonable.

During the night in 2007, we heard a commotion upstairs, and I discussed it briefly with Geza, but we were too tired to pay more attention and went back to sleep. It was Shame who had had an altercation with his 'wife' and beat him to a pulp. He hid the boy from the guards in the morning, but news of the beating leaked through the grapevine, and there was tension. A deathly silence followed when security arrived in the hall from admin block, and Shame's name was called.

All 400 listened to the threats until the guards left to return for him shortly after that with the head of security. I was standing beside Moyo, and we watched Shame, thinking about how he must be feeling knowing what was coming. I felt for him as the guards seemed very fired up to deal with him. Sullen and arrogant as always, he was in a frenzy, and we knew he was up to something.

As I was the senior security staff, responsible for keeping order generally amongst inmates, any prohibited activity would come back on me first. Moyo was a respected staff member too, so we kept Shame in our sights. Three of us saw him hiding a six-inch spike that was strapped to his leg, under *sadza* in a lunchbox in the corner of the courtyard, where they guys usually burnt the cloth for making *skwerekweres*.

Someone alerted us that the guards were on their way, armed and in force, igniting a buzz of anticipation and sending terror through the hall. All I knew was that I had to remove the spike because if it were used in any way, we would all suffer.

At the sound of the gates opening, Shame ran for his lunchbox in the corner of the exercise yard, but I had beaten him to it. Without his spike, he had to change strategy. Wild with animal-like panic, he ran through the gathered crowd, heading for the staircase, which was off limits, with four of us chasing after him knowing he was about to do something crazy.

On reaching the first floor, we heard glass breaking further up followed by growling and screaming as he stood there like an enraged beast, slashing huge deep cuts across his upper forearms with a shard of glass. He had four cuts on one arm and three on the other, blood pumped out everywhere. As we approached, he dropped his white drawstring shorts, took hold of his manhood with one hand and slashed it several times as well.

He was facing the window with his back to the steps. I knew we had to go for him, and before he could turn on us Moyo and I had him pinned down. It was quite a struggle on top of the blood now pooling on the bare concrete floor amongst the shattered glass. He was swearing and threatening us, kicking and wriggling to break free, but we held him until the guards came up, cuffed him and escorted him away. The guards seldom thanked us for any good deed, but this time they did. Shame received his punishment, a merciless beating in the centre-court two days later despite many stitches.

A week later, during feeding with everyone seated on the tarred exercise yard floor, Shame was made to walk around the 400 seated prisoners naked with his equipment in one hand berating himself while proclaiming to all that his organ was his problem. I thought long and hard about Shame. It bothered me that I could not fathom what was going on in his head to get to where he was in life. Why had he beaten the kid so badly, knowing the consequences? I thought about how he had been driven to such fear that he would do something so destructive to himself, to avoid what he knew was coming. It was one of many puzzles I battled with.

Another shocking incident happened on a cold winter's morning in June 2007. There was a deathly scream in the eerie silence around 4 a.m. It startled all 36 of us in our barren cement and steel cell. For security reasons, four bright lights were left on, and I saw Geza jump up at the far corner of the cell. In the opposite corner, standing naked, still screaming was a kid around 20 years old. Blood poured through his thin fingers covering his right eye while his man, Marabba, viciously assaulted him with slaps, kicks, and punches.

Marabba was tall, his face pockmarked with acne pimples, and thin with rounded shoulders and a hunched back; he was always active in the gangs. He had just stabbed his 'wife' and was now trying to silence the kid, but the guards had heard it. Within minutes we listened to the pounding of boots up the stairs to our floor.

Like a disturbed swarm of bees, the complex came alive as over two thousand men woke hall by hall and guards streamed up from all over. The youngster had refused sex and had been promptly stabbed in the eye with the point of a rusted compass. Luckily the spike had passed below the eyeball, but the wound was deep.

As the story unfolded through the steel mesh wall, so the threats increased from the guards, who changed shift at 6 a.m. but left a report for the next lot. Everyone waited anxiously. Eventually, about an hour later, no less than 30 stormed up, unlocked the door and put them both in handcuffs and leg irons.

They were marched into the centre-court, where all 2,200 of us could witness the price of bad behaviour. We had all seen it many times, but this day my heart went out to the kid who had just been stabbed in the eye. Cuffed and leg-ironed, pinned on his stomach by boots and a chair straddling his torso, he was beaten on the soles of his feet severely. They hit him for 20 minutes then made him run around the centre-court gutter-trench twice, a distance of about 400 metres, to get the blood flowing in his feet, then 20 more minutes of beatings. That was the routine for his two sessions. They put all their strength into each stroke, jostling and laughing for a turn. Once again, I asked myself how such brutal barbarism could be happening. How could anyone leave this hellhole in a better mental state than when they came in?

The kid hobbled back to our hall, but for Marabba, worse was to come. He was an orphan from childhood and had spent almost his entire adult life inside prison, with 22 years to go. He was mercilessly hammered under the feet, whipped across his back and buttocks, kicked in the ribs repeatedly, and slapped across the face until his mouth and nose were bleeding. This went on for two hours. He crawled back on hands and knees, his feet badly bent with bleeding welts all over. For days he crawled, up and down stairs, and everywhere he had to go. Nobody was allowed to help him. After day three, huge sores mushroomed, oozing pus from the tops of both enormously swollen feet, which gave him problems for years.

Marabba was a thief and a predatory homosexual. He was always at the meetings where they decided who their victims were going to be and who would do what to whom. It was cold, callous and calculating. Marabba was capable of great evil. I was never sure whether I should feel sorry for him or not. It was a tough place trying to make sense of all these strange minds at work, but I tried to take something out of all the madness.

Two days after this incident, Geza walked out of prison as a free man. It was an emotional farewell. He was a good man and had stood by me for many years. We hugged and said our goodbyes and I reminded him that he had promised to remain straight and leave crime behind. The vision of him limping out the gate, a beaming smile across his face and waving wildly, is still so clear to me. Seeing him leave me behind was tough, I was happy for him, but it set me back feeling lonelier than ever.

CHAPTER 56

Attacked

We had our in-hall soccer league, and then an inter-hall competition when there was an OIC who allowed movement between halls. When these games took place, there was massive excitement.

Fatso was one of the first people I met in Chikurubi, and we had become good friends, but we were on opposing sides when we played soccer. Shortly after Geza left, during an exceptionally vigorous in-house league final, things got very ugly.

It was a rough, hotly contested game and Fatso and I went at each other hard. At one point, I rammed him into a wall, which was a bit excessive, but I had the hammer down and wanted to win. As I nailed him, he swung backwards wildly and hit me in the mouth with his elbow and nearly took a few teeth out, but I figured I deserved it, so ignored it.

Things were getting tense with scores even and the pace unrelenting. Minutes later, I tackled him hard again, and the whistle blared, bringing the game to a stop. I apologised; the intensity had got the better of me and a free kick was given. But tempers remained hot, and the next time we clashed, he struck me with a blatantly illegal tackle, that sent me sprawling on the hot tar. The referee chose to ignore the transgression and play continued, which infuriated me.

I could sense this was becoming racial, but there was no way I was backing down, and when he got too close to our goals, I flattened him in pretty much the same way he had hit me. This brought the confrontation to a head; he was enraged, and so was I. Both of us were of similar weight and stature, we squared off, and he punched me hard in the mouth, then immediately started backing away fast. I was fuming and went after him, intending to return the punch when the racial invective flew loud and clear. It was unlike any I had ever heard, and it gutted me: 'We'll kill you, you white dog! Just like your forefathers killed ours, we'll kill you. You're the only white in here, we'll kill you! You all dogs, this country doesn't need white pigs like you.'

That was all the hyped-up crowd needed, and suddenly, apart from Chichoni (another good friend), Moyo and my mate George who were trying to quell the mob, I stood alone against an enraged, racially-pumped mob of over 70 dangerous criminals who charged at me roaring for my blood.

Elisha, the captain of Fatso's team, someone I considered a friend and the guy I trained with daily on the steps, attacked first. He went for my throat from behind, swearing the whole time. My only thought was: 'Stay on your feet no matter what, keep fighting with everything you've got, but just don't go down, or it will all be over.'

I found the strength to pull Elisha over my shoulder and threw him to the ground in front of me, then continued to battle the mob with fists flying in every direction. Somehow my flailing fists kept them at bay long enough for the guards to hear the uproar, and they came running into the mêlée and stopped the attack before I went down.

In the end, three of us needed stitches, but what hurt the most was the verbal attack from Fatso. This was an educated, articulate man whom I had considered a friend and a confidant, with whom I had bonded across the racial divide and this belief had cheered me and given me confidence. With this attack, I realised I had been fooling myself; no matter how hard I tried to be kind and fair to all my fellow prisoners and to be accepted for what I was, I was still seen, by most, as some sort of threat. I think, under the surface, those people hated me just because of the colour of my skin. I had to remind myself that I was surrounded by people who might turn on me at the flick of a mental switch, simply because of my race. Phil and I had been separated, and Geza had just gone, which left me feeling desperately alone, although Moyo and George were amazing. Chichoni surprised me the most that day, and I had a different respect for him after that.

After three of us had received our stitches, I made a report to the OIC through the HIC and demanded Fatso be moved to another hall. The OIC came to our hall and asked me to forgive and make peace as we all had to live together, but I was in no mood for reconciliation. I insisted that he be moved away from me. It was a Sunday and Elisha had had time to reflect on his actions. He took the time out to come and speak to me about what had happened. He asked me to please make peace and said it was all part of the game, and we needed to coexist, but I had had enough. Too much damage had been done, and I wanted to see the back of Fatso. He was moved to another cell and never received another thing from me. Elisha and I continued running the steps, but I had become more aware of who he was deep down.

Ironically, Fatso spoke glowingly of the European community and all that they had done for him, yet under the veneer he remained a dangerous racist. In 2008, Fatso got bail, pending an appeal and was released. Only a few months later he was shot in the legs three times during an armed robbery and was sent back to prison, where he remains today. I guess his soccer days are over now.

After the incident on the soccer pitch, I spent most of my days with George and Moyo. George and I had our mornings taken up selecting the critically sick to go to the hospital, then we'd walk and chat unless I was playing sport. There were three particularly nasty guards who made it their business to make our lives hell: Makorudzo, Chihambakwe and Ngerazi.

Ngerazi was thin and hunched, with bulging eyes and a wicked, ragged-toothed smile. He just loved beating prisoners. He worked in the reception away from the halls, which kept him isolated from us, but his cruelty was boundless. Trying to keep our clothes as clean as possible was a constant challenge especially during the icy cold winters. The only way we could dry our clothes by the morning was to hang them on the wire mesh front wall of the cell, in the circulating air. If they hung off the walls there was little air movement to dry them, so the mesh was our best option, but, strictly speaking, this was not allowed because it interfered with the guards' ability to see into the cell. Most guards were happy to turn a blind eye, but not Ngerazi. Even though he was not one of the regular night-duty guards, he would do surprise inspections at around 3 a.m. and make a note of which cells were hanging garments on the mesh and how many were hanging on each.

Then from 10 a.m. to 11 a.m. during his tea break, he would go around to each hall with his list and make each of the unlucky culprits sit in formation. Then he would beat the palms of each hand extremely hard with a rubber baton, five on each hand per garment, smiling the whole time. Sometimes he would make you hold your fingertips together facing upright and beat you on the tips of the fingers with his baton instead. I would often watch him enjoying himself and feel sorry that he needed to stoop to such levels for pleasure. He was a sadist, and one of the many whom I battled to forgive. It upset all the inmates and George would shake his head in disbelief making his disapproval visible. I decided to leave it to God to make him realise one day how much anger and senseless pain he was causing. Moyo would just say, 'He's mad.'

I heard later that he was transferred to a farm prison and continued his behaviour until he went to a local beer hall where relatives of a prisoner he had beaten were waiting for him. They returned the favour and gave him a terrible thrashing.

Throughout my four-and-a-half years at Chikurubi Max, there was one guard who stood out amongst the rest: of all the guards, Chihambakwe was the cruellest – and worse than Ngerazi because I had to deal with him daily.

He was also the toughest to deal with because we had to see him every time we had visitors, and he relished being as unpleasant as he could be to them. Because he oversaw visits, this malevolent man invariably spoiled those rare moments of joy. He hated anyone getting their stipulated 15 minutes every two weeks, and could disconnect our conversations at any time. George had visitors regularly, and he would curse Chihambakwe after every visit.

At Khami we spoke through wire mesh that they would cake with mud to give you less visibility. In Chikurubi we spoke on a phone through several panes of thick glass. Not a single visit during my entire time there went on for the full allowable time. Invariably, after five or six minutes, Chihambakwe would say, 'One more minute,' then wait a minute and either turn the phone off or snatch the receiver away. No matter how hard we tried to comply with the regulations, he would always find an excuse to confiscate some of what my visitors brought me.

His arrogance and rudeness was flabbergasting. Regularly, women would be in tears when chatting to me after passing him. Obviously, his behaviour left them thinking this must be how I was treated inside there, and in many ways, it was, but that was something I didn't want my loved ones to know. I felt I had already caused them enough pain and hardship and they had their own problems to deal with. It was a hard system with no real intention to rehabilitate at all, just a straightforward punishment-based ideology.

When I read about the prisons with a bed, mattress, bedding and decent food, it didn't come close in comparison to the barbaric conditions we were facing. Even when Mugabe was in Chikurubi during the Rhodesian years, he slept on a bed with bedding, regular laundry, a balanced diet and working ablutions.

Because I had a lawyer and an advocate who visited regularly, I was never seriously beaten, but they made up for it with mental torture. Moyo wasn't feeling well with an upset stomach, and I wanted to collect some tins of food for him. I asked to be escorted to the censor's office, and the guard said he would take me later. He purposefully delayed and delayed. Because we were only allowed out our cells for four hours a day, I knew if someone did not take me, I would run out of time and have to wait another day. I became so desperate with him that I threatened to break a window or do something stupid to cause a commotion and suddenly, with just 30 minutes left until lock-up, I was taken to collect some food. It was a constant uphill battle in there.

CHAPTER 57

Escape

To pass the time and ease the pain, I had a gorgeous fantasy girlfriend named Sheree. She was the most perfect, magnificent woman of my wildest dreams. We would fly all over the world in our private jet, catch marlin in Mexico, make love on secluded beaches, laugh and party with our friends without end, spend money freely and provide limitless help to those in financial distress.

I would lie for hours every day with Sheree. It took me to a place far from the pain, where I could smile and laugh again wholeheartedly. It felt fantastic and gave me a deep sense of hope and freedom, which helped me cope with the soul-destroying circumstances. I would also dream of all my aspirations and goals that had pushed me so hard over the decades. To have hope and dream felt better than having nothing at all. In the mornings, Moyo would often ask how my night with Sheree went, and I'd give him some wonderful, passionate story, and we'd laugh out loud. He slept in a different cell to me, and we'd meet downstairs every morning and chat in the sun.

Walking in the yard with George, I was called to visitors. Lyn delivered my daily food and her devotion and loyalty were critical in keeping my spirits up. She mentioned that I should expect a visit from some officials. She couldn't

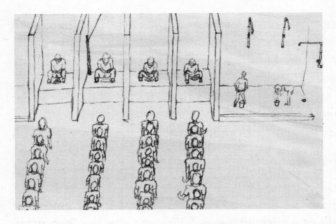

ABOVE Queues waiting for the toilet and washing out of buckets

RIGHT Receiving food from Lyn with Chihambakwe

say more with Chihambakwe listening in. The following day I had a very encouraging visit from a group of retired judges, church elders, and high-ranking war veterans. They came to Chikurubi to tell me they knew all about my plight, believed I had been wronged and would apply to the president for clemency and have me pardoned. They said to me in no uncertain terms to have no further contact with Justice Paradza and to keep our meeting secret.

My spirits soared when the promised attorney arrived and helped me fill in the required clemency forms. That week the application went to the minister of justice. What happened after that is not very clear. Many stories were circulating.

I saw Simon Mann after this visit and he noticed my excitement. He warned me that these people were untrustworthy and suggested I should not get too confident about my chances. By this time, the mercenary pilots had been released and sent back to South Africa, but Simon was still serving and down in the dumps. He had been told he was going to be released, but was terrified that they would send him to Equatorial Guinea to stand trial there. The last I heard from him was a note wishing me well and a message to say he was praying hard not to be sent to Equatorial Guinea.

Well nothing came of my hopes, and I never went anywhere. Exactly what transpired is still a mystery. Two days later the guards came to tell me that Simon had been taken away and had been sent to stand trial in Equatorial Guinea. (He spent two years in Equatorial Guinea's notorious Black Beach Prison before receiving a presidential pardon.) I felt terribly sad for him, but there was yet another inmate headed my way who would also give me the hope that I might one day be able to leave this terrible place.

A group of ZANU PF guys were imprisoned for the murder of opposition MDC activists. One of them was a man named Albert. He was in line for a ministerial post and close to the minister of justice. He was tall, handsome and well-educated. We shared many hours walking and talking because he appeared genuinely interested in my case. I told him my whole story in detail. He said to me that it would not be long before his politically connected friends had him released. He assured me that once he was free, he would use his political influence to have me set free.

Once again, I got excited, as Albert only served a short time before he was released, and I heard I was to be moved to Harare Central Prison.

True to his word, on his release Albert phoned my sister Lyn and told her he wanted to take her to meet the minister. Lyn went with Albert to see the minister but was unable to do so. The minister told Albert that I could now be released from prison. Albert told Lyn to have my lawyers draw up the clemency application again, have me sign it, and bring it to him. A lawyer came to the prison, and we completed all the forms once more. I thought this might be my lucky break, but then I heard nothing. Frustrated, I got Lyn to phone Albert and ask what had happened. He told her the application was at a very high political level, and it would take some time, but he assured her I would be released very soon. Every time she spoke to him, she received the same assurances. Again, nothing happened.

Three months later, I had another approach offering to organise my release on medical grounds, but I turned it down. I insisted I wanted to be released because I was innocent, not because I was sick.

There had been several occasions when I had over-trained and gone down with a chest infection even while on cortisone tablets, but reading through a *Men's Health* magazine one day I saw how terrible cortisone is for you. I had been on 20 mg a day for two years, and the side effects were: a weakening of the immune system, crumbling bones, vision problems, dangerously high blood pressure, stomach and back pain and more. My eyesight had deteriorated badly, and I was experiencing severe stomach and back pain. I immediately approached the nurse that was visiting our hall that day, and he asked me who had prescribed cortisone for that long. When I explained that he was one of the nurses who had prescribed it, he denied it and cancelled my doses without weaning me off them. This set me off on another string of antibiotics to cure my chest of infection. I eventually had cortisone smuggled into the hall by hospital staff, at a price, and slowly weaned myself off until I recovered, but I never played any sport or trained again until I left Chikurubi.

After watching hundreds die over the years, my friend and washer Nyere's health began to deteriorate, which worried me deeply. Nyere had chest pains and a continuous cough and had been on two different antibiotics already, but his condition remained poor.

George and I sent him to the hospital, only for him to return with the antibiotics he had been given in the first instance. Within a week he declined seriously. We then had to carry him to the hospital and told the nurses that his condition was critical and pleaded with them to look more carefully at his problem. We were only able to apply this modicum of pressure because we were senior inmates and had positions of responsibility. After pleading with them, we were escorted back to our hall. To our astonishment, Nyere was not hospitalised and was carried back to our hall. He said he tried to tell them what was wrong, and they said that he still has plenty of strength and gave him more antibiotics.

One of Nyere's faults was his stubborn streak, which annoyed the guards; he would never back down if he felt he was right, even when guards were severely beating him. The next day his condition was grave, and George and I carried him back to the hospital, leaving strict orders that once we left, he was not to say a word to anyone. He was admitted, put on a TB trial and tested that day. His TB count showed full-blown TB. Very sadly for the entire prison, as Nyere was quite a legend, he died that night. I felt sick to the core. He was a good man, honest and down-to-earth. He had been my loyal washer for four years and I had taken care of him during tough times. I could only take comfort in the fact that he had escaped the horrors of that prison and gone on to a better place.

CHAPTER 58

Rock Bottom

t was 2008, and the death rate was horrific. Phil had been reclassified to a C-class prisoner and been transferred to Harare Central Prison. The water crisis had worsened. Lyn was doing her best to have me moved to join Phil, but things weren't happening. My chest was playing up, and I wasn't in good health. I could feel there were more significant health issues underneath. What followed set me back even more.

I had served over five years of my sentence, which meant I had less than five left, and they were refusing to reclassify me.

In the categorisation of prisoners, on top of the pile, were the condemned men, who were in single cells, naked, and locked up for all but one hour a day, when they could exercise in a tiny yard. They waited for the knock on the door that would be the signal that they were on their way to the gallows.

Prisoners like me, with more than five years to serve, were D class. We were subjected to heavy security and our movements severely curtailed. Convicts with between two-and-a-half and five years remaining of their sentence were C class and were given menial jobs to do. They were sent to a medium-security prison. The prison workshops were derelict, so there was not much to do there but C-class prisoners made all the prison uniforms, did some plumbing and electrical work, and worked on the prison vehicles.

B class had less than two-and-a-half years to serve. There were several prison farms around the country where only B-class prisoners were accommodated to assist with the agricultural activities such as growing crops and raising cattle, pigs and chickens. They could regularly be seen in public carrying out cleaning duties at courthouses or government buildings as well.

A class were prisoners over 60 years old with less than six months remaining. On their shirts, they had a large A marked front and back in red. They were only locked up at 7 p.m. and were free to move during the day. They were used a lot to run errands for the guards and prison staff in large prison complexes like Chikurubi, which had a maximum security, women's prison and a farm prison.

To walk out of Chikurubi maximum, one had to pass through seven locked and guarded gates or heavy doors and questions were asked at each entrance. A Mozambican national was with us, serving 25 years for armed robbery and murder. Somehow, he very secretively acquired an extra shirt through connections of his in reception. With several smuggled red pens, he marked As on both sides of the spare shirt. It was on a summer's morning when he put it on inside out, followed by his usual shirt, and asked to go to reception to check something on his warrant. He was escorted there at 9.30 a.m. which was perfect timing. His escort told him to wait there, because he had something he wanted to do, and disappeared. At 10 a.m. shifts changed at all posts. The prisoner went to the toilets, offloaded the covering shirt, turned the other to show the As and sauntered through all seven gates to freedom! At 3 p.m. during lock-up, his absence was discovered.

At this point, there were hundreds of prisoners perishing annually, attracting no attention or concern from HQ, but that night and throughout the next day, over 20 furious, top-brass prison officials arrived to deal with it.

The next day was probably the worst of my ten years in prison. A terrifying onslaught was ordered. The cells were ransacked, virtually everyone was beaten, everything we owned was confiscated including our clothes and books, and we were locked up naked with lice-ridden blankets for 23 hours a day. From lock-up, at 3 p.m. until 8 a.m. (17 hours), we did not eat. The two feeding staff, the head staff, an assistant, and I, went downstairs at 8.30 a.m. to carry the sugarless mielie-meal porridge straight back up to each cell. Then we were locked up again, until 2 p.m.

Lunch and dinner were combined: boiled cabbage mixed with sugar beans and *sadza*, which had to be eaten immediately in the cells. Plates were then removed and all locked up again. There was no running water, and as our pleas for relief in the regimen were ignored, it turned the place into a stinking nightmare with inmates dying all around us. I worked hard on getting messages out to my contacts and lawyers and eventually there was intervention from human-rights groups and lawyers. Conditions were finally relaxed after three of the worst months of my term. It set hundreds back physically, leading up to a catastrophic cholera outbreak later that year. In the four-and-a-half years I was locked up at Chikurubi I estimate 1,400 inmates died of disease, starvation and, in some cases, of abuse.

I was not spared from health problems there either. While I was never as close to death as some of the inmates, I nevertheless understood my body well and knew how hard it was struggling under those conditions.

In October 2008, I was finally reclassified as C class and told I was moving to Harare Central Medium Security Prison. The shock and excitement were invigorating. I was bubbling inside, but not wanting to be disappointed again, I kept my excitement to myself. The morning I left, I found George and Moyo and gave them as much as I could of my books, containers and food, and wished them well. We had shared some horrific times and had become very close friends. I felt their pain as I walked out the gate of that hall. I had experienced that pain every time one of my other friends had left for happier places.

CHAPTER 59

Candid Camera

B y the time I arrived at Central, I was in very poor health, and my chest was giving me terrible trouble. The cortisone had taken its toll. The day I was transferred I had four large polystyrene sacks to carry. They dropped me off at the remand section and told me to walk 600 metres to the convicted section. I was dizzy, weak and sweating profusely. I had never experienced such physical weakness and became quite concerned about overexerting myself carrying all that baggage in the boiling hot October heat.

The first person I saw at Harare Central was Malagas, the guy I had first befriended in Chikurubi, who was instrumental in the mob justice attack I witnessed. It was great to see him again, and we chatted briefly about what he had been up to over the past four years.

Unbeknown to me, he had been in Khami Max and was now a red stage. He was quick to inform me that Phil had arranged for me to join him in his cell.

The joy of seeing Phil again helped my spirits enormously. We embraced each other with great elation. He was such a boon to my emotional wellbeing. We gathered up my belongings and set off to my new quarters.

The cells were similar to those in Khami. On the bottom floor were mostly single cells, interspersed with five-man cells. The five-man cells in Central generally held between six and nine people, so they were stacked up pretty close, but Phil had made a plan for me to join him and only three other guys in his cell. The other three were good guys we had been with in Chikurubi, so it was like a happy reunion. It was fantastic to be back with old friends and in a cell where we had some room to move.

In comparison to where I had been, it was like being in a luxury hotel. We were only locked up for 16 hours a day, rather than 20. In Harare Central, unlike Chikurubi, there were no high security walls, which allowed more sunlight while we were in the large communal courtyard. Seeing old friends with whom I had shared many tough years was wonderful, and we had a lot of fun exchanging stories under relatively relaxed security conditions.

Lyn was beside herself with not having to walk that one kilometre up to Chikurubi and back carrying our food, and Phil was also permitted to join me and see her. We spoke through a thick steel wire mesh, so our hands were only a centimetre apart. Being that much closer to her felt fantastic.

During one of her daily visits, about three months after I had arrived there, she asked me if I would like an iPod. I asked what an iPod was. She said, 'It's a thing that plays music.' Knowing anything like that would be contraband, I asked how big it was. With her fingers she indicated the size of this tiny little thing.

'How many songs does it play?' I asked.

'About a thousand,' she said.

'No way, so where do you put all the CDs?'

That's how far technology had advanced in just six years that I had been away. We laughed until tears were rolling down our cheeks.

The following day the iPod came in under the salad along with the charger, a headset, and instructions. Phil and I were like hysterical kids at Christmas trying to figure out how to use it. After six years of no music or even knowing what time it was (watches were not allowed) the pleasure that that device brought is difficult to describe. We soon smuggled wires through from the kitchen and connected the charger to the light. We would take turns in enjoying the beautiful memories that music brings.

About a week later Joe Wright, a close friend for many years, visited and asked me if I would like his spare Nokia phone. I was ecstatic. He also kindly offered to pay the monthly phone bills. It was exciting, risky business, which you could not dream of in a maximum security prison. But I had grown accustomed to living on the edge and breaking the boring routine in there. I soon had two more iPods from my old mate Martin Pieters and his wife Candy, and my sister managed to get me another phone. We now had a device each to play with, in our happy little cell.

Although it was dangerous, I had my back covered by Joe, Graham Hingeston (with whom I shared many happy memories from the safari business), and Lyn, all of whom were taking care of guards in the right places.

Another special high-school friend of mine, Calvin Maughan, visited soon after that and offered to buy me an electric toothbrush. It was as if I had died and gone to heaven when I used it for the first time. These luxuries made up for the downside of our harsh living conditions. Within a month the toothbrush was confiscated in a search, but after threats that I would take legal action, it was grudgingly returned.

It was indescribably wonderful to be able to connect with the outside world again. But I soon discovered that, to protect my feelings, sensitive information from home had been withheld from me for years.

I remember the moment so distinctly. I was next to Phil, lying on a blanket listening to music on the iPod when I received a call from Dusty, who was living in Durban at the time. It was exhilarating chatting to him privately on a phone. Eventually, I asked him if he had a girlfriend and if so, I wanted to know the details.

I had touched on this subject in previous conversations during his visits to see me, but he was always evasive. I put that down to him being a little shy in other company. On this occasion, there was complete silence, and then he said in an apprehensive voice, 'Dad, I'm gay!'

My immediate reply was, 'That's okay, boy, I love you as you are. Being gay doesn't change a thing.'

All he said was, 'Thanks, Dad.'

It did throw me for a moment; my love for him was far too deep and sincere to be affected, but I instantly began questioning myself.

I was brought up in a staunchly heterosexual environment, and tried to bring him up in a similar manner. Had I worked too hard to make him what I wanted him to be, rather than what he wanted to be? After the call, my mind was a confused mess for a few days, but our bond was far too powerful, and soon it was a thing of the past. We remain exceptionally close today.

Even though he could never bring himself to return to Chikurubi, my friend John Sharp visited me many times at

Harare Central. All of his visits were wonderful, but one was particularly memorable.

A friend of John's was visiting from Florida, and agreed to keep him company on the 860 km drive. Sully said he was happy to wait in the car with John's fox terrier and read a book while John came inside.

John was still waiting to see me when he heard a commotion by the entrance. Glancing over in idle curiosity, he was shocked to see Sully being frog-marched towards the prison door! He rushed over to see what was going on. It turned out that Sully had left the vehicle, probably to stretch his legs, and decided to take a photograph of the prison. All photography around or near a prison or military base is strictly forbidden, and to make matters worse, he had snapped a photo just as the OIC of the prison was exiting the gates on his way home.

Two belligerent guards marched Sully into the prison grounds. Initially, they said, they would release him if the photos were deleted from the camera, but Sully could not do this – he barely knew how to switch it on and off. John then also tried and failed – it was a rather old camera. One of the guards snatched the camera away from him, saying that he was not stupid and knew how to do it. He failed too. Next thing they grabbed Sully and steered him through the front door of the prison, the OIC right behind them and still shouting threats. There was nothing John could do at this stage except wait.

Phil and I were just approaching the visiting area and could see Sully being led out from the bowels of the prison. John asked him what was happening, but he said he didn't know.

When our visiting time was up, Sully emerged and he, John and the OIC walked out together. Apparently the OIC delivered a lecture to Sully about how he had the power to lock him up for seven years, despite Sully's US citizenship.

He then reached into his pocket and brought out Sully's camera. He handed it to him and instructed Sully to take a few photographs to exonerate the prison of any damage that the camera might have sustained at their hands. Sully was flabbergasted. He had been arrested for taking a photo of the prison, and now the OIC was ordering him to take more! Sully calmly took three more close-ups of the prison. After confirming that there was nothing wrong with the camera, he was allowed to leave.

Since they had failed in their attempts to erase the original photo from the camera, it now contained four illegal shots of the prison. In the offices, he had handed over $40 for his freedom to his two guards, and this had seemingly nullified his offence.

CHAPTER 60

Solitary Confinement

Unbeknown to me, a jealous prisoner got word to Prison HQ that I was running a business by phone from prison. I had good standing in the pecking order, and direct access to senior officers, but he made his report directly to HQ and not to the prison guards who were looking after me, so they were not aware of what was happening.

Out of the blue at 11 a.m. a delegation arrived from HQ to do a search. Suddenly one of the friendly guards was standing at the entrance to my hall, and everyone was told to get outside. I asked the guard what was going on, and he said there'd been a directive from HQ to search my hall. He was on the payroll, so I told him where all my gadgets were hidden. As I turned around, I saw four HQ guards marching across the courtyard towards me wearing face masks and white rubber gloves.

Another guard in the hall was locking prisoners out of their cells so he could search without distraction.

My guard called him to throw the keys over. He had locked about seven cells before throwing across the long chains with dozens of keys attached to it. My guard knew exactly which key it was and headed straight for my cell. The HQ guards were just five metres away. They burst past me, knowing exactly where they were going. About three seconds later, my guard came out with pockets bulging, and as he passed me, he gave me a wink. It was a very close shave, one which would have had me sent back to Chikurubi.

It cost my sister US$100 to get the gadgets back, but the downside was that the HQ guards were convinced I was up to something and that I needed to be monitored. The same suspicion fell on Phil. We were informed that both of us were being sent to solitary confinement for two years.

Solitary means you are put in a 3 m X 1 m X 3 m cell, that has a solid door with a spy-hole, and a vent too high to see out of. In solitary you are locked up and let out at the same time as all the inmates. We could still have all the other privileges that other inmates were allowed, but we were locked up for sixteen hours a day from 3 p.m. onwards. The loneliness was tough. It's a long time alone in a cell daily.

On the plus side, it gave us more control of the lice that drove us crazy, and we would be isolated from the cholera infection which had broken out in prison. Having experienced that precious little link to the outside world, however, I had to get my phone back. When I did, it made a huge difference. As a precaution, I had my sister find me two spare batteries, which I had friendly guards charge for me. I also had two iPods, one for the guard to listen to and return charged the next day, and one for Phil and me to share. The music on those iPods was a significant factor in keeping us in good spirits and sane. I used to listen to old songs and let my mind wander back to better days when I was free and happy. I was able to communicate from 3 p.m. until 10 p.m. but this had to be under my blankets in case a guard looked through the spy hole in my door.

The constant communication made it feel like I was getting my life back. My best friend Max Rosenfels called me every single day without fail, whether he was in Zimbabwe, South Africa, or even once in Mauritius. He was unbelievable, and our friendship since school has always remained unchanged.

CHAPTER 61

Cholera

The initial stages of a cholera epidemic started three months before my arrival. Several guys had contracted it, but they were confined to one hall. We all became incredibly hygiene conscious, and thankfully the water pipes to that prison were still operating, so showering was not an issue. (If you resided on the same water line as an influential government official, then water was never a problem.)

Food was in short supply, though, and I asked Lyn to ask friends to assist so I could help some of the other guys who were starving. The only way to ensure the food got to the prisoners was for her and a few friends to bring huge pots and deliver it to me personally. Phil and I would then dish it out, to keep it from being stolen.

Towards the beginning of the cholera epidemic, a few weeks after we had been sent to solitary, I walked into the bathroom area and saw a kid in his late teens in the shower. He had his back to me and looked like a skeleton covered in wrinkled old skin. It shocked me deeply, but what was worse still was when I noticed the area around his rear-end was one huge festering pink and red sore, as if someone had stuck a red-hot poker in there. When he turned and saw me, he immediately covered his backside with his hands. He was embarrassed and had a pitiful look on his face that is still stuck in my mind. He died a few days later like hundreds of others during that time.

There was an old man named Admire who had been in Chikurubi with us for many years, and we chatted often. I liked his pride and steadfastness. He was honourable and unafraid and regularly stood up to the guards and prisoners alike. He loved reading, and Phil and I always shared our magazines with him. One evening he came to my cell to collect a magazine, and after he had not returned it the next day like he always did, I thought I would surprise him with a visit in the cholera hall. I hardly ever went in there, and he was only in there as a staff member, but I decided to go anyway. Phil was dead against me going, but I wanted to see how bad it was. I walked up to his space on the floor to find him lying there, stone dead.

It made my blood run cold. Apparently Admire started rushing to the toilet early in the evening, and within six hours he died. It was another significant loss to us all; he was one of the good men in there.

Having been starved of sunshine for so many years, we couldn't get enough of it. We would often suntan to pass the time, and started looking healthy again. I still wasn't strong enough to do any sort of exercise. One day Phil and I were playing UNO on the tarred floor of the crowded exercise yard, and a guy rolled over on the floor close to where I was sitting and died. Nobody around us moved. It was bizarre: death had become so commonplace. Phil and I just turned a little, so we couldn't see him and carried on dealing cards until hospital prisoner-staff collected him. That is how terrible it was in there; we could smell dead people continuously, day and night. We became entirely desensitised.

That incident hit me hard and left me wondering why that guy died and I didn't. I had had the support of friends and family, tirelessly bringing vital nutrition, but, even so, I will still never know why so many others lost their lives, and I had the privilege of living. What I do know is that it taught me to be humble, and grateful for every little thing about my life.

We have all in some way become desensitised to things in our community at one time or another. It is a survival mechanism, but it also reduces compassion and humanity. It is a fine line to tread, but if you have lost the ability to empathise, then you have forgotten what it means to be human. Phil sat there and just said, 'This is not right, Russ. They must do something about these guys dying, it's not correct.'

The weekend that followed, 22 inmates died. Every dead body in that prison had to be carried, wrapped in blankets, by hospital staff to the mortuary. To get there they had to pass through the corner of the exercise yard. We were always summoned into our cells as if we didn't know what was happening, and they would be carried out one at a time.

The following afternoon before lock-up at 3 p.m. a young prisoner was sitting on the tarred floor of the exercise yard, leaning in a slouching position against the library wall. His plate of food had been placed on his lap by one of the feeding staff assigned to help the sick inmates. I was assisting the guys in getting to their respective cells that day and went to help this particular prisoner. After taking him gently by the arm and telling him that it was lock-up time, I noticed he was dead. It was a terrible feeling. To see these young men perishing daily was soul destroying. I called the hospital staff to take his lifeless body to the hospital.

There were quite a few street kids in there with us, and they would scavenge food from the most unhygienic places. I was returning from collecting Phil and my daily food delivery from my sister one day, and as I entered the exercise yard, one of the street kids bumped my arm, sending the lunchbox flying to the floor. Food was splattered all over the filthy tarred floor, that hundreds of cholera-riddled inmates had walked and sat on. Within seconds, about five street kids had shovelled handfuls of every scrap into their mouths. There was not a thing left. I stood there gobsmacked and just shook my head with pity for these poor guys. I learned to hold my lunch tight from that day on. Phil thought it was hilarious until he had to give me half of his food!

From the unused soccer ground, one could see that the refrigeration units in the mortuary had been removed. Apparently, after they stopped working years previously, no effort had been made to fix them because there was no money. As the number of deaths rose, and bodies were not collected within weeks, they just stacked the corpses up in an ever-growing pile. I was told there were huge, hairy, orange, flesh-eating caterpillars swarming around the bodies and gorging themselves on the rotting flesh, which left the bones snow white.

Every few months they conducted paupers' burials, and all the bones were shovelled into polystyrene sacks by inmates and buried in massive graves. These were all reported in the government-controlled newspapers. The thought of shovelling your fellow inmates' bones into a bag did my head in.

One afternoon I walked into the showers after a few hours playing UNO in the sun with Phil. There were six showerheads, and around 40 inmates showering. There was a moment when I looked up, and five metres away, the shock of the dreadful physical condition that the inmates were in hit me hard. It reminded me of photos of the German concentration camps during the Second World War. The guys were just skin and bone, like wrinkled skin pulled over skeletons. Some were standing sideways and had absolutely no backside, just skin hanging where there used to be a butt. It's a vision that will live with me until my dying day.

One small mercy was that the practice of beating prisoners on a whim calmed down a little as the death toll climbed.

For eight months leading up to March 2009, 432 prisoners out of 1,200 at Harare Central, died. That's more than one-third in eight months. I estimate that in the six years I was incarcerated, over 2,200 prisoners died in the prisons I was in. Just how many died in prisons countrywide would have been staggering. After compiling information received from inmates transferred from other prisons, Phil and I estimated that between 2002 and 2009, more than 15,000 prisoners died in the country.

Sadly, people were dying of starvation outside of prison too, so little sympathy was shown to the prisoners. The country was going through an economic meltdown, and there was no food on the grocery store shelves. News of the horrendous death rates in the prison system had become public after several complaints were made, through smuggled letters from inmates – including myself – to legal practitioners. These, coupled with reports by sympathetic guards, had finally reached the newspapers. President Mugabe flatly denied to the international community, that there was cholera, saying it was a bad spree of diarrhoea. Following international pressure as a result of leaked footage of skeletal inmates, the authorities finally agreed to the Red Cross intervening for the first time in Zimbabwe's history.

CHAPTER 62

Red Cross Rescue

The difference it made when the Red Cross took over managing the food was astonishing.

We were overjoyed to see them. They immediately began weighing and measuring every inmate in several places on our bodies. We were then put into categories and put onto courses of 'Plumpy Nut' nutrition bars. The more serious your condition was, the more bars you got at intervals during the day. They were about 10 cm long by 5 cm wide and 1 cm thick, tasting much like a healthy peanut butter bar and toffy-like in texture. The positive effect on the death rate was unbelievable. Within a month, from losing up to 11 inmates in a day, there was only one death in April and then no more after that.

After the Red Cross started feeding us the Plumpy Nut protein bars, a remarkable woman by the name of Theresa Wilson, together with Father Fryer from the Catholic Church, also became involved in supplying oranges and bread at Harare Central. Father Fryer arranged finance from the church for many inmates' education. He was an unbelievable human being. Theresa was incredibly helpful and capable, but she grew frustrated with being unable to control the theft. She was entirely at her wits' end with the thieving antics of the prisoners who appeared to be stealing on behalf of the guards. They made her task tough and exhausting.

Carefully selected prisoner-staff were permitted to assist her in the offloading and carrying of goods to the kitchen. She could not be at the delivery truck and in the kitchen at the same time, and despite her frantic efforts to oversee the process, she would end up almost in tears with frustration. It was too much to see food carried off in different directions by prisoners with guards watching. When she caught someone, even during the confrontation in front of the guards, goods would disappear behind her back. She was an absolute saint, and even though she was struggling for funds to buy food, she would always return., She was subject to the same treatment every time. The truth was, the guards and their families were starving too.

Now that the Red Cross had taken over feeding and normality had returned, we began a soccer league. I was delighted to make the prison squad; it gave me the privilege of walking, under strict escort, to play against the officers' side on a field in their compound. During our joyful march there, singing all the way with fellow players, I asked a guard if I could touch my first tree in six-and-a-half years. Granted permission, I joyously broke formation. I instantly caught the memorable smell of the jacaranda tree I was touching and the freshness of the vegetation. The feeling of the bark reminded me of rubbing my grandfather's rough forearms as a little boy. I stood there watching the termites moving on the bark. It was so beautiful and uplifting to touch that tree and feel green grass again.

Being on a soccer field back in the prison grounds revitalised me, physically and mentally, but after almost a year the broken tar field was taking its toll on us players. I sent a request through my sister to ask Mike Fowler, a water polo friend from school days, to visit me. It was a thrill seeing him again, and by then the OIC and I were friends again, so we all met in his office. Mike offered to buy the prison team playing kit, to pay for grass purchased from the Trade Fair grounds, and to organise the transport to bring it to the prison for our soccer field. We were elated beyond belief.

It was a mammoth task to first uplift, and then carry by hand, tons of thick tar to a section against the soccer grounds. Every prisoner participated, and after two months of blisters, sweat, and exhaustion, the field was complete. We eventually had several ex-national soccer players visit the tournaments they generously sponsored for us. By then I was not only playing several games a week, but also training hard in my daily gym routine with Phil, and we started getting into great shape. I formed my own club, and called it 'Plumpy Nut' in honour of the Red Cross.

Mike kindly donated kit for my team, too, and our caring community from Bulawayo donated 26 pairs of soccer boots. When they arrived, a few of us systematically counted out aloud every pair and wrote down the numbers of each size. The following morning, I was called by the rehab office and told that I could take my boots to hand out to my players. Lo and behold, there were only 25 pairs. I was furious and argued for ages with the guards and staff, but the one pair had vanished. It became apparent after many months that the deputy OIC had instructed that a pair in his size, be put aside. I was shocked, but not surprised.

I had many opportunities to speak with guards about their brutality to inmates. Many were very pleasant to be around and laughed and joked with us, then turned into sadistic animals when beatings were happening. They were always immediately defensive up front. But after I explained how I was beaten as a child by my father and the effect it had on me and went on to what damage they were doing to some of these kids, they started reasoning. I think mainly due to the frustrations of their personal predicaments and the country's economic crisis, they all began changing their attitudes towards the violence. In Chikurubi, Elisha and I actually stopped one officer from beating a prisoner in front of the entire hall one day. He was entirely out of control, hitting the inmate all over his body with his baton and kicking him as he rolled around on the ground trying to avoid further blows. I addressed him straight on about his behaviour. When that same officer was transferred to Harare Central, I never saw him beat a single prisoner, and his demeanour changed completely. I switched the mindset of many guards in there, reminding them that all these people have families and feelings just like them. It is my dream one day, to try to make a difference to the prison system in Zimbabwe. The current system is fuelling our violent crime and draining our economy.

CHAPTER 63

Death Row

Playing soccer one day I was called to a visit with my old friend Wayne Williams and his colossal son Mike. They brought me some protein powder to supplement my diet. I had never seen this stuff before, but I noticed that when I broke the silver foil seal carefully, tasted the powder with my fingertip, and replaced the seal and lid, the next time I opened the lid, the silver foil had re-sealed itself. This got my attention as a potential place to hide contraband.

At 5 a.m. one morning, 18 months after being sent to solitary and having had no issues up until then, one of the guards who was on my side, knocked on my cell door, and quietly called through the spy hole, 'Rust, Rust, they are coming for your phone!' There was no way of getting it out of there, but I had the container of protein powder. I opened it, peeled the silver seal back, removed half the powder, wrapped the phone in a plastic packet, threw it into the container, replaced the powder then the silver seal and the lid.

Sure enough, at 6 a.m. they arrived in force. As per normal routine, they made us strip naked, then ordered us to do star-jumps in case we were hiding something somewhere. Then all the prisoners in our hall, a few hundred of us, walked out stark naked into the exercise yard in full view of all the guards, both male, and female, while they searched the cells. Eventually, we were ordered back to find everything upside down. Lunchboxes and containers were emptied out on the floor, sugar all over the place, even honey spilled on the blankets, but my protein powder was still in good shape. I was not amused but knew I could not complain in fear of them searching further.

While I was sitting glumly on my pile of blankets wondering where to start cleaning up, the new head of security came into my cell. He looked very frustrated.

'Where's your phone?' he said. 'I have no phone,' I answered.

'I know you've got a phone,' he said, then abruptly turned and walked away.

Five minutes later a prisoner came to tell me that I was wanted in the security office. Four guards were standing and one was seated behind a large desk. On my side of the desk was an empty chair. The guard sitting down said, 'Take a seat.' I had not sat in a chair for seven-and-a-half years.

I took a seat, and the questioning started.

'Do you have a girlfriend called Karen?' This took me a little by surprise.

'No, I had a girlfriend called Karen before prison,' I replied. 'Okay, when did you last speak to her?'

'Long ago. Before I went to prison,' I said.

'Are you sure?'

To which I answered, 'Yes.'

With that, they pulled out a letter addressed to me from Karen. My heart missed a beat when they handed it to me, and I read: 'It was so nice talking to you on the phone the other night. You sounded so positive.' I went cold and was speechless. My first thought was to just stuff the letter into my mouth and swallow it. Then I thought the OIC and I were on good terms and that would upset him, so I decided to play it calm.

Years in prison had taught me that, when cornered, say as little as possible. I remained silent through a barrage of questions, while trying to figure out how on earth I was going to get out of this one. After about five minutes they asked me if I wanted time to think about this, which I said I did. With that, the senior officer told them to take me away and lock me in the empty teaching hall.

My mind was in a whirl while I dug deep for a story that would work. Then, like divine intervention, the story came to me that Karen was having lunch in Bulawayo one day and befriended a woman. After chatting for a while, they realised that they both had boyfriends in the same prison, so the woman offered to call her boyfriend, who was a guard in there, and he could call me, and Karen and I could chat. I had a story. After 20 minutes they returned and escorted me back, and I gave them my account.

'So, who is the officer?' they asked.

'I can't remember,' I said. Clearly stuck for words but knowing they could not prove me wrong.

'You can't remember! You know all the guards well so how come you can't remember one that trusted you with his phone?' the senior officer asked angrily.

The room heated up, they were getting upset. 'What rank was he? How many bars did he have?' pointing to his sleeve.

'He had no bars,' I said.

'How long ago was this?'

'About three months ago.'

'Where did this take place?'

'In the hospital.'

Frustration crept in, and the senior officer spoke: 'This is a national security issue, and the CIO (Central Intelligence Organisation) will be sent to see your friend Karen in Bulawayo to find out more. We want to know who this officer is, and we will stop at nothing to find out!'

The CIO people arrived and were in an aggressive mood. They pushed me to the floor and told me to sit there, then the threats and the abuse started.

I told them I wanted my lawyer and wanted this matter settled in court. This only made them angrier, but it made them think. I was left alone for about an hour then summoned upstairs to the OIC. There were about 15 high-ranking prison officials standing in a semicircle and the OIC seated behind his large desk. Now I knew beyond any doubt that I was in grave trouble.

I knew my story was a tough one for them to disprove, but if they visited Karen, I knew I would battle to get out of this one.

'If you don't tell me who the guard is, your life in this prison is going to change,' he said looking me straight in the face.

Then the questions came from all around, getting more forceful and louder by the minute. I answered what I could until one pleasant officer said, 'Do you want to talk to the OIC on your own?'

'Yes, please,' I answered immediately.

When they left, I pleaded with him, 'Officer, we've been through hell together. We've watched hundreds of guys die. I've donated endless stuff to the prison service, soccer balls, volleyballs, a volleyball net, soccer uniforms and boots for the squad! Can't we just let this one go?'

'Rust, I don't care about you, but I want the guard's name now.' He was angry.

'I don't know his name, officer.'

With that, his whole attitude changed. He called out the dreaded command, 'Officer, put him on death row – in the dark cell.'

I was escorted out and over to the condemned section. The cell was the same size as my one in solitary, (3 m X 1 m), but it was pitch dark. A staircase outside covered the only air vent, and the electric light did not work. I was made to strip naked, given a plastic five-litre container cut off at the top as a toilet (the same as in solitary confinement), three filthy lice-ridden blankets and a bottle of water. They locked me in there for 23 hours and 45 minutes a day. I was allowed out for five minutes in the morning to clean my teeth, five minutes at 10 a.m. to have a shower and five minutes at 3 p.m. to prepare for lock-up. It was freezing, lonely and dark, I couldn't even see my hand. I was being eaten alive by lice that I could not see and therefore couldn't kill. I felt like I'd been buried alive.

I was not sure how much of it I would be able to take. Every now and then there would be a knock and a voice: 'Are you ready with the name yet?' they would ask, and I would say, 'No.' Mentally I had reached rock bottom. I had no idea where to find the strength to continue. I walked holding the walls and did press-ups and sit-ups regularly.

What troubled me deeply was the fact that members of the CIO were going to see Karen, to find out more about the lunch that had never happened. I had to get a message to her. The staff for the condemned section was an old man called Simon. I needed to get a message to him to tell Phil, who would then be able to pass the message to my sister Lyn. Simon was a very amiable guy, white-haired from age, who I knew well from Chikurubi. We had been together there for four years.

The condemned cells faced each other, and the death row prisoners were always watching my cell through their spy holes. If they noticed something untoward, they would snitch, and that would get them a reward of extra food or better blankets.

Simon came to my door, and I quietly told him through my spy hole, that I needed a pen and paper urgently. He said okay and was gone. At 9 a.m. he was back and said, 'Russ, second toilet, on top of the wall.' At 10 a.m. they came to take me for a shower and left. The toilets were opposite the showers. I entered the second one and on the cement wall, was a 20 Madison cigarette box opened flat, and a pen refill. I wrote instructions as fast as I could and left it where I had found it. I then jumped under the freezing shower. I was tense waiting for Simon to report after I had been locked up again, but around 11 a.m. he passed by my cell and just said, 'All good.'

The relief was immense. Now it remained for Phil to get the note to my sister to call Karen and explain what had happened and what she must say. That day Lyn came with food, and Phil handed her the empty ones with the note hidden between them. While Phil was trying to explain in more detail what had happened the OIC arrived and shouted at the guards. 'No more food for these white men,' he said, 'give all the food back!' Phil had to hand all the food back to Lyn, but the message had been passed. Thank God.

Prison Intelligence went to Karen, and she was prepared for the interview. I could not believe that there was not enough money to buy food for the prisoners, but there was enough to buy fuel to drive 860 km to Bulawayo and back about a pathetic phone call!

Then they started taking me out for identification parades. At the first one, over 60 guards lined up, and I was asked to point out the culprit. On the other, there were about 40 guards. By day six I was desperate. My vision was going in the constant dark, and the lice were driving me insane. Utterly desperate, I got on my knees and prayed to God to help me. I knew I could not last much longer. Never will I forget the feeling of calmness that then overcame me. It was like warm water washing gently over my body, and I felt like an invisible hand was reaching out to me. It was exactly the same feeling I had when I was lost during the war.

I sat down on the cement floor leaning against the wall and within 30 minutes, I faintly heard my old mate Phil shouting from the soccer ground against the condemned section.

'Hey Russ, don't worry my mate. Everything is okay. Don't worry!' 'Hey, Phil!' I jumped to my feet and shouted back.

'Don't worry my mate, everything is okay!' he replied.

I lay down looking up at the darkness, and within 10 minutes, they unlocked my door. 'Ka-Ka-Ka,' that unforgettable clunking sound goes right through you. They threw me my clothes and said, 'The OIC wants to see you.'

Covering my eyes from the glare, I crossed the exercise yard with my escorts, climbed the stairs and stood at the OIC's door.

'Hello, Rust,' he said.

'Hello, officer,' I replied.

'Have you remembered the guard's name yet?'

'No, officer.'

'Okay, I'll tell you what I'm going to do. I'm going to leave it in God's hands, you can go back to your cell.'

As it turned out, at the exact moment that I was on my knees praying, my sister was paying him US$200 to get me off death row and back to my cell.

That was a turning point in my life. I always believed in God, but it was only the second time I had reached out. I always figured other people needed help more than I did; I felt I could look after myself. I felt very blessed and remained extra humble for many days after that.

CHAPTER 64

Positive Power

Towards the end of 2010, news leaked out that Joyce Meyer, an American Christian, was visiting the prison. I had read one of her books and was extremely impressed, but nobody else knew who she was. Her husband addressed us first, all seated on the tarred exercise yard floor. He impressed me too, but when Joyce walked up, I was blown away. At the end of her delivery, the most potent message was the value and power of hope. Unfortunately, I was not able to talk to her, but we made eye contact and shared a smile, and that was enough. Those small moments of hope helped me through the darkest times.

'Hope' became the most valuable word in my vocabulary in prison. I believed then and still do, that it is better to have hope and have that magic day not arrive than to have had no hope at all. When you are removed from the rat race we all get caught up in, you see life from a very different perspective. I had all the time in the world to look at my past under a microscope and assess what I had done right and what I had done wrong. I realised how different my perspective was. Mistakes I had made, money I had wasted, opportunities I had lost, and people I had neglected ... I now have a very different vision of where I want to go and what I want out of life. Life, I learned, is about your journey and the people in it, not your assets and wealth alone.

Without hope, you stood the risk of dying. It happened regularly. After the cholera outbreak had ended, a guy by the name of Wally was incarcerated in Harare Central. His crime was not paying alimony, which I felt was the lowest form of revenge an ex-wife could ever stoop to. He was serving, if I recall correctly, about nine months. Although the conditions had improved dramatically, it was still hell on earth – sleeping on the floor, the lice, washing clothes in toilets, and the deep humiliation that followed being incarcerated under those conditions.

I could see that Wally was a broken man before entering prison. He had been put through hell by his 'ex' and her lawyers, and he was not a strong character. I helped him as much as I could by introducing him to the senior prisoners and guards and offering him food daily. Nothing seemed to cheer him up though. I warned him of the dangers of stress often and tried to bring more humour into his days. No matter what I tried, he got progressively worse.

I kept up with how Wally was doing after I left Harare Central. It was a huge shock to learn that Wally eventually died. I am of the firm opinion that his death was from the effects of being incarcerated and his negative mindset. It confirmed my belief that your thoughts control your future physically, in every way. What you think is what you will become. Wally let his situation get to him, despite my efforts to cheer him up. Instead of standing tall and refusing to lower himself, he allowed himself to be affected by his predicament.

It was a struggle to stay positive in the face of challenges both within the prison, and in my life 'outside'. By this time my financial affairs had deteriorated markedly. Charlie

(Sue's brother-in-law), who was managing my affairs, visited to inform me that my businesses were effectively insolvent. Our debt now outweighed the money owed to us. I took into account that they had taken over running the businesses in 2004 when the Zimbabwe dollar crash began, followed by the world financial crash of 2008. It was tough for everyone during that cut-throat period, and the tax authorities ruthlessly targeted safari operators and other foreign currency earning businesses. The nightmares that some people endured were horrific, and Charlie and Lara were no exception.

The problem was that, in the safari industry, you are the business. Clients came to photograph, hunt and fish with me, and because I was absent our ability to generate revenue was severely curtailed. On top of all the other problems, the country ran out of fuel, so hard currency had to be sourced and imported to stay operational. Unfortunately, 'borrowing from Peter to pay Paul' had gotten out of control and in the end, after all their desperate efforts, my companies went broke; all vehicles, boats, safari-lodge equipment and a huge warehouse full of other equipment were sold with a substantial debt remaining for me to take care of.

One positive for Phil was that he finally got his wish to spend his last years of prison life on a farm. When he was classified as a B-class prisoner, he applied to be transferred to Pendenese Prison in Banket. Initially, they sent him to Mazoe Prison instead. Mazoe was hell, and he was poorly treated by the guards. As a sixty-three-year-old As a sixty-three-year-old, he was made to work for ten hours a day in the blazing sun with a hoe in the fields. He was a tough man, but after five days his back could not take any more, and he applied to be transferred to Pendenese Prison.

They sent him to Chinoi for two weeks, and then finally to Pendenese. It was a Tobacco Research Board prison, and it was the next best thing to an open prison. He was delighted and immediately started studying for a diploma in how to grow tobacco seedlings on a floating-tray system. He obtained his diploma and moved to Karoi Prison twenty months later where he was in command of the tobacco section. The crop that he produced, reaped and cured, according to the OIC there, was the best they had ever produced.

After I was released from solitary, I was re-classified as a B-class prisoner. Leaving the confines of that lonely solitary cell brought me a sense of liberation. I had spent two years there, and apart from the connections by phone, the only other company were the cockroaches. It was a constant battle to keep them out of my lunchboxes containing the food Lyn had brought me. I had never seen such huge ones in my life. They got up to 2 inches long and could fly. During the day we would try and kill as many as we could on the cement ceiling above the toilets. They'd congregate in their hundreds, and as soon as you struck once, they would all fly into the closest crack. Being aware that they were feeding off what they could find in the toilets, was a sobering thought. I would lie in my cell as still as possible with my lunchbox within striking range and wait until they were close enough, then lash out with a carefully prepared piece of rolled-up old blanket. Being in isolation for so long, it was these trivial activities that kept you sane. I felt closer to freedom and the real world.

My new cell, 3 m X 6 m, was in a different section. We were 12 prisoners in there, which gave us plenty of room. I had become accustomed to my space being clean and tidy, with a certain amount of control over the lice. That changed dramatically. The lice were uncontrollable again, and the untidiness drove me crazy. Over the years you accumulate a certain number of belongings – hand-made shoes and hats, non-perishable groceries, water containers, books and magazines and so on. We stored these in bags made from polystyrene sacks. This was all exposed to the thieves while you were working. If you covered your belongings with a blanket, you had a chance, but anything left visible would invariably get stolen. The feeling of living with untrustworthy people, purporting to be your friends, was very unsettling.

Most B-class prisoners were sent to work on the prison farms around the country. The thought of being a farm labourer did not excite me, and I really wanted to work in the kitchens – that way I could still get food from Lyn daily. The officer in charge of the kitchen was a wonderful old man and wanted me to work there because I was healthy and prepared to work hard. I put in a request to be transferred, and it was approved. I have never worked so hard in my life! I was up at 2 a.m. to start cooking the *sadza*. We cooked it in huge stainless-steel electric pots, one metre in diameter, for 1,200 inmates. We had to prepare six pots a day, and most guys only managed one, sometimes two. Three of us prisoners were assigned to cook *sadza*, and I never cooked less than three because I wanted to stay fit. During a power failure, we would have to cook in cast-iron pots over wood fires.

We had to stir the porridge with a two-metre-long, 15-cm-thick pole, which made it physically demanding and the sweat just poured off our bodies. After breakfast, we would head off to collect firewood in Mbare township, or we had to chop firewood for hours. The wood had to be used the following morning for the wood stoves to cook the relish for the inmates.

Rural Zimbabweans were chopping down trees on the farms abandoned by the farmers who had been evicted. They were bringing it to town to sell for firewood. We would arrive with armed guards and merely steal the wood they had stolen from the farms. The sellers used to plead with us to speak to the guards and not take too much of what they had stolen, but we would load up 10 tons at a time and head off back to the prison. It was a very tough regimen that lasted for the six months I was in the kitchens, but on the plus side, I was in terrific physical condition.

In 2010, the minister of health came to visit the prison. Before he arrived, the OIC went to the exercise yard and asked me to prepare a speech for the minister. I asked him if I could tell everything and he said, 'Yes, tell them everything.'

When the minister arrived, I told him about the dreadful unsanitary conditions, washing our clothes in the toilets, no food, leaking sewage pipes and the number of needless deaths caused by wanton neglect and indifference to the plight of the inmates.

My speech went down very well with plenty of cheering from the inmates. After I had finished, he thanked me kindly and asked me for my notes that I had used to talk from. I gladly handed them to him. About 10 days after this a group of 10 senators came to the prison. The OIC asked me to deliver the same speech, but the senators did not seem impressed or interested in what I had to say and kept telling me to hurry up as they were running late. They did, however, ask me for my piece of paper I had used to talk from, and I think my speech made an impact. It was the first time I considered myself a good speechwriter, a skill that would come in handy later on.

A group of guards from an open prison called Connemara visited Harare Central to interview inmates who qualified to go there. I had been trying to get there for months and for the first time was accepted for an interview. All went well, and they said they would advise us when the transfer would take place and who qualified. The following morning, two of us were called and informed that we were leaving within an hour. The excitement was unbelievable. The other prisoner was Hendry, who I had been with in Chikurubi, and was in the cell with Phil and me before we were sent to solitary confinement. My sister Lyn had been instrumental in co-ordinating the transfer details and was waiting outside the gate for us. The vehicle to transport us was parked outside, and while being escorted out by the rehabilitation officer to board, I saw my sister. I asked if I could give her a hug and they granted permission. We hugged and laughed. I was overjoyed at the new freedom.

It was my first hug since I had embraced Sandy in my first year.

CHAPTER 65

Farm Boy Again

C onnemara Open Prison is a farm prison near the town
of KweKwe, in the Zimbabwe Midlands, with a very
relaxed regimen. I was transferred in May 2011, and
was lucky to be there. I will forever be indebted to Mike
Fowler, Tony Sapo and many other loyal friends for their
combined efforts to convince the authorities that I would
be a tremendous asset to the farm. My duties would consist
of repairing and driving tractors, ploughing, planting crops,
assisting with beef and dairy cattle and chickens, as well as
repairing boreholes and farm machinery. It was a massive
and welcome change.

There were roughly 100 inmates, most of them over 60
years old, and the place was run on trust. There were no
high fences, razor wire or bars. The complex consisted of
eight dormitories, four of which had been subdivided inside
to form nine cubicles to house one inmate in each. After
three months' probation in one of the regular dormitories,
we could apply for a transfer to a cubicle room, if one was
available.

This was the only prison in the country with beds; however, mattresses were scarce and in bad condition. We were
permitted to bring our own mattresses and bedding from
home, and that was a godsend for me. After arranging for

bedding to be delivered, I had my first comfortable sleep in eight years.

Mirrors were also permitted, and I got to see my face and have a decent shave for the first time in eight years. It seemed like I had died and gone to heaven. Another privilege of the open-prison system was that, after a three-month probationary period, we were permitted five days at home, totally free, and then again, every 30 days after that. So, it was 30 days inside and five days at home, until my release. We were permitted visits at any time during my two years there, and over weekends visitors could stay from noon on Saturday until 5 p.m. and all day on Sunday.

I spent my first night at Connemara sitting around an open fire on logs and bleached cattle skulls, chatting with old Ndebele inmates. It took me straight back to what I'd loved so dearly as a child. By this time, I was completely fluent in both Ndebele and Shona. I got lost in their stories, the beauty of the sunset, the dancing flames, the tranquil call of a nightjar, the bright stars and the moon, which I hadn't seen for eight long, lonely years. I was reminded then, that while I enjoyed life's luxuries, the bush remained in my blood. The sense of being back with nature had my spirits soaring to a level I had not experienced in the eight years since I shuffled through the gates of Khami Prison.

Under the bright stars in the still darkness, I paced along on soft damp soil. My feet were bare, and I had just climbed out of a cold shower, wearing my own tracksuit bottoms, on my way to empty my garbage can. Looking up, I thought about how perfect and surreal it all felt. Imagine eight years with no stars, the moon, a sunset or sunrise. I realised how meaningful the little things in life are, like a hot bath, a soft bed, a sip of good wine, or a spontaneous cuddle from a loved one, because those are the things I missed most when

I had them all taken away. Never again would I take these gifts of God for granted.

In the mornings, I would relax around the same mopane log fire, with three or four of the old guys in their well-worn clothes, warming our hands. We would stir our mielie-meal porridge and check our boiling eggs in the clear, chilly calmness of the mornings. I seldom tired of conversing with these wise, uncomplicated souls. Three of them were from the West Nicholson area where I was born and raised, so we shared endless childhood adventures.

I loved the gentle humour that flowed in the evenings around that campfire. My favourite, Ndebele, was an avid draughts player, who always won. I loved to watch and listen to him. He was well over 60 years old, but quick on the board. I can still see the juices from the watermelon running down his unshaven chin, dropping into the sand as he chatted away, covering subjects few people would ever think to dwell on. He shared hunting stories about how cunning bushpigs are. Being a proud woodcutter, he would go into great detail about the art of chopping trees quickly, cleanly and effectively. He always threw in something to laugh at. I loved the simplicity of it all and was reminded that we often complicate our lives needlessly. The traditional African way is simple and stress-free. Have little, but want little. These days we tend to have a lot and spend our lives wanting more.

I had only been at Connemara a few days when Captain arrived, still wearing that big bright smile of a young, energetic kid. At 24 years of age, he had been conned by two older friends into an escapade deep in a remote range of his impoverished homeland. They stole a cow, were apprehended and he received the mandatory nine-year sentence, serving six. When he arrived at Connemara, he had done five years of his time. I knew him from Chikurubi and Harare Central and had liked him immediately; having moved high up the pecking order by then, I took him under my wing, knowing what would happen if I didn't. I spent much time over the years teaching Captain, in his language as he could not speak English, about leading a respectable life. While I feel he learned a lot from me, I too learned from him. He was loyal, helpful and fun to be around, so it was fantastic to see him again after 21 months apart.

On the first Sunday, my sister Bev, her husband Mark and their children Sharna and Maison visited me. It was the first time in eight years that I had seen their children and couldn't believe how much of their lives I'd missed out on. Bev brought a delicious lunch, and we spoke for ages about how their lives had changed. Most families were severely affected by the land-grab and economic crash, and Bev and Mark were no exception. Mark is a veterinarian, and he and Maison had been involved in translocating a family of elephant. It was an incredible achievement for Mark, a wonderful experience for Maison, and a fascinating story for me.

The following weekend, Spike, Chris, Brebs, and all their wives and children arrived for a *braai* (barbecue) at the prison. It was an unbelievable feeling: as if time had stood still, except that there were children everywhere. We laughed and joked the whole five hours together and caught up on all the whisky that had flowed under the bridge for eight long years. The *braai* was just like old times, eaten by hand around the plough disc with kids and all piling in.

Spike had not lost his dry sense of humour, and I could feel the deep bond that we shared was still there. He had married Corneli, an attractive woman from an Afrikaans background, who was very much a home-maker. They had a daughter and a son, both of them good-natured, bright and inquisitive.

Chris had married bubbly and vivacious Ash, and they'd produced two adorable bush-happy blond sons. I was instrumental in their getting together from the beginning, and Ash wrote me letters monthly without fail for all those years.

Daisy and Brebs married the year I went to prison and have a lovely son. Brebs and Chris together were always non-stop entertainment, and saying goodbye that day was tough. I felt the loss of time together profoundly that day.

One hard, hot day after I'd repaired a tractor, officer Majaura, the prison farm manager, told me to hop into the rusted back of his battered old pick-up truck. I had only been in the open prison for about a month by this point. Being my first outing since the beginning, there was no hesitation. I vividly recall the pleasure of clattering down the eroded sandy farm road, ducking overhanging branches and breathing in the fresh evening bush smell I knew so well.

Memories of fun-filled days in the bush flooded my mind, and I felt so happy and free; I wanted to shout out to the heavens. I had little idea where we were or where we were going. Suddenly glimpses of glistening water flashed through the trees, and my heart rate doubled with excitement.

We came to a halt beside a shining mass of beautiful water. I stood and gaped in wonderment. It had been an awfully long time since I had seen a spectacle so pristine and gorgeous. Dried trees, bulrushes, and granite boulders broke the surface, and the water was alive with birds: lily-trotters, coots, cormorants, dabchicks, ducks, geese and herons all on the move in their busy search for food. Crowning it all were the magical calls of the African fish eagle. I was in my element, bubbling with the joys only nature can bring. Unable to contain my excitement while walking on the dam wall, I asked Majaura if I could take my first swim in eight years.

'No, no!' he frowned, 'If you drown, they will hang me; it's very deep, this water.'

'I promise I will stay on the surface,' I pleaded with him. 'I'm a strong swimmer.'

As soon as he gave his uncertain 'Okay', I tore off my clothes, ran down to the water's edge and launched myself at the gently lapping waves. It was almost surreal, gliding across the surface, feeling freer than I had since walking down the stairs of the Bulawayo High Court. It was a sublime moment I will treasure forever.

The dam was on the KweKwe River, and I would return there frequently to fish in the months ahead, with the OIC and others. I only caught one decent bass, but I never tired of the thrill of losing myself in the little wilderness that it was.

On a chilly evening, Farai approached me dressed in a heavy, dark-green jacket, and wearing his naughty smile as he told me of the mischief he was planning. Farai was from an area close to the prison. He knew where some beehives were and needed help. I had a flashlight, which was essential, so he asked if I would accompany him and bring it. I was delighted and sprang into action immediately. It would be the first of many adventures we'd have together on the farm.

We sneaked off through the rough country in the dark; about an hour later we came across an old mineshaft. Down we went and there they were: a thick mass of busy bees, humming gently in the quiet night. Looking closer, I saw nine large honeycombs in parallel lines hanging from the rock ceiling. An experienced honey-hunter, Farai wasted no time. Handing me the flashlight, he unpacked the pile of borrowed lunchboxes he had brought in an old cream polystyrene sack and went in with skilful hands. The bees fell off in lumps getting angrier by the second, but he worked quickly and fearlessly, scraping them off the combs while quickly filling the lunchboxes. The bees hammered us, but they were large combs, and we were not going anywhere until we had filled our boxes. After taking three combs, we sprinted out to distance ourselves from the angry bees. We laughed all the way back, happy with our booty. Although we were seriously stung, it was an exciting little adventure and an outing I will always remember.

Having been a farm boy, driving a tractor was second nature to me. The prison had an old weather-beaten Massey-Ferguson 4X4. She was painted red but years in the sun had taken her shine away. She powered on, though, and I spent many happy hours at the wheel of the old girl. She was used for collecting firewood, ploughing, and with a trailer attached, she was the mainstay of the prison transport.

Most days I was tasked with taking the sturdy old tractor out to get firewood. I enjoyed the outings and was always happy to get busy chopping, stacking and loading the wood. Mornings after the rains were always my best with the distinctive freshness in the air. With some pride, I wore a dirty blue baseball cap, an oil-stained, grey, long-sleeved shirt and faded jeans. We had to wear either grey prison trousers or a grey prison shirt, then whatever civilian clothes we wished. It was such a welcome change compared to the short-sleeved shirts and drawstring white shorts I had worn for the last eight years.

I used to stop at will and stand high on the footrest looking for signs of wildlife. Often spotting Swainson's francolin scurrying off into the undergrowth to hide as my mind raced back to good old days on the cattle ranches.

One day a year was the prison community service day, when we did our good deed cleaning up the streets and public places of KweKwe. It was a bit humiliating, but I climbed in with the rest.

Passing through the town on our return, I searched for faces I might recognise, and a head peered out of the driver's window of a small white pick-up truck. Our eyes locked, and I recognised the beaming smile right away – it was Mike Goosen, who'd been part of the childhood circle that included Bush, Di, and Wayne Stanton. We were only five metres apart, but moving in opposite directions. We shouted greetings as quickly as possible, and his last words were, 'I'll come and visit you!'

The return trip was memorable. The men were singing beautifully as I gazed up at a crimson sky, behind broken puffs of cloud, while smelling the wild scents that Africa is blessed with. The ability of the prisoners to harmonise so beautifully, accompanied by crude but lovingly fashioned instruments, was incredible. Usually, there would be a high-pitched lead, a deep, low chorus, and rhythmic hand clapping.

Back at the prison, it was always incredibly silent at night. In the quietness, seven of us gathered and chatted, seated on cracked hand-carved stools, well-worn logs and bleached ox skulls. And there before us our 'bush TV'; we all stared contentedly at the blue and orange flames flickering in the dark. It was an extraordinary end to a peaceful and happy day.

True to his word, Mike visited regularly. The first time was a memorable *braai* with some down-to-earth folk from KweKwe town. These are the kind of people who epitomise

Zimbabweans: they had given up their Sunday, spent a small fortune on outstanding meat, food, and drinks, taken hours to prepare delicious snacks and travelled 32 km out with their children in tow to make me feel at home. They returned many times after that, always calling ahead on my illegal phone to make sure I didn't need anything. On their departure that day, I remember feeling wholly chilled and happy knowing that I had such good people close by.

CHAPTER 66

Poisoned

Three months in and I was as close to paradise in prison as I could get. Friends and family were supplying me generously, I was eating like a king and my three, friendly inmates kept us all content and healthy. I supplied them with food and other luxuries, and in return, they helped me. Roger did our laundry, Farai was our cook, and Kafupi swept and cleaned the cells.

On a cold and clear winter's night, 26 June 2011, we had tasty rump steak grilled on the fire and *sadza*. I was feeling relaxed and happy lying on my bed reading a magazine when, suddenly, everything went wrong. My fingers went numb, my throat began closing, and saliva poured into my mouth. I headed outside knowing that I needed to vomit, hoping the fresh air would help, but it worsened fast. As I turned to make my way to the bathroom, I saw an inmate walking past the TV room, where all the others were watching soccer. Somehow, I instinctively knew I had been poisoned and shouted to him, 'Call the OIC quick, I've been poisoned,' then took a few steps into the corridor of our dormitory and collapsed.

The shock hit me then; I was alone and terrified I was going to die. After all the hardships I'd been through, with freedom not far off, I lay there feeling life was slipping away and thought: 'They've got me this time.' The worst part was I felt this was now beyond my control. Before I had fought or muscled my way out of trouble but now, I felt utterly powerless. I could feel myself getting worse by the second and summoned all my strength to stagger down the passage to the toilet where I collapsed and began violent, vomiting convulsions. On my knees, I shook uncontrollably, my skin felt like it was on fire and bursts of pain exploded through my stomach while sweat poured off me. Vomit spewed out until it became only dribbles of saliva and orange bitter-tasting fluid, then it started to pour out the other end too. A crowd soon gathered. Some held me on the toilet while I continued to heave into the bucket.

Despite it being a freezing cold winter's evening, I continued to sweat profusely. This continued for almost an hour, and my head felt like it was going to explode. I desperately wanted to hold on to life, but at the time it was just a matter of fighting something inside me, trying with all my strength to break down the attack. In my mind, I kept telling my body, time and again, that we had won all the other battles and we were not going to lose this one.

They carried me, exhausted and listless, to my room where I continued to shiver and sweat. I curled up under the covers but was still freezing with my head thumping and skin burning, but the stabs of abdominal pain had subsided. The OIC and medical orderly arrived 90 minutes later. I was carried to the clinic where they tried to put a saline drip in, but my veins had collapsed, so I swallowed rehydration and headache tablets as the shivering and shaking continued. Some time after midnight I was carried back to bed.

I had a terrible night, so when the OIC and the doctor woke me at 8 a.m., I asked them to leave. When Farai woke me at 2 p.m. and advised me of the time, I knew something was very wrong. I ran my fingers over my face, which felt extremely swollen. Stumbling out of bed I reached a mirror and looked at myself in horror. My eyes were so puffed up they were almost shut, my cheeks had ballooned, my lips were swollen, and even my ears were huge and thick. I looked like a physical freak.

I sent for the OIC who took one look and called my mate Grant Locke in Gweru and told him to come immediately to take me to hospital. They admitted me to Gweru General in a private ward, put me on a drip and started courses of antibiotics and cortisone. Two days later I managed my first meal; the third day I held down more food and felt better, so I took a slow stroll in the garden thinking the worst was behind me. Within 30 minutes I went down again, but this time worse than the first. It lasted two hours, and the terrible pain that came with the violent convulsions left me exhausted and bereft of hope; I felt I was losing this battle – now it was simply time to let go. Within hours, my body was completely covered in millions of tiny blood blisters, everywhere.

The next day, a dear friend of mine, Suzette Saunders, transferred me to an intensive care unit at the AMI Hospital in Harare, where a specialist took over. They put me on a cortisone drip in one arm and another drip in the other with a ventilator over my face. Fourteen vials of blood, stool and urine samples were taken and sent off to Lancet Laboratories. A day later, the prison doctor general arrived. His first question was about who was going to pay the hospital bill. After I assured him that I would be taking care of it, he asked what had happened. I gave him a detailed rundown of events, and then he left. The following day, the chaplin general arrived with two other prison pastors to pray for me. Their first words were begging for the poison to be removed from my body. Interestingly, at this stage I had said nothing about poison to anyone from HQ, I had only discussed my symptoms. Clearly, they knew something more than I did.

Two weeks later, still on drugs and a drip, I was informed all samples had to be retaken as the tests were 'inconclusive'. The next round of tests all showed little; only my S-immunoglobulin E count was ridiculously out of control. The normal range is 0–100, mine was 5,000. The specialist was shocked and said he shuddered to think what it must have been at the time I ingested the poison. The count measures the level of antibodies produced due to allergies or a substance my body was sensitive to. I spent seven weeks in that hospital trying to determine what it was. They tested for botulism, typhoid, anthrax, HIV and an array of other possible causes but no answers were forthcoming.

I took four months to recuperate, but my kidneys have never recovered, and my physical performance has never reached the same levels since.

From the day I returned to the prison, I supervised the cooking of my food and carefully watched everything I ate and drank. I have also had to take preventative asthma treatment daily ever since. Whenever I trained too hard or had a good party, within two days I'd get a sore throat followed by flu and invariably a chest infection. The worst was during my five-day trips home with plenty of partying and then training hard on my return to prison. It would be five days of partying and 30 days recovering, without thinking about what I was doing to my body.

I began trying to get to the bottom of what had happened and who might have been responsible for poisoning me. I was told by the authorities that it was probably not a good idea to continue this line of inquiry, because it might be deemed necessary to return me to a closed prison where they could better monitor the food that I was fed. My only suspicion of the poisoning is that I exposed too much of what I knew to the minister of health and senators during my last month at Harare Central.

CHAPTER 67

Five Free Days

After my three-month probation was up, I was entitled to my first five-day trip home. The excitement was unimaginable. My precious sister Lyn came to collect me. I struggle to describe the feeling of driving towards my home, passing all the familiar sights I had not seen for eight years. The saddest part was the destruction of the land caused by the violent, lawless land invasions. Acres of beautiful trees had been hacked down for sale. But the trees along the 600-metre driveway to my home were still there, and all of them had been tied with yellow ribbons. We arrived at my house to a very emotional gathering of my closest friends, while the song, 'Tie a Yellow Ribbon Around the Old Oak Tree', blared in the background.

As I opened the car door, Sandy came boiling out of the front door like a steam train. She ran past the swimming pool and leaped into my arms with legs wrapped around my waist and arms around my neck, squeezing me so tight I could hardly breathe, all the while, sobbing uncontrollably. There was no holding back the tears. We laughed and cried for what seemed like forever, then it was tearful welcomes all around. Max's wife 'Chicken' had arranged a delicious *braai*, the pool was glistening, and my beautiful gazebo came alive with laughter and happiness. It was a day of pure bliss. The only one missing was Dusty, who was bound by business commitments and could not make it.

Despite the hell I had gone through, physically and mentally, the worst part of being locked away in prison was the knowledge that my beloved children were growing up without me. Being with Sandy again brought it all back so strongly. Not living under the same roof as them, when Mary and I separated, was hard, but nothing compared to the heartbreak I felt when I went to prison. The bond I have with them is something I will cherish and protect until my dying day.

It still pains me to know they went through first loves, crushes, dances, 21st birthdays and entered the wide world, and I wasn't there to see any of it. I am their father and should have been there, but I couldn't be. I don't want anyone reading this ever to have to feel that way. Make enough time for your loved ones and never take them for granted.

Max is known for his exceptional generosity, but now he and Chicken outdid themselves. With nobody on the property for over a year the sun had taken its toll, leaving everything looking overgrown, bleached and dull. They had gone to great expense and effort to have my house restored as close to its original state as possible. Chicken, her dad 'Flogdog', and 16 workers worked like machines with Max overseeing everything. Ian Hodgson (Hotdog) and his wife Karen had kindly donated paint to repaint the entire house. It was a monumental task, but they transformed the house back to its sparkling former glory within two weeks. The sight of the lovely old stone house under thatch with the Rhodesian teak windows and doors filled me with unbridled delight.

The generosity and consideration the community showed me was unbelievable. Hundreds of people showed up to my homecoming party at Busters Sports Club the following day. The place vibrated while we danced to Gary Stanley's sensational singing. (Gary's sister Karen was the one who wrote the letter that put me on death row in the dark cell.) The night was electrifying!

I obviously had to do a speech, which had everyone captivated. I think many were wondering if I was still sane after the reports of conditions and death rates had leaked out, but my rugby mentors, Bucky Buchanan and Freddy Jocks, told me I changed lives that night. It was an occasion that is deeply etched in my memory.

What struck me the hardest after being away for eight years, was that it was not the streets, trees, and houses that had changed, but the people and their physical conditions. It became very evident who had gotten off their butts and made a success of their lives and who had sat in the bars and sports pubs, complaining about how tough times were. It reminded me, once again, how important health and positivity are.

I also realised how much my self-confidence had been crushed during my time in prison. It was a blow realising how much had happened without me since I had been taken away. I was, in a sense, now at the back of the pack I once led, and to top it all off, the full coffers were long empty, and all that was left in their place was debt. It came as quite a shock to realise how much work I would have to do to get anywhere close to where I was before I went away.

CHAPTER 68

Final Seasons

It was a real pleasure for me to be aboard a tractor again after my hospital ordeal. I felt a wonderful sense of release grinding through the woodland, the wind in my face, the rising sun in my eyes and only the growling sound of the old diesel engine in my ears. The area set aside for the prison was pristine, and in winter the grass still stood dry and high, the bush a pastel-coloured carpet of dry leaves below the trees.

The morning excursions with tractor and trailer were always special, but being winter, it was damn cold. My eyes watered profusely, and my nose never stopped dribbling, but it was refreshing and exhilarating. Often the going got tough with a heavy load in soft soil, causing the old diesel engine to roar along belching clouds of black smoke while I dodged stumps in my path as the men on the trailer behind laughed and cheered me on. Loading up those old logs, I often thought, what a shame they couldn't talk and tell me their history. Some of them were large leadwood tree trunks full of character from hundreds of years living through harsh conditions. On the return journeys, we raced home through long golden grass leaving a welcome feeling of inner peace only a bush-lover fully understands.

When planting season came around the old red trac-tor broke down, so we all had to make our way into the ploughed fields to plant maize by hand for days in intense heat while we waited for spare parts to arrive. It was tortur-ous stuff. On the third day, one of the prisoners carelessly flicked a hand-rolled cigarette onto the soil, which was cov-ered by fine dry grass and maize-storks, and moments later there were flames. This happened just as a hot wind gusted strongly across us and dust billowed. It was frightening how fast it spread and, despite our frantic efforts to stamp it out, we suddenly found ourselves fighting a major fire.

It reached a gum plantation in no time, rendering us helpless. The flames soared high in the trees and getting close enough to have any effect was impossible. It was suffocating and blistering hot. Fortunately, the wind was blowing consistently, and we were able to back-burn and beat around the edges of the line of fire until we brought it under control. We finally snuffed out the last flames at pre-cisely 11.11 a.m. on 11 November 2011. After all the com-motion there was a sudden quietness, and I took myself away and prayed to God under the shade of a huge acacia tree. The spiritual connection felt more powerful than ever.

My 50th birthday party coincided with a home-leave period, and Max and Chicken laid it on again. Hundreds of people were invited to the same venue as my homecom-ing party. Chicken arranged a delicious help-yourself din-ner, Gary Stanley once again played for free, and the place rocked until the early hours. My darling little sister drove from Harare, and Dusty and Sandy flew in from South Africa.

Dusty had graduated from hotel school and was doing exceptionally well as the manager of the Bushman's Nek Hotel in South Africa, but after the weekend of my 50th he felt he really belonged in Zimbabwe. It wasn't long before he called to inform me that he was coming home. It had been over nine painful, lonely long years since we had spent quality time together, and my five-day home leave trips were wonderful. I had forgotten what a warm, easy-going, beautiful person he was. I can't express the happiness I felt being father and son again.

There were treasured moments I vividly recall during my last two years as a prisoner. Getting into the field in the early mornings was always a special treat, and I came to know where the wild game would most likely be. We started work early in the mornings and finished at 4 p.m. After that and on weekends we were free to roam the five-thousand acre farm. We had to be back by sundown and roll call was at 9 p.m.

At the slightest opportunity, I was off tracking and scouting, getting lost in the wonders of nature. One early spring morning with the sun creeping over the horizon, I was moving down a sandy streambed in the crisp cool of dawn, savouring the sharp smells of mopane woodland. Russet coloured newly budded leaves appeared in patches from the early summer shine in the rising sun's beams. On a carpet of green, a pair of spirited steenbok danced away almost as an opening performance before the main act, which was the appearance of a majestic kudu bull which stood motionless only a stone's throw away. His wild beauty froze me in my stride. We stared at each other for a special moment, before he swung his enormous head around, took two great bounds and melted silently into the bush.

After the early rains was always a significant time for us. The thousands of flying ants provided a rich bounty of protein for the prisoners, which we scooped by the handful from under the security lights at night into buckets, to be turned into a tasty relish to eat with our *sadza*. The smell of fresh rain on dry land fuelled our spirits and lifted morale. On special occasions, we got bream from the dam, and I savoured the moments watching it cook slowly in an old cast-iron pot on the grill while Ndebele chatted away. The laughter during these gatherings was therapeutic. I always had one ear tuned to the trees and the bush, listening for the trill of the guinea fowl and rattle of the francolin.

A few weeks later, I tracked down the edge of a belt of mopane trees bordering a drying stream sprinkled with pools where I frequently saw fresh spoor. I knew they were close, then I saw three kudu cows looking jittery, their tails flicking before they turned and bolted away. They knew, and I knew, danger lurked nearby.

No more than a minute later, I heard an unfamiliar noise and moved fast to get closer. I broke into a sprint across an open grassy plain while staying on their tracks and saw only two kudu in the distance in full stride. The thrashing sound was now clear and off to my right. I veered towards it, and there the kudu cow lay on her side in a helpless frenzy. She tried to tear her neck away from the trees, but she was lashed to a thick steel wire snare that was strangling her to death. Her body shook in paroxysms of pain, her eyes rolled back so only the whites showed and her purple tongue quivered in her mouth. I knew she was dying.

Instinctively and recklessly, I tried to release the tension around her neck by dislodging her front feet, and in an instant, her left shoulder hit me squarely in the chest, sending me reeling, with her head and neck still tight against the tree. Our bodies rolled in a heap with her sharp hooves flying dangerously close to my head. One kick in the wrong place would have killed me. I was winded and dizzy but determined to release her and inched closer to where the wire was tied. Being steel wire, it seemed to take forever, and I could see her life was ebbing away as her convulsions slowed with the lack of air going into her lungs. Sweating, struggling for breath, my muscles straining, I finally got it undone and pulled the noose from around her neck with all my might. She didn't move.

I grabbed her neck and felt a faint pulse in her jugular but no breathing. She was motionless, and her eyes had a deathly glaze. I massaged her throat, trying to open the airway then placed both hands on her ribs near her heart and pushed with all my weight. To my surprise, stomach fluids blew out her nostrils almost like an exhaust as an engine ignites; she took a deep breath, then another and then blinked back into life like a light coming on. I was breathless as I watched her roll over onto her chest and hold her head up in a daze. I looked on anxiously, and minutes later, to my absolute delight, she came giddily to her feet and walked off back into the trees. I could barely contain my joy.

When the rains arrived, we were sent off after bushpig that were ripping the maize fields to pieces. Waking up at 5 a.m. three of us headed for the prison guard gun-carriers hut, organised a rendezvous and then collected Spot, the OIC's dog, for tracking. The destruction the night before was serious and soon Spot was off following a scent with us thundering behind, but his inexperience showed, as he lost the trail regularly until nothing was found. We returned to where we had started, and one of my colleagues motioned excitedly in the direction of a dry reed-bed. The gun-bearer was right there, and, in a flash, a blast rang out as he fired randomly into the cover.

To my dismay, a terrified little kudu calf bolted away with a yelping dog in furious pursuit, followed closely by the rest of the hunting party. Being the furthest from the direction they headed, I bellowed to them to stop but was ignored. Breathless, I arrived at the scene to find a heavy boot on the crying calf's head, while the dog tore at its slender back legs. Cursing loudly, I went flying in and knocked the man with the offending boot off the tiny animal, then pried the dog's jaws open and off the leg before embracing her. She was shaking uncontrollably, but I was relieved to see the bullet had only nicked the tip of an ear and no serious damage was done. It had a bit of velvet-like fur on its head missing, a slightly bloody nose, a few puncture marks and a small tear on the back legs, but was otherwise fine. I sent the others off with the dog and carried the beautiful baby back to where we had disturbed her, hoping the mother would find her again. Only then did I notice the umbilical cord remained attached. She tried to take off again when I placed her down, but I held her and whispered soothingly while stroking her gently until she calmed down. I returned three hours later and from a distance could see she was still there. The next day I returned, and she was gone with no sign of disturbance, so I hoped for the best, and that she was back with her mom.

After so long spent inside walls, every moment in the open felt like a special occasion. The sights, smell, and sounds of the bush intoxicated me and my spirits soared. Whenever I had the chance, I wound my way up into the granite hills, through the long grass and explored the crevices and crannies for signs of wildlife. Wearing my favourite Courteney safari boots back on my feet was a treat in itself. I had covered hundreds of miles in them during the safari days, and I planned on covering many more.

Up in the hills, I found myself a rocky ledge with a view that I would frequently visit. The solitude gave me a chance to breathe deeply and search my soul for answers, and my mind for the way forward back into a happy and prosperous world, where I would be able to care for the people I loved and enjoy the precious company of friends so forcibly lost for so long. The more I let my mind meander through the maze that is life, the more I felt I would find the answers and would soon be back where I was before being snatched away. I have so many delightful memories of times in the wild with some incredible people and the unique gifts that only nature can provide.

Sitting around our favourite firepit surrounded by hard, well-swept red earth, I listened to the sounds. The calming call of a black cuckoo and the gruff grunts of an old Brahman bull nearby. On the horizon, rays of orange light raked through the cracks in the rain clouds. A sense of precious calmness overcame me as my mind wandered while I kept one ear on the gentle chatter of my fellow inmates around the fire. I could now release my fantasy girlfriend Sheree and take in these magical wonders of nature instead. It almost felt like freedom again.

CHAPTER 69

An Emotional Reunion

My 'illegal' phone gave me a chance to get onto Facebook and reconnect with long-lost friends who had mostly dispersed all over the world after the Zimbabwe dollar crash. I had been on Facebook for about five months when another great friend, Barry King, posted a photo of our rugby days with Sue in it.

I had built a strong wall deep down against her to protect my feelings, but the picture hit me hard. Then she commented on it, saying that they were the best years of her life. It had been a long time, and plenty had happened, but my emotions, deep down, were still powerful. We had been ripped apart, still madly in love and it became apparent right away, that I was not over her. No matter what she had done, my feelings were still there.

I replied to her comment saying that they were the best years of my life, too. I knew she had become a mother and had built another life in the United Kingdom, but had not married. We began e-mailing each other after that but nothing seriously emotional, just about our lives in general.

The unconditional love we share with our parents, siblings, and children, is very different from that with the person we choose to share our life with. Family will always be there, no matter what, but the love you share with the one you sleep beside every night is stronger and more profound than any other. The pain that followed the rejection I went through from Sue, during horrific hardships, can never be explained. Letting her in again made me extremely nervous and emotionally unstable.

About two months later I met a woman in Harare. Photos posted on Facebook upset Sue, and in fairness to everyone, we stopped all contact. During many of my trips home, several people had informed me of Sue's infidelity during the second year of my incarceration. It certainly hurt. I put myself in her shoes and knew that I would probably have behaved no differently. As hard as it was, I still loved her for what we had shared. My new relationship ended after about three months, and soon Sue and I were e-mailing again.

Towards the end of my time at Connemara, Sue asked me if I would mind if she visited me while I was on my five-day 'home leave'. I felt delighted but apprehensive. We planned for her to meet me at my house at 3 p.m. on a Friday. I arrived home at around 11 a.m. and could hardly contain myself waiting for four hours. I cleaned my teeth, made sure my hair was properly combed, straightened my kit. I had planned for all my staff to take the afternoon off and was alone when she drove into my driveway and parked in front of my office block. Feeling apprehensive but bubbling inside, I strolled out, a huge smile on my face, not knowing what to expect. As soon as she saw me, she started running my way, her long silky brown hair bouncing in the wind, as slim and gorgeous as ever, calling out, 'Baby, baby, baby!' We were wrapped in each other's arms again. It felt like yesterday. We kissed, cried and hugged for ages, then walked hand in hand, full of smiles into the house.

Once she had looked around the house she had built and furnished with me, we lay down and spoke about us. She broke down in tears immediately and confessed to having slept with only one guy. I quizzed her about other rumours, which she flatly denied, and I believed her. She had no reason to lie and her stories correlated precisely with what I had been told by trusted friends who I had looked to for the truth, just because it was the truth I so desperately needed for my own peace of mind.

I forgave her right away. If we were going to try and pick up the pieces, then we needed to put the past behind us. The five days went off fantastically, and I was head over heels in love again. Max and Chicken came out to the prison the following Sunday and brought Sue with them. We spent a fabulous day with plenty of laughter and made plans for Sue to return for my release. It was a tough goodbye, and we called one another often after that. I would take walks into the bush with my phone and chat to her in Manchester at least every week, and we messaged daily.

The OIC at Connemara, Superintendent Matonhodze, was a fantastic man, one of the best I encountered during my time as an inmate. It was such a pity more were not like him. He had promised to take me fishing one Sunday on the dam where I had taken my first swim; I was over the moon as always. I knew we had to grind maize first for the prison, but he said we would go after I had done that. I got the work done and, being fishing crazy, was anxious to get to the water. He was, as usual, moving at his own casual speed. I was still a prisoner, so I contained my anxiety. Eventually, we were on the road, but had little daylight left. Just as we neared the main road to the dam, there was an old army vehicle with a few soldiers standing around. To my dismay, he screeched to a halt and said we must try and help them. I really had to bite my tongue as I stood by watching him have a long chat with the soldiers as if time was endless. Eventually, we made it to the dam with 30 minutes left before dark in perfect conditions, but the fish weren't interested in our lures at all. It was still beautiful out there, and we fished until dark with not a touch. I liked him very much and thought I needed to share this lesson I had just learned from him.

I said, 'You know, officer, when you stopped to help those soldiers, I was upset, I really was. I'd been waiting all week to fish today, and time was running out, but you have taught me something. You stopped to help people in distress, and I am sure you made some friends who will help you one day. The fishing can always wait for another day. I always told my children that if you ever want something too much in life, it's likely to turn out a disappointment ... and look what happened.'

I was about to have that revelation challenged one last time.

CHAPTER 70

The Final Hurdle

My final year in prison came to an end close to what was known as the airstrip, which was an old airforce base from the Rhodesian era. It was almost totally flat and bordered, in the summer months, by lush green mopane trees on two sides and mimosa forest on the rest. I loved listening to the calming, sunset sounds – the sharp 'gwapp' of breeding frogs from muddy pools nearby and the cuckoo's melodious 'Piet-my-vrou' call in the distance. I felt the frogs and birds had become accustomed to my regular solitary presence. I sometimes saw kudu there as well, their keen eyes glued to me and ears like radar scanners honed into my footsteps. On most evenings during the summer, there was a crimson sky with thick rain clouds in the distance. It was another one of those places where I found peace in natural beauty as the curtain started to come down on my life as a prisoner.

Leading up to my release, I had organised with Max and about 50 friends from Bulawayo to come out and collect me in the back of Max's 10-ton truck with hay bales and cooler boxes. It was going to be a day we would never forget. But three months before my release date, the OIC told me there was a potential problem. He said I might have to do another 60 days for the mobile phone issue.

I protested and told him that it had been sorted out. I reminded him that I had asked for an appeal, but had received no response, so had assumed the matter was closed. I requested to have my records checked at the courts. A week later, I was very relieved when he told me he had done so, and they did not know anything about a mobile phone issue or 60 extra days. He was of the opinion that it was probably not a problem. He confirmed my date of release as 3 April 2013. I could not stop smiling – but not for long.

The day before my release I was called to the OIC's office. 'Rust,' he said, 'we have a problem.' My heart sank. 'You have to go back to Harare Central to deal with the issue of the 60 days you were given for the phone.'

I felt sick, but I kept calm. 'But it was sorted out.'

'No, you have to go back and deal with the officer who gave you the punishment in person.'

'But he's left,' I said.

'Well, all I can tell you is they are coming for you today. They will be here in two hours, so you better prepare yourself.'

This had me in a spin. I had to message my sister, so she could inform every one about the new arrangements, and contact people in high places to find out what was going on. Then I had to start packing my belongings, with my phones appropriately hidden. I called my old friend Ndebele and gave him my room, the bed with all the bedding, crockery, cutlery, and cooking utensils. He was shaking with excitement. Farai got heaps of my clothes and shoes, I left my refrigerator for the prison service and all my fishing rods, reels and tackle for the OIC. Sure enough, that afternoon they arrived, and I was on my way back to Harare Central in a slump.

Everything was going wrong, but my spirits lifted a little when I was taken into the holding cell to find my good friend George, the armed robber from Chikurubi days, waiting for me. He greeted me warmly, and we wasted little time catching up on where we had been and what we had done over the last four years. Shame, the guy who had slashed his manhood with the glass, was also there. Another guy I was shocked to see was Amos, an armed robber we had been with for all the years in Chikurubi who was released and had since had his arm shot off by police in another armed robbery. He showed me his stump just below the shoulder. He seemed very sorry for himself, but no doubt would be out soon robbing, innocent people again.

The next morning my worst fear looked like a reality: I was called to the main office and told that I had to do another 60 days. I pleaded with them, explaining once again what had transpired. I reminded them that I had asked to appeal the sentence and was never given the opportunity to do so. There was a shrug of shoulders. It was quite simple: Prison HQ had sent an instruction that I was to do the 60 days.

I advised them that I was a free man being held illegally and was going to take the matter further. I was sent back into the exercise yard and told that I would be called after they had consulted with HQ. At 11 a.m. I was called again. They said that I was required to sign an admission of guilt, which I flatly refused to do and requested they call my lawyer. Again, the OIC said he needed to find out more from HQ and would call me later. I was escorted back to the yard and managed to get one of the friendly guards who used to help charge my phone to contact my sister Lyn, who had been rushing around in meetings trying to get me released. She left instructions that I was not to sign anything. At 2 p.m. I was summoned back upstairs to the OIC's office. He looked me square in the eyes, with no expression.

'Rust,' he said, 'I have spoken to HQ, and they say you have to stay another 60 days.'

I wanted to die. I looked at him in complete despair.

'You must be joking, officer,' I pleaded. A silence followed, and then he smiled.

'Yes, I am joking, you are a free man, your sister is waiting for you outside.'

My heart leaped into my mouth, I jumped into the air cheering, gave him a big bear-hug and took off down the stairs.

My ten years of hell was over.

CHAPTER 71

Closure

I wish I had the words to express the happy, bubbly, exciting, beautiful, feeling I felt as I walked out of those prison gates to freedom, after 10 years of hell. People don't appreciate freedom, and I have realised, that even when we are not in prison, there are ways in which we imprison ourselves – in sour business partnerships, poorly selected careers, being obsessed with money and ambition in the corporate world, even in unhappy marriages. Only when you have your freedom completely taken away do you realise that, in many ways, you were already in some form of prison. When I look back on it all, it makes me wish I could somehow get through to people just how precious and priceless freedom is. If you look at your life as it is, how free are you within your circumstances? Freedom is more than just not being in prison. Freedom is the ability to make a choice and act on it. Freedom is letting go of what you cannot control. Freedom is forgiveness. Freedom is being free from negativity. Freedom brings health. If you can be free in all areas of your life, then you will reach your full potential.

That said, 3 April 2013 is a day I will cherish forever.

Sue flew in from the UK to be there for me. It was as if my life had just stood still for 10 years. Nobody could stop smiling. My darling sisters were there, Lyn with her new man Ed and children Tara and Kassie, Bev with her husband Mark and their children Sharna and Maison. We hugged and laughed and drove in three cars to Lyn's house in Harare where champagne was waiting on ice.

After a few glasses and a bite to eat, full of the spirit of freedom, we left for Bulawayo where Dusty was preparing a party at my house. The joys of true freedom were exhilarating. We danced, laughed, sang and partied late into the night at my beautiful home.

On Friday, people turned up by the hundreds to my official release party. Instead of a speech, I delivered a poem I'd prepared. The last lines read:

> *It broke all our hearts when life seemed so grand,*
> *But maybe it's for a reason, that we'll one day understand.*
> *Still, to me the meanest thing, that they could ever do,*
> *Was take me from my adorable children, and beloved Sue.*
> *Now that it's all behind me, I'm well on my way,*
> *To enjoy my freedom and cherish every moment of each day.*
> *All settled back home again, in this caring, considerate society,*
> *I'll take whatever life throws at me and make happiness my priority!*

I looked around me at the people who had stood by me for ten long years and thought about how we all were back in the 70s and 80s. We were such a close, caring community, enjoying the simple things in life, but things had changed. Hundreds had moved all over the world in the wake of the chaos caused by the farm invasions. Some ruffians in their wild youth had reformed and become hugely successful businessmen while others had let their health dictate their limits. Others had sadly, passed on.

There is a unique, unwritten code that bonds friends in Zimbabwe. The warm, caring and considerate society that we live in, made up of all races, can never be equalled, anywhere! I share treasured memories with almost all who were there that weekend, and it was those memories, and the endless generosity, consideration, and knowing what a fantastic bunch of people we still have left there, that kept me going all those years in hell. I had dreamed that one day I would be travelling the globe reminding people never to forget what they have, because only when they have it all taken away, will they realise what they had. I've always lived by the motto, 'Live every moment for the pleasure of the moment'. Now I would add one thing: but don't neglect your health, your loved ones, or your friends.

The celebrations carried on through the weekend, with *jukskei* (a traditional game in which the wooden pins from the yoke of an ox wagon are thrown at a stick in the ground) and a *braai* on Saturday, and another *braai* and drinks on Sunday. My first weekend of freedom was fantastic, but it ended too soon. My precious children and other family left on Sunday, leaving me, Sue and her daughter Emily for two weeks of bonding before they returned to the United Kingdom. The plan was for Sue and Emily to settle in Bulawayo with me. However, she needed to get consent from Emily's father first.

During those two weeks together, Emily spent every night with her cousins, whom she adored, giving Sue and me time to get to know one another again. I was very unsettled emotionally. My spirit and confidence had taken a huge knock, and my financial position was a constant source of stress.

Being an ex-national rugby player and prominent business-man, I was well known before my conviction and became even better known with all the publicity that my incarceration had attracted. On my release, all eyes were on me. I would go into a restaurant, and there would be a sudden silence, and everybody would be looking at me – mostly in admiration, but it was terribly unnerving to be a constant focus of attention. In a community that I was once central to, I now felt unsure if I belonged at all and, if I did, I was not sure of my place. It came as quite a shock to realise how much confidence I had actually lost, and it would take some time for me to recover that.

My insecurity triggered two arguments between Sue and me during those two weeks, and I saw a side to her that I didn't know existed. She appeared very bitter deep inside and attacked me in a way I had never experienced before. Her instant ferocious reactions on both occasions left a seed in me that I needed to deal with. Was this going to happen every time we had a dispute? Would she ever forgive me for indirectly messing up her perfect life before prison? Would she resent me for the years she had grudgingly spent in the UK because there was no other option? Was this the real Sue and was the Sue I had known before only perfect because the situation was perfect?

When Sue and Emily left to go back home, it became evident that this was our closure that we both badly needed. She and Emily had a new life in the UK, and I lived in Zimbabwe. I wanted to share my life with someone and make love, and sleep beside that person, every night. I missed that dearly for 10 years. I also needed to put the past behind me in every way to find myself again. We decided to call it quits and move on with our lives.

Phil was released after his ten years, which ended seven months before my sentence, and started working on a tobacco farm in Karoi in the Mashonaland Province. Three months after my release I drove 700 km to see him. It was a great reunion catching up on all the old characters we had shared so many traumatic years with. Over a few beers, he asked me if I had heard about George, my friend of all the years in Chikurubi Max. I told him I had been sending George airtime weekly on his smuggled phone but had not heard from him in a few months. Then Phil informed me that two months earlier George had started to become very ill. He was suffering from high blood pressure, and while standing in line for the hospital, he had a heart attack and died. It was very sad news; he was a great friend and someone I wanted to see again after prison.

I left Phil with a saddened heart the following day, wondering what would become of the rest of us who had had our lives turned upside down. We still keep in touch. He was an absolute godsend for me and someone who will always remain special in my life.

CHAPTER 72

New Life

A month after my release, my old deputy headmaster and national rugby commentator Keith Swales, asked if I would go up to Harare and give a talk to about 100 farmers who had lost their farms and were battling emotionally to deal with it.

I immediately said, 'I don't do that, Mr Swales.'

But he had heard about some of the speeches I had given in the last year and persuaded me. I prepared a long speech and two weeks later, went up to the Harare Royal Golf Club to a sit-down dinner for about 120 guests, and read out my talk. It had a huge impact, but I did not realise that this speech would later be the start of a new career for me.

I applied for my hunter and guide's licence and within six weeks I was back in the safari business. I could not get enough of the beauty in the countryside and the feeling it left in me. I needed to find Kermit and any of the staff who had been part of my operation, as soon as possible. As if by divine intervention, Modrick phoned me asking for a job a few weeks after I obtained my licence. I was thrilled and sent him money to catch a train to Bulawayo. Kermit also agreed to come immediately and a driver was dispatched to collect him and bring him to the safari camp. When I walked up to him, sitting around the staff fireplace, it was as if I had been with him the day before. In respect, he never stood up, remaining below me. I sat opposite him for hours, as we laughed and caught up on the last ten years in excellent spirits. Having him and Modrick back in my life was unbelievable. I felt truly free and happy deep inside being in the bush like old times.

At the end of the safari season, Kermit and Modrick requested to return home with their season's funds, and I enjoyed a few trips with old mates – Brebs, Russ Herbert, Billy Mitchell, and five other mates fishing at Mana Pools. Another to Sun City as a marshall for the Million Dollar Golf Tournament with Mike Burns, Lee McNab and several other mates, and a rugby tour with the Zimbabwe Legends team playing against the Springbok Legends at the Shark Tank (Kings Park Stadium) in Durban, where I reunited with Ian Mac who kindly wrote the foreword for this book. They were a huge part of my healing; I was gaining confidence weekly and loving life again.

During my second year in the safari business, while on a safari with Johann Vorster, the CEO of Clover Industries in South Africa, he asked me to tell him my whole life story. After three hours and plenty of red wine, I told him about the speech that I had done for the farmers who had lost their farms. He asked if I had a copy of that talk and I told him it was on my phone right there. He read it in no time. Turning to me after he was done, he said, 'I've got a new life for you my friend, this is your calling, and I'm going to sponsor you.'

Within eighteen months, my life had taken an enormous turn. Dusty was working for a private game resort outside Harare, and Sandy came home and soon had a steady boyfriend, Dayne Pigors. I liked him right away, and they seemed wonderfully happy. Dayne and Sandy were living in my house, which gave me peace of mind in terms of security while I was away. Having always wanted to set my children up in their own businesses, I offered Dayne and Sandy free use of the large warehouse on the property to run events in and to start marketing the property as a venue for functions such as weddings.

Sandy was my first audience as I practised my new public speaking career. She must have heard my talk a hundred times, giving me feedback after each one and helping me tune my voice and body language, along with the content.

During one of my trips home, I was upstairs in my bedroom when I heard Sandy call out to me. I found her shivering at the bottom of the stairs, looking at something in her hand.

'What's wrong, lovey?' I said, running down to her.

'We have a problem,' she answered. 'I'm pregnant!'

She started sobbing. I held her and assured her all would be well. At last, I was able to be there, as a father, for my child when she needed me. Before dinner ended, both their moms had been called, and there was a new vibe in the family. She was only five weeks along then, but the baby list began right away.

Around that time I reconnected with another old mate from the 80s, Andy Conolly, who owned and managed an absolute paradise. During my few days with him there, interacting with elephants, walking with lions, and going on game drives in sensational mule-drawn carriages, Andy could sense my passion for wildlife and conservation was still alive. He planted a seed in my head of his dreams to revive an educational training facility in wildlife conservation. I had found my conservation path again.

Over six months, working with his fantastic team, we established a new organisation called Pathfinders, providing unique and premium outdoor experiences and training in Africa's great wildernesses. We partnered with Brian Serrao of FGASA (Field Guides Association of Southern Africa) to set up an organisation that believes that being in nature has great power to educate, and that nature holds the key to a sustainable future. Our core belief is that when we embrace nature, we start to understand it, and then we care for it. We share and celebrate this passion with every participant who joins us, whether for a professional qualification, or a leisure experience. We see the preservation of our natural resources as a collaborative approach that starts first with an igniting of wonder in our surroundings, and the more we learn, the greater our desire becomes to protect that which is so precious.

I dedicated my life to wildlife before prison, and my heart will always be there. Andy and I were part of a drive to reintegrate wildlife into Zimbabwe, which resulted in our beautiful country having more wildlife than it had ever had in its history. It was a monumental achievement. Having been wrongly convicted for an anti-poaching incident and having seen the destruction of wildlife and nature through the land invasions and rampant rhino and elephant poaching, I knew we needed to try and make a positive impact in other ways. The land and animal populations we had built up and nurtured are gone. It will take decades to ever come close to how it was, but Pathfinders will educate people far and wide so they can spread the word about the importance of conservation and the delicate balance that is in nature.

My first paid-for talk was for the Association of Certified Chartered Accountants at their annual breakfast conference at the Hyatt Hotel in Johannesburg on 16 April 2016. It was a sit-down breakfast for about 180 guests, and it went off fantastically. Two weeks later Russell Ashley-Cooper, who I had played international rugby with and love like a brother, offered me his hangar at Virginia Airport in Durban to do another talk. He had arranged many celebrities to attend: the first Miss World from South Africa, Penny Coelen; Springbok rugby coach, Ian McIntosh; and Springbok legends Gary Teichmann, Adrian Garvey, and John Allen. The keynote was 55 minutes long, but questions and answers went on for another hour. My good friend Jason Marshall filmed the events and offered to create a promotional video for me. My professional public-speaking career had begun.

I found it extremely therapeutic, and it helped me regain my confidence and inner strength. I now do masterclasses in the lessons I learned from my experience to help corporates, which is going exceptionally well.

I began to travel extensively around South Africa between talks. One day in 2016, late for a meeting at Centurion Mall between Johannesburg and Pretoria, I jumped out of my vehicle, rushed over to the first car guard I could see and asked where Fishmongers restaurant was. I was looking up at the colossal mall for clues, but something sparked deep down and I spun around and locked eyes with the car guard. It was Masango, one of the *mapolishers* in Chikurubi Max who had been with me for four-and-a-half years of living hell.

His smile was a mile wide, we jumped and hugged warmly before I had to rush off, assuring him I would be back in an hour to catch up. When I returned we laughed and spoke for ages. I gave him some money and promised I would help him when I got my life back together. We are currently working on a project together. He was an armed robber and, I am delighted to say, one of the ones I helped to reform.

I had found a balance between public speaking and conservation. Then, finally, I found true love.

CHAPTER 73

New Love

I n July 2016, Bella Shaw of Zulu Nyala Game Lodge in KwaZulu- Natal invited me to be in a wildlife documentary on poaching for American television. *Expedition Safari* was about a rhino calf which had been wounded in the leg when poachers tried to shoot its mother. A veterinarian team had its leg put in plaster of Paris, the first operation of this kind. Bella and I had become good friends, and she knew I was looking for a woman in my life.

In October that year, Bella called to say she had met someone special and thought we might suit one another. But when she put the idea to Sandra, she flatly refused as she had had a bad experience with her divorce two years before and was not interested. Bella begged her to 'just meet the guy at least'. Sandra agreed, and we texted for six days before she finally took a call from me.

After my experience of being lost during the war and on death row in the dark cell, I understood that there definitely is a God and He cares about me. The fact that I had to go through what I went through was very confusing, but it all started to make sense slowly after meeting Sandra. She is a very spiritual person and has an incredible connection with God.

During our conversation, she appeared a little aloof but accepted my invitation for lunch at Dainfern Golf Estate. We then walked around the golf course for four hours, talking. Being gorgeous, smart, and funny, she was a pleasure to be around. She had my attention for sure, being quite tall with long wavy blonde hair and olive skin, but told me repeatedly that she was not interested in a relationship. We were enjoying each other's company and I could feel a very strong connection developing, so I persisted.

The following day I gave a presentation at Picolino's Guest House in Johannesburg, and Sandra said she would attend. She arrived with a friend and was very moved by my talk. We planned to meet the following day.

We walked and talked for hours and I presumed the talk had made a difference. She prepared a delicious salmon dish, and we shared a divine bottle of wine by candlelight. Things were looking better. While we were dining, I asked her once again if she really wasn't ready for a relationship. She adamantly refused, so I tried another approach. I asked if she had any friends like her that she could introduce me to. She just ignored me.

Our dinner was magical, so we decided to go on a moon-lit walk around the golf course again. Strolling along aimlessly about five minutes into our walk, with me now walking slightly ahead and clearly showing no interest, she asked if I still wanted her to find me a friend like her. Looking straight ahead with a polite uninterested manner, I said, 'That's up to you,' and carried on walking, looking up into the moonlight.

She sidled up close real quick and slipped her hand into mine. We continued hand in hand for hours, laughing and smiling with a feeling that only new love can bring. A few hours later, sitting on the lush green grass watching the water flowing over rapids in the river below, we had our first passionate kiss. Since that day, we have been inseparable.

How do I begin to describe my relationship with Sandra? To start with, Sandra met me at my lowest, when I was broken, trying to piece together the fragments of my life. Yet, she saw something in me that she fell in love with, not my money (there was none), not my status (which I had lost), but me. Our relationship is built on a deep love and profoundly spiritual closeness. No woman that I could ever have conjured up in prison could have been as warm and beautiful as Sandra. What's fascinating about a relationship that is right is that everything else falls into place. When I met her I had scars I never believed would ever heal. I had an emptiness deep inside that I didn't think would ever go away. But her love, support, and faith have made me whole again. And I have dedicated my life to our future together.

Sandra has embraced my children as I have hers. She is a giver in every sense of the word, my true soulmate, and every day I'm reminded of how blessed we are to have found each other. We are partners in our speaking business, and she manages the marketing and media, while I share my story.

My talk at Picolino's Guest House opened a door to the professional speaking circuit, and I was signed up with a reputable speaking bureau the following day. My world was suddenly opened to corporate stages and platforms. The response I have experienced from this broad new audience has been phenomenal and way beyond what I ever thought or imagined. My keynotes have expanded exponentially, talking to corporates at Sun City and other prestigious venues around southern Africa and live virtual talks worldwide.

In February 2017, my grandson Jesse Reinhold Pigors was born. We were all there for Sandy: Dayne, me, Sandra, Dusty, and the new grannies and grandfathers. It was an unbelievable feeling to hold this little bundle of nature so innocent and reliant on us all. My baby had had a baby, I couldn't get my head around it. To say he has turned our world upside down would be an understatement. This gorgeous, charismatic, energetic, loving little boy is the apple of his granddad's eye.

Sandy and Dayne have developed their events business on the Bulawayo property. Dayne is a talented chef, and every Thursday evening, they hold a dinner for fifty in the warehouse or in different locations in the garden, and they also host weddings and other celebrations. 'The Barn' has become a sought-after venue and popular Airbnb. We have also gone into fish breeding on the property; Kermit, Modrick, Hasane, Rom and Gombise all work with Dayne and Sandy in the new venture to create a prosperous future for us all.

Whenever Sandra and I return home, we continue the ritual of the plough-disc *braai* on the lawn. Sitting around it, eating in the traditional way with our hands is always a jovial bonding occasion.

On 6 December 2018, Sandra and I spent a week in Durban, where I was giving some talks. Because we're always stretched for time to see our friends, I suggested we invite some to meet us at the Oyster Box in Umhlanga. There were eighteen of us on the balcony overlooking the lighthouse at 6 p.m.

I sneaked downstairs and called Sandra to come down, telling her I wanted to introduce her to some close friends of mine who were on the beach. In front of the lighthouse I got on one knee, and the crowd on the balcony – who were all in on the plan – went crazy!

'Baby, will you marry me?' I asked as the velvet box opened with a beautiful ring.

'What are they all shouting about, babe?' was her response. 'Forget about them,' I said with a wide smile. 'Will you marry me?'

She said yes.

A month before our wedding, our second grandson Jay Rusty Pigors was born on 8 February 2019. Now there were two little angels to enjoy many years of the outdoors, fishing and fun. We were dying to meet Jay and planned to leave for Bulawayo soon after our wedding.

Being so excited about having found true love, I wanted a big wedding to share with those precious people in my life who had been so good to me over the years, but some important friends couldn't make the date, so we organised two ceremonies.

The first was a small intimate wedding at Casalinga Restaurant just outside Johannesburg. Sandra's best friend Genevieve flew in from Durban, and our three amazing sons, Dusty, Gideon, and Daniel came up from Cape Town. I stood beside Dusty with tears in my eyes as Sandra walked towards me, glowing in the evening sunlight, with Gideon and Daniel at her side. She looked unbelievably beautiful, and her sons overflowed with pride. The service was wonderful and the speeches evoked happy tears and a deep sense of spiritual connection – followed by a lot of vibrant dancing!

Within two days we were in Bulawayo. Preparations were trying thanks to fuel shortages and limited supplies, but we were ecstatic meeting little Jay and seeing what a beautiful little boy Jesse had developed into. Sandy and Dayne had done me proud caring for this paradise I loved so dearly. The garden was radiant with rolling lush lawns leading down to the dam full of purple and white water lilies surrounded by massive evergreen trees. The venue was magnificent.

Sandra's three closest friends, Genevieve, Liane and Liz, flew in from Durban and Cape Town to be her bridesmaids.

I decided not to have a best man but 12 groomsmen. There were so many great guys from childhood days that had been unbelievably good to me over the years, and I wanted them all to be part of my new happiness.

On the day, 300 people turned out at this loving festive occasion. The crowded service on the banks of the lovely dam started at 4.30 p.m. and the party was still reverberating at 4 a.m.! I never saw the dance-floor empty once. Chris Burton was our master of ceremonies and gave a very moving speech, along with myself, Sandra and our four children, all around the pre-arranged theme of love and the value of true friendship.

Sandra and I snuck off at 2.30 a.m. knowing that we were leaving on a 6-hour drive to begin our honeymoon the next morning. My special friends Martin and Candy Pieters had offered us a houseboat in Elephant Bay as a wedding present.

We caught plenty of fish and soaked up the beauty that only Lake Kariba can offer. It was magical in every way with beautiful sunsets to boot. Three days later we were at the magnificent Victoria Falls. We enjoyed a night at the luxurious Chundu Island Lodge above the falls, and ended the trip at Ganda Lodge near Hwange National Park. The pristine lodges were spectacular with surreal Zambezi River cruises and memorable bush walks.

We were surrounded by elephants at one point, the regular call of the African fish eagle and magnificent weather and sunsets were an absolute blessing.

CHAPTER 74

New Body

Every year after prison, my allergies dictated my fitness, training and partying. Every time I trained too hard or for too long, no matter how fit I got, my chest would play up, and invariably I would end up on antibiotics, which most doctors were quick to hand out. The same thing happened after a fishing trip involving plenty of drinking with the boys or a few rough nights in a row. All the while I remained on my asthma pump and nasal spray.

In March 2017, I went on a fishing trip to Mozambique for a week with some heavy drinkers. Naturally, I tried to keep up and ended up on repeated antibiotics and cortisone courses, as I could not shake off a chest infection. I had been on six courses, which included cortisone four times, up until October, with vitamin C doses daily. After my last course the doctor said if that did not work, I would need my lungs flushed.

The course was 2,000 mg of Augmentin morning and evening and ten cortisone tablets a day. The doctors said they needed to blast it out of my chest once and for all or I would end up with pneumonia. It worked, but I was shaking continuously from the drugs.

I did a showcase talk in Cape Town and learned of a doctor who had cured people of asthma completely, using a metatronic scanning machine. I was sceptical, but desperate, and prepared to give it a go.

I met Dr Jonathan Brinkman, a tough, athletic and knowledgeable man covered in tattoos. He asked me about my health history, then sat me down, put a set of headphones connected to a computer screen on my head, and told me he would be back in 20 minutes. I was not to touch the headset. I watched my body being scanned inch by inch on the screen, every little part. Cross sections of specific organs were scanned several times, and different-coloured small triangles would appear randomly on each body part. I was transfixed by the screen. He returned when all was done and said, 'Right let's see what's going on inside you.'

He flicked through sections of data, organ after organ, periodically stopping and concentrating on the odd one. Watching his facial expressions for hints, he did not look happy. Then he sat back and said, 'Okay, we have a few problems, but nothing that can't be sorted out.'

I had four dead tissue patches in my thyroid area. 'We can put you on homoeopathic treatment and see if the tissue grows back, but if not, it could be a problem.' My kidneys were not functioning properly. 'But that might be from all the drugs. Your liver and adrenal glands don't look good but the big problem, and I'm not sure if you want to hear this …'

I thought I must have cancer or something, when he said, 'Your heart is like a champagne bottle about to explode. The walls of your heart are four times thicker than they should be and the chambers are about to collapse.'

I was gobsmacked. Every time I had been anaesthetised in the past, they had always remarked how powerful my heart was. 'If you work with me, we can get through this,' he said. I said I would do whatever it took.

He told me I had chronic PTSD (Post Traumatic Stress Disorder). My cortisol levels were sky-high, and my immune system was totally finished from the drugs.

He put me on a serious detox flush, powerful probiotics, and a high-dose vitamin regimen, and told me to throw all my other mediation in the bin.

I did exactly as he told me to do, and, thank God, despite training hard daily and partying when I wanted to, I have not touched any medicine since. I've had three more scans, and all my organs are back to normal.

Epilogue

When I reflect on my time in prison, there are a few key principles which stand out for me. They are things I learned, or things I already knew but came to have a deeper understanding and appreciation of from having to practise them to survive. These are: the power of forgiveness, a positive mental attitude, building resilience, the importance of dignity, the value of gratitude, the potential of ingenuity, and, underlying it all, the enormous spiritual strength and comfort that comes with a connection to God.

The power of forgiveness

Resentment ate away at me during my first year in prison, more than the lice ever could. The humiliation of being labelled a murderer and the terrible conditions were extremely hard to deal with, as was the pain of my bitterness, anger, hatred, frustration and desire for revenge for what they had done, and were doing to me. I hated them bitterly.

Initially, I would lie there for hours wishing every terrible thing on each of them in turn: the poacher, the police, the judge, and all who were involved in my conviction. Then one day, I was struck by the realisation that they had all forgotten about me long ago. There I was, consumed by the unfairness of it all, while they were blissfully unaware of the evil I wished on them every day. In the end, I was only hurting myself. I was carrying all of it in my head and beating myself up for nothing.

The single biggest lesson I learned in prison, was true forgiveness. And for me, it was bigger than anything I could have achieved on my own. True forgiveness was inspired by God Almighty, as was letting go. It was a huge weight off my shoulders, and I learned to live in the moment from then on. The past was too painful, and the future full of broken promises – so, I just dealt with each day as it was. I learned to have faith because no amount of worrying was going to change what I was going through. If you have anger or resentment towards anyone, in any way, it will eventually destroy you, because that is what those emotions do. They steal from you; they steal happiness and freedom. You can look at it in two ways: you can forgive, forget, and move forward or, you can retain, remember, and regret. The choice is yours, and if you say, 'I'll forgive, but I'll never forget,' then you will still remember, and never move forward. You can't bounce back from anything unless you forgive those who you believe have done you wrong; only when you forgive and let go of the past, can you be entirely free to move forward with your full potential.

People often ask if I still resent them for what they did to me. I spent US$42,000 in one year with private investigators trying to find the assumed deceased. It was like looking for a needle in a haystack. As soon as a stranger entered the remote area where he was living, the word spread like wildfire, and he would go into hiding. They had taken 10 years of my life; all my companies went broke, and I realised that I was just giving them more and more. So, I do not give them one more second of my thoughts any more. That's all behind me. I still have my health, a beautiful wife, a wonderful family, fantastic friends, a magnificent home and a brilliant future ahead of me. I do not entertain negativity at all today, and surround myself with positive people, love and happiness.

Positive mental attitude

There was one thing I kept telling myself in prison: I was not going to be a prisoner of my past, or be a prisoner to them mentally. They had imprisoned my body, but I refused to give them my mind.

I have mentioned how I detached myself mentally from life in prison, by living in a fantasy world with my gorgeous girl-friend, Sheree. But I wanted to know scientifically how the mind deals with those horrific conditions. I wanted to know how I got through there without being affected mentally and physically. So, I did some research on it with communication pathologist and cognitive neuroscientist Dr Caroline Leaf.

Whenever we think, feel and see, our mind generates a signal that affects every cell in our bodies – about 75–100 trillion cells in total. Thinking is 98 per cent of that signal. So, what you think actually affects every cell in your body and brain, physically.

Research shows that 75–95 per cent of illnesses come from our thought life and we have an average of 30,000 thoughts a day. So, thoughts play a massive role in caus-ing diseases in our bodies. By the same token, it can be just the opposite; when you are thinking correct thoughts, you generate very healthy signals, which affect your blood chemistry and build more healthy cells. So, our thoughts create who we are, physically, and it was my happy thought life, even though it had to be a fantasy, that kept me healthy and sane in there. That is the power of posi-tive thinking.

Often, we are so caught up in our circumstances that we only see problems. In prison, we had nothing but difficulties. If you give yourself over to them, they will literally kill you: kill your spirit, your soul, drain your strength, and lead to sickness. Scientists say that negative emotions lead to excessive excretion of cortisol, a stress hormone in your brain. Cortisol is good, but too much of it can lead to chronic disease. I watched hundreds of guys die from stress in prison. They hadn't contracted any illness, yet they died from the worry of possibly perishing like so many others. Never give in to negative emotions.

Building resilience

Purely from a physical point of view, I learned how much hardship humans could withstand. People complain about the most pathetic things in life. I notice it more and more every day. 'I have nothing to wear!' yet the walk-in closet is full, or, 'I'm not sure if I can take any more – they've delayed the flight again!'

People have lost sight of what hardship means in the comfort of mansions and designer label clothes. There have been people shipwrecked for 48 days without food, others left bobbing in the ocean for 29 hours, and countless numbers who withstood horrendous torture. As long as we have air to breathe and water to drink, we can endure enormous physical abuse. But it is how we get through that mentally, by clicking into survival mode and living in the moment, that makes the difference.

Setbacks are part of life, but how you handle them is a big test of your character. There was nothing I could do about being incarcerated, but I had to fight against them imprisoning my mind. While I needed a positive mindset, I also needed to maintain my physical strength to protect myself in the face of threats from men I had, in most cases, considered my friends. To find the effort and resolve to get up and exercise daily, with no running water, very little food, and so many dying around me, boiled down to resilience. Many will argue that you are either born with it or you don't have it. I believe you can become resilient through your state of mind. What you think, you become. If you have the resolve to stay fit, physically and mentally, you will survive under the harshest conditions.

The importance of dignity

Retaining my personal dignity was a big issue for me. I knew it was essential for my survival that I didn't lose pride in myself, even though I was a convict surrounded by what are assumed to be the dregs of society. Prison visits were always terrific but at the back of my mind lurked a sense of helplessness. All my visitors had seen me in the prime of my life when I was flying high, a dominant member of the community, and here I was, dressed in rags, behind bars and a convicted murderer. It was never easy to deal with, and having the guards constantly belittling you made it harder.

There will always be people who will try to break you, and if you let them, they will. A negative word, a cold stare, a false accusation, or the guards smashing precious water bottles during the no water days in Chikurubi, these things seem simple, but they can affect you. They can break your confidence and spirit. The guards revelled in mentally torturing prisoners. Like when you spoke to them, they would immediately say, '*Gara pasi!*' ('Sit down!') and refuse to acknowledge you until you crouched down at their feet. Initially, it really got to me; then I realised that the more upset I got, the more they enjoyed it. You learn not to lower yourself to being affected by them. We all get hurt sometimes, that is part of life, but if you have lost a piece of yourself because of it, then you need to take up the fight to get you back. You are the only person who knows your own value. Nobody should be allowed to alter who you are. If you have let someone dictate your value, then you need to redefine who you really are.

The value of gratitude

One of the biggest and earliest lessons I learned in prison was to be grateful for what I had. Even though I worked hard for it, I was taken away from a life of plenty where I had more than most people could ever wish for, and yet I always wanted more. I had lost sight of the simple blessings in life. I do think the root cause of many of the world's problems lies in the fact that too many people take too much for granted because they don't appreciate what they have. We should all take stock every day of what we have to be grateful for before we start complaining about what we don't have.

For me, giving thanks to God every day goes a long way. Having gratitude for my health, a loving family, a beautiful home, a soft bed, running water and so on. When there is no food, no water, and people are dying all around you, you become grateful for the fact that you are still breathing, and you realise that another day is a blessing. When you lie in a cell with 78 other people and not even your breath is your own, gratitude suddenly has a different meaning altogether.

Prison was a form of shock treatment in reminding me how important the basics are for being able to live a happy, healthy life, and how much there is out there that we yearn for that we don't really need. Being ever needy quickly turns to greed, and greed is an unfortunate and destructive human condition. Greedy people are never content and probably never really experience true happiness. And there is some truth in the assertion that the best things in life are free. I think it is fair to say I am a warm and affectionate person who craves the pure embrace of loved ones and this was a component that I missed dearly.

Gratitude opens up the motivation, reward and connection centres of the brain, which makes us more receptive to new possibilities and gives us a deeper level of meaning and purpose. Think about that for a minute. When we wake up feeling grateful about who we are, what we have and what we have achieved in our lives, it is uplifting and invigorating, it motivates us to go out there and reach for greater things. The reward centres of our brain are also known as the 'pleasure centres' and are what give us a feeling of wellbeing and make us want to do that thing again. When we stimulate our reward circuits with healthy pursuits, like laughter, play, sex, creativity, we release endorphins and neurochemicals that can regulate emotion, decrease pain, and increase trust and connection. All these emotions affect how we communicate and form relationships. The healthiest of all human emotions is gratitude, remember that: the healthiest of all human emotions is gratitude. Practise it. Having an attitude of gratitude is one of the most impactful habits for a fulfilling and healthy life. Those simple happenings are free and priceless and what so many take for granted. God has come into my life, and when I communicate with Him, I thank Him for who I am, what I have, and for what I have been able to achieve.

The potential ingenuity brings

I learned something about the resilience of the human spirit while in prison. When faced with such harrowing conditions, there is an optimistic ingenuity that springs to life and introduces some of the comforts of home. Like ironing clothes, and boiling water, and making soccer balls, and jewellery. I believe that this is something we are all capable of. Ingenuity. In business and life. We get so comfortable though that it seems that our ingenuity is reserved for getting ourselves out of trouble only. It is a skill we all have. We need to develop it, without being pushed to do so. Because the reality is that one great idea or using something for a purpose other than what it was intended for – like tin lids for boiling water – can change your life. Hell, in my case, it can even save your life.

In business and in life, ingenuity is what sets you apart from the rest. What is it that you are bringing to the table that is unique and different? What processes can you think of that will improve your business? The thing is, we all have the ability to be great in whatever it is that we do, from the tea server to the board executive. So, if you are not on the road to reaching your full potential, then you are bound by whichever fear is holding you back. You are not free, and you need to address that.

Final thoughts

I'd like to close with a word of caution. We have all at some stage in our lives, pushed things a little close to the edge of the law, and gotten away with it. I did it many times, with forex deals, overstepping boundaries during safari days, or driving home well tanked after a good party. We have all done it, but may my lesson – of chasing poachers carelessly as a proud citizen of my beloved country – be a lesson to you all, not to act carelessly or push the boundaries of the law. It is easy to go to prison, trust me, but to get out, is a very different story.

Another piece of advice, and I was guilty of it before prison too, is that unless you were present during an incident, do not always assume someone is guilty, no matter how qualified you may think you are. We all read about stuff in the press and assume that if someone has been to trial, then his judgement must be correct. There were many innocent men in prison with me, including Phil, and very sadly, not everything you read, nor every judgement made, is correct.

In conclusion, I was fortunate. I had made it big, was very successful, and possibly during that time, I became a bit arrogant. But that experience has made me realise that I am just a normal human being.

You can't value your life based on your title, your success, or your material possessions. If everything was taken away from you right now, who would be left? What would people see, looking at you as a person?

We need to look at our core values more deeply and see how we can change lives and maybe make a difference in this world. There were times when I felt I had come to the end, I didn't have the mental strength to overcome the never-ending challenges. But from the bowels of despair came this realisation that, just as my mind had helped drag me through those depths that far, so it could it pull me out of them.

Each and every one of us, when we dig deep enough, can find this inner strength to get through life's toughest times and deepest holes. Every one of you reading this is faced with challenges, day in and day out. Some are challenges you look for, and some sneak up on you from behind. But who you are, and the depth of your determination, is what is going to elevate you to become someone that people will look up to and forever remember.

So, if you struggle to see the light that there is at the end of the tunnel, think about what I have been through. Because I can assure you, no matter how dark the tunnel, or how long the dark tunnel continues for, there will be light at the end of it.

Map of Zimbabwe

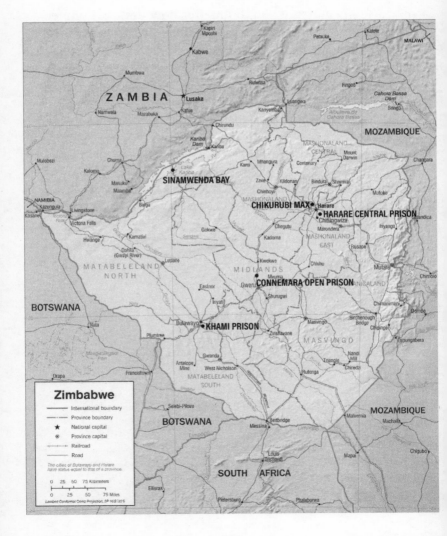

372

Acknowledgements

I wrote about 70 per cent of this book on a prohibited iPhone during my last two years in prison, emailing myself each script as I went along. Many thanks to Hannes Wessels for initially assisting with the structure and expanding on descriptive literature. The cover photos were done by my American friend Mark Frapwell in the USA. Thank you, Mark. A huge thank you to Pierre Behr for his incredible graphic design work on the cover. For the layout of photos, sketches, and letters, special thanks to Chad Laybourne. To Jacqui L'Ange, my sincere gratitude for her phenomenal restructuring and editing. For the passionate vision of the potential of my story, a big thank you to Ingeborg Pelser. And lastly, to my precious wife Sandra, who saw my calling, walked with me, and has relived my story every day. I love you with all my heart.

If you would like to book Rusty to speak at your event, he can be contacted via:
rusty@beatingchains.com